JOSHUA

~ AND ~

THE LAND OF PROMISE

Tabernacle Sermons - VIII

BY

Rev. A. B. SIMPSON

PASTOR GOSPEL TABERNACLE, NEW YORK.

Originally Published By:

Christ In The Bible Joshua:
CHRISTIAN ALLIANCE PUBLISHING CO.
692 Eighth Avenue, New York
September 1893 – February 1894

The Land Of Promise:
CHRISTIAN ALLIANCE PUBLISHING CO.
692 Eighth Avenue, New York
September - November 1888

Vol. 8 Tabernacle Sermons

Authored by A. B. Simpson

Republished under Public Domain rights by:

Empowered Publications Inc.

529 County Road 31

Millry, Al 36558

ISBN: 978-1-943033-28-7

Tabernacle Sermons

Beginning in 1886 A.B. Simpson began publishing a series of books called "Tabernacle Sermons." These books contained messages that he had preached in the Gospel Tabernacle, New York City, New York and subsequently published in eleven volumes.

These books are reprints of their original volumes. The content has been kept as close to the original as possible. Spelling was modernized in a few places, and where there were obvious errors in the text (one or two), comparisons were made to later editions of the books to keep the author's intent. Some of the original eleven volumes were combined, and some of the author's other books were added into the series.

VOLUME 1

The King's Business

VOLUME 2

The Fullness Of Jesus

VOLUME 3

The Gospel Of The Kingdom

VOLUME 4

Natural Emblems Of Spiritual Life

VOLUME 5

In Christ

Containing Three Volumes: The Four-Fold Gospel, The Christ Life, & The Christ Life And The Self Life (This book was originally printed as three separate books: The Four-Fold Gospel, Volume 5 of Tabernacle Sermons; The Christ Life, Volume 8 of Tabernacle Sermons; and The Christ Life And The Self Life, which was printed as an individual book.)

These three small volumes were combined as their contents relate to each other, and also to give the reader the most content for their purchase.

VOLUME 6

Divine Emblems In Genesis And Exodus

(This book was originally printed as two separate volumes: Volume 6, and Volume 7, in the original Tabernacle Sermons.)

VOLUME 7

Christ In The Tabernacle And Leviticus

(This book was originally printed as two separate books Volume 9 Christ in the Tabernacle – part of the Tabernacle Sermons Series; and Christ in Leviticus – part of the Christ in the Bible Series.)

VOLUME 8

Joshua & The Land Of Promise

(This book was originally printed as two separate books: The Land Of Promise Volume 10 of Tabernacle Sermons; and Christ in Joshua – part of the Christ in the Bible Series.

VOLUME 9

Walking In The Spirit & When The Comforter Came

(This book was originally printed as two separate books: "Walking In The Spirit," Volume 11 of Tabernacle Sermons, and "When The Comforter Came" was printed as a thirty-one day devotional dealing with the Holy Spirit.

CONTENTS.

JOSHUA

THE LAND OF PROMISE

CHRIST

- IN -

THE BIBLE.

- BY -

REV. A. B. SIMPSON.

VOLUME III.

JOSHUA.

ORIGINAL PREFACE.

THIS VOLUME is the third in the series of "CHRIST IN THE BIBLE," a work whose publication was begun several years ago, but has been delayed for many months by the great pressure upon the time of the author, and his inability to give proper attention, in the multiplicity of public duties, to the preparation of the matter for the press and the superintendence of its passage through the process of book-making.

He now hopes to continue the publication of these volumes at the rate of one or two yearly, if the Lord should spare his life, until the whole series shall have been completed.

PREFACE TO THIS EDITION.

This book was originally printed as two separate books: The Land Of Promise Volume 10 of Tabernacle Sermons; and Christ in Joshua – Volume 3 of the Christ in the Bible Series. The two books are printed together as their contents are similar and to give the reader the most for their purchase.

THE BOOK OF JOSHUA.

INTRODUCTION.

The following chapters contain the substance of a series of discourses on the book of Joshua, designed to unfold the deeper spiritual teachings of this Book as a revelation of Christ in His fullness, and as a type of the higher inheritance of faith and peace into which our Divine Joshua waits to introduce His faithful people.

They do not claim to be so much an exegetical commentary on words and phrases, as a more comprehensive analysis of the general plan and spiritual teachings of the volume, and an exposition of the mind of the Spirit, as He, through these ancient types, unfolds to us our privileges under the Gospel and our full inheritance in Christ.

Other volumes sufficiently expound the questions of history, geography, textual criticism, skeptical objections, and allusions to manners and customs, and other matters connected with Biblical illustration.

Our object, in harmony with the general purpose of these volumes – namely, to unfold "Christ in the Bible," is, to bring the hearts of our readers into touch, at all points, with the Lord Himself, and the lessons which He designs for their own spiritual life.

There is in all things, a good, a better, and a best. That is especially true in our spiritual life. The story of Exodus, Leviticus, and Numbers is *the good*, unfolding Israel's redemption from Egypt, and foreshadowing our salvation through the Lord Jesus Christ.

Deuteronomy and the earlier chapters of Joshua introduce us to *the better*, Israel's entrance upon the Land of Promise, the type of our sanctification through the Lord Jesus, and by the power of the Holy Ghost.

But there is something more than even this, and the later chapters of the Book of Joshua unfold *the highest and the best* possibilities of our spiritual life.

There were choice possessions in the Land of Promise. There were victories to be won, even after all the land was subdued and the thirty-one kings were conquered. Hebron, Kirjath-sepher, and Timnath-serah represented something more than ordinary victory, and point us forward to the prizes of Christian life and the special inheritance of glory awaiting the few, even in the sanctified host of God who are willing to be more than conquerors through Him that loved them.

If this volume shall be used of God to inspire any of God's wandering children to turn from the good to the better, we shall feel deeply thankful.

But if we shall have the joy of finding, in the day of harvest, that it has stimulated some of God's consecrated children to press on from the better to the best, and to win some Hebron of love, or Timnath-serah of cloudless light and incorruptible joy in the heavenly places which await us even here, we shall feel that the highest purpose of this beautiful, inspired volume which we have sought to unfold has been in some measure accomplished, and that we have not been disappointed in our own humble, and most earnest hope and prayer.

CHAPTER I.

OUR FULL INHERITANCE IN CHRIST.

"Now after the death of Moses, the servant of the Lord, it came to pass that the Lord spake unto Joshua, the son of Nun, Moses' minister saying: Moses my servant is dead; now therefore arise, go over this Jordan, thou, and all this people, unto the land which I do give to them, even to the children of Israel. Every place that the soul of your foot shall tread upon, that have I given unto you, as I said unto Moses. From the wilderness and this Lebanon even unto the great river, the river Euphrates, all the land of the Hittites, and unto the great sea toward the going down of the sun, shall be your coast." – Josh. 1:1-4.

IN the plan of Divine revelation there is a deep, logical and Christological order of conception and thought; and while, of course, we find at every step the usual freedom and diffusiveness of the Oriental style, yet there is one great definite idea that moves steadily onwards in clear development and grand progression.

THE BOOKS OF MOSES.

The Book of Genesis is the Book of Beginnings, and everything that comes in the later books has, in some sense, its source and foundation here. Exodus is the Book of Redemption, and all that the later Scriptures reveal with respect to the grand plan of human redemption, has here its roots and germs. Leviticus is the Book of Reconciliation, and unfolds the teachings of the Holy Ghost respecting our access to God, and our life in the holy place of His sanctuary. Numbers is the story of the wilderness, and the picture of our wanderings below; and especially of the failure of God's people to enter into their inheritance. Then Deuteronomy comes as the second or new departure of the people of God, after the sad experience of failure and sin, and rehearses afresh God's covenant and His charges to His people, as the second generation look forward to enter into the rest which their fathers had refused.

JOSHUA.

The culmination of all this is reached in the Book of Joshua. As Numbers is the story of failure, and Deuteronomy of renewed preparation, so Joshua tells us of the actual entering into the land of promise. It marks the highest point in the history of the covenant people hitherto, and necessarily suggests some deeper lessons in its higher spiritual significance as respects the New Testament revelation, and the spiritual people of whom ancient Israel was but the type.

Therefore, we find the Apostle in his letter to the Hebrews, saying: "If Joshua had given them rest, then would he not have spoken of another day," – "there remaineth, therefore, a rest for the people of God." It is evident, therefore, that Canaan was not designed to be the permanent inheritance of Israel, but a type of the higher heritage of faith and holiness which still remained for God's covenant people.

NOT HEAVEN.

That inheritance cannot be the heaven that awaits us after death, or even the earthly kingdom of glory and righteousness which the coming of Christ is to bring. Our hymnology is laden with this conception and its appropriate phraseology, but it is all contrary to the real idea of the Holy Ghost; for we shall not find in heaven, or even in the Millennial state, anything to correspond with the enemies in the land, whom Joshua had to fight, with the years of conflict through which Israel passed, with the shame and sin of Achan, or the subsequent backsliding of Israel. Into that land "shall enter nothing that defileth," and there shall be no foe or fear of conflict; and even Satan – the great leader of all the adverse host shall be utterly cast out.

The spiritual kingdom must, therefore, be some experience and condition here. What it means, the Apostle very distinctly expresses when he tells us: "He that has entered into his rest hath ceased from his own works, even as God did from His;" and yet again, "Let us, therefore, fear, lest a promise having been given us of entering into His rest, any of you should seem to come short of it." God's rest is something here; a condition and experience of spiritual victory, power, and satisfaction which corresponds with the experience of Israel in Canaan; just as the wretched experience of failure and inconstancy so often found in Christians corresponds with the story of the Book of Numbers and the forty years of wandering in the wilderness.

TWO TYPES OF CHRISTIANS.

Even the most superficial observer must have noticed in the records of Christian experience, and the observation of life, that there are two very distinct types of Christians in the world, in every age; one representing an experience of despondency, anxiety, doubt, inconstancy and frequent declension; a life so unsatisfying as to make one question whether it is really worth all it costs; and the other full of confidence, victory, joy, satisfaction, power and stability.

The difference between these two types is more marked than even the experience of conversion; or the contrast between the man of the world and the professing Christian. Those who have passed into this second stage of Christian life have uniformly testified that their second blessing marked a far greater change in their experience than their first.

There has been no period in the history of the church without these two classes of disciples. Even the apostles themselves passed from one stage into the other; and their experience before the coming of the Holy Ghost was the realization of the Book of Numbers, and their subsequent life, after the day of Pentecost, was a repetition of the Book of Joshua. There is not a congregation of Christians on earth today but contains the same two classes; the people who have simply come out of Egypt and are wandering in the wilderness, with a hope of salvation and a measure of grace sufficient to separate them from the world; and, on the other hand, the people who have been filled with the Spirit, and are walking in the light and joy of the Lord.

Taking the lowest view of it, who is there who has not felt the need of something deeper and higher in his Christian life? Who is there who has not wept over his failures and humiliations, and reached out for the purity and the power worthy of the cost and the grandeur of God's great salvation? Who is there who has not felt that there must be something higher than a life of sinning and repenting, and longed to rise above the evil that he hated, and realize the holy aspirations which constantly struggled in his breast?

Sometimes men have grown so weary and dissatisfied that they have thrown up the little religion they possessed, and said, "If I cannot have something better than this, I will have nothing;" and after years of struggling, have found the full salvation of God, and accepted it and been brought into the full experience of the sanctification of the Holy Ghost. It is the natural instinct of a newborn soul to expect such a life from the beginning, and it is a strange disappointment, when the first fall comes and the soul is overwhelmed with its insufficiency and helplessness, and pours out for the first time the bitter cry, "O! wretched man that I am; who shall deliver me from the body of this death?"

We read as early as the 13th chapter of Genesis, that God gave to Abram a vision of this Land of Promise, long centuries before it was fulfilled; and so God has been giving to us, all our lives, a vision of a larger, richer blessing than we have ever enjoyed. Sometimes we have seen it in the lives of God's saints with whom we have come in contact, and their shining faces have made us hunger for what we did not possess, and wonder why we did not have it too. Sometimes we have seen it in the promises of God, and asked ourselves why we should not realize these great words, if God really meant them. Sometimes the vision has seemed to be a vague outreaching, quite indefinable, and then sometimes the light has grown clearer, and the land has stood out in its great landmarks and headlands, until we understood more definitely what the promise meant, and what the fullness of our inheritance involved. This is the Apostle's prayer for his friends in Ephesus, and it is the prayer of the Spirit for each of us, that "the eyes of our understanding may be enlightened that we may know the riches of the glory of His inheritance in the saints." May God so open our eyes that, as we read these lines, we may understand the meaning of the inheritance of the saints, and the fullness of the blessing of Christ!

VICTORY.

The first definite landmark in the inheritance is VICTORY. Canaan meant to ancient Israel, triumph over their enemies, and our first great spiritual need is power to overcome the evil within us, and the evil around us. We are not anywhere promised that we shall be delivered from the conflict, but it is our privilege to be victorious in it.

Sin shall not cease to exist, in this present dispensation, but we may be dead to sin, and claim the mighty premise

– “Sin shall not have dominion over you, for ye are not under the law, but under grace.” It is the covenant and oath of Jesus that we “being delivered from all our enemies, and the hands of them that hate us, might serve Him without fear, in righteousness and holiness before Him, all the days of our life.” Victory over the sin within us, over the self that dominated us; over the temptations that beset us – this is the promise of Christ; this is the purchase of His blood; this is the sanctification which the Holy Spirit comes to give to every surrendered heart.

“I will put My Spirit within you, and I will cause you to walk within My statutes, and ye shall keep My judgments and do them.”

REST

Canaan is called “God’s REST.” Following, as it did, forty years of weary wandering, it was, indeed, a delightful repose. It tells of something in Christian experience which is as precious as it is rare – deliverance not only from sin and temptation, but from care and fear; the peace that passeth all understanding, and garrisons the heart and mind through Christ Jesus; the trust that is careful for nothing; the confidence that casts all care on Him; the perfect peace in which God keeps those whose mind is stayed on Him; the great peace of those who love His law, and nothing shall offend them. Christ had this perfect peace Himself, and His last bequest to His disciples was: “Peace I leave (or bequeath) to you; My peace give I unto you; Let not your heart be troubled, neither let it be afraid.”

Greater than to be saved from the ills of earth, is it to be kept from their shadow and their fear. This is the privilege of the heart that fully trusts and wholly yields itself to God. It is the heaven of the soul, and the blood-bought inheritance of all who are willing to enter into the promised land.

REALIZATION.

The land of Canaan was to them the realization of many former promises. It made actual to them things which had been only hopes. And so to us, in our Christian life, there is a stage of faith and promise, and there is the experience of full realization and blessed satisfaction. "The law was given by Moses; but grace and reality came by Jesus Christ."

The Holy Spirit is an earnest and a seal; and these figures express most emphatically the deep impress of living realities in our heart and life. There is for us the actual consciousness of Divine things, the personal and intimate knowledge of God; the utter satisfaction of every longing of the soul; love so rooted and grounded that it cannot be moved, and blessings "exceeding abundantly above all that we ask or think." The inheritance, beloved, is for you. God wants to make the things of the Spirit more actual in your life than the things of sense are in the lower world of the material, and to quicken every inward sense until you shall know and see the invisible realities of the world to come with a vividness that the things of earth can never have.

POWER.

How men long for power! How weak and ineffectual are the lives of our Christians; how little they tell for God and man! Christ is the Almighty One, and there is no sphere in which His almightiness should be so strongly felt as in the spiritual realm, where the Holy Ghost supremely rules.

The experience of Joshua in Canaan expresses victorious power. It was the march of God, through His people, in continual triumph, until every earthly foe and every material force acknowledged this supremacy. The same power has been embodied in the Lord Jesus Christ, and His almighty Spirit, and it awaits the trust of every fully surrendered heart. "Ye shall receive power after the Holy Spirit is come upon you; and ye shall be witnesses unto Me;" "He that believeth on Me, the works that I do shall he do also; and greater works than these shall he do."

YOUR OWN INHERITANCE.

But there is something higher than all this. The land of promise has a personal meaning for each of us. No man can occupy the whole world, or live in a whole city; there is one spot which each of us calls home. That is a personal location and possession, and expresses our own individual residence. And so there is a sense in which God has a special inheritance for each of His children. God's promises have a meaning for you that they cannot have for me; and God has a plan for you which is distinct and individual.

That plan He is ever unfolding to our faith, as we are able and willing to receive it. This is what David meant when he said, "The lines have fallen to me in pleasant places; yea, I have a goodly heritage."

The inheritance of every Christian is the highest will of God for Him. It includes both our internal and our external life and it means for each of us the revelation of Christ in our own heart in all His fullness of grace and power, and the ordering of God's providence in our life, so as to develop us in the highest manner and use us for the greatest good.

All our life long, God has been speaking to us about this plan. Some of us remember the distant vision of our childhood, as we knelt in our earliest prayers, and the light of heaven first began to illumine the firmament of our souls, and open them to the thoughts and plans of God. More and more clearly, as we have come into His more immediate presence, has He made plain to us His thoughts for us, and added promise unto promise. And as He has fulfilled them successively, He has led us on to a larger vision, vaster hopes and bolder advances, and we have begun to walk through the land in all the length and breadth of it.

The measuring lines of this land are the promises of God. Every New Year's eve, every day of special waiting upon Him; every time of renewed dedication; every birthday and every anniversary, has He enlarged these promises and expanded this vision and every successive year that faith and expectation have been turned to thanksgiving and praise, as we have found His promises fulfilled and His word proved sure and true.

A LARGER LAND.

But for most of us there is a larger land than we have yet realized, and God is speaking to us as He did to Abram of old, and saying, "Look, now, from the place where thou standest, northward and southward, and eastward and westward, for all the land which thou seest, to thee will I give it and to thy seed forever. And I will make thy seed as the dust of the earth; so that if a man can number the dust of the earth, then shall thy seed also be numbered. Arise, arise, walk through the land in the length of it and in the breadth of it; for I will give it unto thee."

And again, He is speaking to some of us in the rich and glorious promises of Deuteronomy 8:7, "For the Lord thy God bringeth thee into a good land, a land of brooks of water, of fountains and depths that spring out of valleys and hills; a land of wheat, and barley, and vines, and fig-trees, and pomegranates; a land of oil, olive and honey; a land wherein thou shalt eat bread without scarceness; thou shalt not lack anything in it; a land whose stones are iron, and out of whose hills thou mayest dig brass. When thou hast eaten and art full, then thou shalt bless the Lord thy God for the good land which He hath given thee."

What a glorious land this is, with its springs of spiritual refreshing, its fountains from which these springs all come in the indwelling life and presence of God; its ample provision for all your spiritual need; its wheat, barley, fig-trees and pomegranates; its bread without scarceness, its honeyed sweetness, its oil and olives, producing in perpetual freshness the anointing of His gladness and His power; the land whose very stones and hills, with their ruggedness and barrenness, are but mines of brass and iron, enabling us to draw strength, out of our very difficulties, and blessing from all our trials.

Beloved, there is such a land for you, if you will but enter in and claim all the fullness of this boundless blessing. Nor need we fear to claim all the fullness of this promised land.

Again, in Jeremiah 32:41, "He says: "I will rejoice over them to do them good, and I will plant them assuredly in this land with My whole heart and with My whole soul."

This was the Apostle's prayer for the Thessalonians, 2Thessalonians 1:11, "Wherefore, also, we pray always for you, that our God would count you worthy of this calling, and fulfill all the good pleasure of His goodness, and the work of faith with power." This was the meaning of the prayer of Epaphras in Colossians 4:12, "That ye may stand perfect and complete in all the will of God." This was the holy confidence of Paul, "that in nothing shall I be ashamed, but that with all boldness, as always, so now also Christ shall be magnified in my body, whether it be by life or by death." And this was his one desire in life, and the only thing that he counted dear, as expressed in Acts 20:24, "That I might finish my course with joy, and the ministry which I have received of the Lord Jesus, to testify the Gospel of the grace of God."

There is for each of us a ministry, according to the will of God; for each of us a plan for reaching His highest thought for us, and the very best that we can do or be for Him and the world, and to even seem to come short of it will be an everlasting disappointment; and so He calls upon us, "Let us labor to enter into that rest, lest any of you be hardened by the deceitfulness of sin."

Beloved, there is nothing in life so important as this, and when the close comes, it will be an unending satisfaction to look back and feel that nothing has failed of all the will of God. But what a bitter disappointment it will be to look back from the light of eternity and realize how very much God had intended for us, and that it is forever lost!

Every moment of our life is adding something to this land or taking something from it. How swiftly the shuttle is flying to and fro with every throb of our heart, and threads are being woven and the pattern being wrought out or ruined. We cannot do it over again; the issues are hastening near, and they are forever. May God help us, that we may not even *seem* to come short!

ITS BOUNDARIES.

In our text, the boundaries of Canaan are given in a very striking manner. They were to extend "from the wilderness unto this Lebanon," and "from the great river Euphrates unto the great sea toward the going down of the sun." The wilderness was its southern limit, and this Lebanon the northern boundary. Joshua was standing at the time on the edge of the wilderness, and Lebanon was far away on the extreme north. It seems very strange to call it "this Lebanon." Humanly speaking, it was "that Lebanon." But Joshua was speaking of it in the language of faith, and faith always overleaps distance, and counts the things that are not as though they were. It was by Abram's faith that he saw the promise afar off and ran to meet it and embrace it. He had such faith in God that he saw the land afar off. Faith brings the distant near, and the far-off things that appear unapproachable, the blessings that seem to be beyond our reach are made so plain to the eye of faith that they are reckoned ours before they come to pass.

So yonder snow-crowned mountain, lost in the clouds, and dim in the distance of more than a hundred miles, is "this Lebanon." The eye of faith loves to gaze upon the distant heights of promise, and say, "this Lebanon." One touch of faith will dissolve the spaces that intervene, and cancel the interval of years, and bring us into God's ever present now, "where one day is as a thousand years and a thousand years as one day." We may get a foretaste of heaven, and dwell in its light, and sing the joyful song of trust:

"Give me the glorious foretaste here, I pray,
Let faith foredate that everlasting day;
And, walking in its glory all the way,
Oh! lead me in the way everlasting."

There is another beautiful suggestion in the description of the eastern and western boundary. Their line was to extend from the river Euphrates unto the great sea "toward the going down of the sun." It was not to reach the going-down of the sun, but to be toward it. In this land the sun never goes down. Away beyond the great sea of God's fullness lies the sunset, but our western boundary never reaches it. It is very striking and beautiful that the last picture in the Book of Joshua is the inheritance of Joshua himself, which was Timnath-serah, which literally means "the city of the sun." So, the picture of Canaan begins and ends with a sunlit sky, whose light and glory shall never fade. This is the inheritance where God's children may all abide. "Their sun need no more go down, for God shall be their everlasting light, and the days of their mourning shall be ended." Are we dwelling in its light?

Perhaps we might regard all these places as, at least, symbols, if not types, of some higher spiritual meaning. Shall we take the wilderness where the survey began as a figure of our life of wandering! Shall we take Lebanon to represent the strength and power of God in the truly consecrated and Christ-filled life, endued with the Holy Ghost and filled with the fullness of God? Shall the river Euphrates represent the rich fruitfulness of which it was a type, and shall the great sea speak to us of the larger fullness of God Himself, unto which all these blessings are intended to lead us?

Such is God's great survey of the Land of Promise? Into it He is waiting to bring His consecrated people. Shall we not listen while He says, in solemn earnestness, to each of our hearts, "Let us, therefore, fear, lest a promise having been left us of entering into His rest, any of you should seem to come short of it."

CHAPTER II.

THE GRAVES AT THE GATEWAY.

"Moses, My servant is dead; now, therefore, arise, go over this Jordan, thou, and all this people, unto the land which I do give them, *even* to the children of Israel." – Josh. 1:2.

WE have looked at the land, now let us look at the gateway. It leads past four solemn graves. Through death we enter into this higher life, and the deeper the death the higher the life will be. There is no principle so profound and so prominent in the plan of redemption as this principle of life through death. Indeed, we find it deeply written in the records of nature. The generations that live today are treading on the dust of former generations. The very plants on which animal and human life is sustained are the outgrowth of death, and they have sprung from the ashes of myriads of beings that once themselves were living creatures.

"Life evermore is fed by death,
And joy by agony:
And that a rose may breathe its breath,
Something must die."

Spring itself, with all its glory, comes from the grave of winter; the waving harvests grow from buried seeds, and the corn and wheat must die before they bear their fruit of golden gain.

The rite of circumcision, which was the initiatory ceremony of Judaism, is the symbol of death – the death of our natural life. Baptism has its chief significance in the same idea. All these symbols find their fulfillment in the cross of Jesus Christ, the cornerstone of redemption and the eternal memorial of life through death and salvation by suffering and sacrifice. The profoundest truths connected with our deeper spiritual life are associated with this idea of death. And so, in introducing the subject of sanctification, in the sixth chapter of Romans, the Apostle teaches us that we must enter into union with the death of Christ, and thus into His resurrection-life, "reckoning ourselves dead indeed unto sin, but alive unto God through Jesus Christ our Lord."

And so, again, in Colossians, we are represented as dead with Christ, and risen again with Him, by virtue of His resurrection from the dead. It is all summed up in these pregnant words: "I have been crucified with Christ; nevertheless I live; yet not I, but Christ within me; and the life I now live in the flesh I live by faith of the Son of God, who loved me and gave Himself for me," – Gal. 2:20.

This is the truth that lies back of the vivid symbolism of the book of Joshua. The Land of Promise, the great type of our full inheritance with Christ, was entered by the gateway of the grave. Four graves stand out before us in these opening chapters.

I. THE GRAVE OF MOSES.

"Moses, My servant, is dead; therefore arise, thou and all this people, and go over this Jordan."

The death of Moses has something very touching about it. Many of us have wept over that lonely grave on the heights of Nebo, and wondered why it should have been necessary for that brave, true heart to sink on the very threshold of his most glorious hopes. And yet the death of Moses was essential to our higher life, for Moses never could lead Israel into the land of promise. This was something that Joshua alone could bring about. Moses represented the law, and "the law made nothing perfect; but the bringing in of a better hope did." Moses represents human effort, and the best that man can do, and man's best can never bring us into the land of victory over sin, and full obedience to God. Therefore, Moses must break his own law, and sink under its condemning blow, to prove forever to the world that all man's efforts are vain to sanctify the soul. And so in every individual life there must come a point where we pass out from under the law, and it becomes true – "Sin shall not have dominion over you, for you are not under the law, but under grace."

There are thousands in the church of Christ who fully believe in salvation by Christ, but they are struggling after sanctification by works. It is as impossible for man to purify his heart as it is to cancel the judgment of God against his sins; and so God has to let us strive and struggle chiefly that we may find out our own inability, and give up the struggle for the better way of Christ and His Divine and complete salvation.

Sanctification is the obtainment of grace, not the attainment of effort. True, it involves the most strenuous and mighty energy on our part, but it is all the Divine fruit of God's working in us "to will and to do of His own pleasure," and we pass out of our works into His working, and from henceforth say: "Whereunto I also labor, striving according to His working, which worketh in me mightily." But there is a deeper death signified by the river Jordan.

II. THE GRAVE OF SELF AND SIN.

"Now, therefore, arise and go over this Jordan." We know that Jordan is the symbol of death and judgment, and the crossing of the Jordan is the symbol of our partnership with the Lord Jesus Christ in that deeper death to self and sin of which the New Testament speaks so fully.

Some very suggestive things are brought out by the detailed account given in these opening chapters of the passage of the Jordan by the children of Israel.

1. We notice that it was a very definite act.

They came up to a real river; they stepped in and passed over; they knew when they crossed it, and they knew that they were on the other side. And so this experience in our life must be very definite. We cannot glide into it, we cannot grow into it; we come to a point where we take a definite step that can never be undone, and can never be done over again. This is not a great marsh that spreads over leagues and miles, and in which we wade along indefinitely for half a lifetime; but it is a real river, which there is no mistaking. There is a moment in every consecrated life when we come to the fords of this Jordan, when we pass sentence of death upon ourselves, and by one blow, one definite act, forever pass out of ourselves into Christ and His fullness; and from that time our Christian life is as different from its former era as that was different from the time prior to our conversion.

2. It was difficult, as well as definite.

We are told that when they crossed the Jordan the river overflowed all its banks, for it was the time of harvest; and it is always flood-time when God calls us into the experience of death. The thing He asks you to do is the most difficult thing He could ask of you, and the time is usually the hardest time when it could happen. When God aims a death-blow at us, He aims at the heart, and His aim is so true and sure that He never wants to repeat the blow. When man tries to crucify himself, he always manages to escape a vital point; but when God undertakes the work, He chooses the thing which is the very key to the situation, and requires the sacrifice in which all your life is most intensely bound up. It is your Isaac that He demands; it is your life He seeks; and if you are wise, you will let Him have it promptly and unreservedly, and by one decisive and final act be done with the agony.

3. It is only possible through Divine enabling. You cannot put yourself to death; God alone can accomplish this work. You are just as unequal to the death as you are to the life. You can mutilate yourself, you can tantalize yourself, you can deny yourselves a thousand things, but you cannot slay your sinful self. God must do that. And soon we read in Romans 8:13, "If ye through the Spirit do mortify the deeds of the body, ye shall live." It must be through the Spirit. And again the Apostle says, "God forbid that I should glory save in the cross of Jesus Christ, by whom the world is crucified unto me, and I unto the world."

No one but Christ can crucify you. You cannot die alone, but must fall into the arms of Jesus, and hang with Him upon His cross, and let Him love your sinful soul to death.

Now, this is all set forth in the symbolism of Jordan. The people could not enter Jordan until the ark – which is ever the type of Christ – had preceded them, and it had to remain in the bed of the Jordan until they had all clean passed over, and then to follow up and finish the work which it had begun.

Jesus must lead us into the waters of death; He must stand with us through them, and must bring us out on the other side. We are helpless to perform any act of self-surrender or true consecration except by Him. We can pass sentence of death upon ourselves, we can yield up ourselves to the death-blow, but He must strike that blow, and we must trust Him to do it.

4. It must be an act of faith.

The symbolism here is very fine. They had to step down to the very edge of the flood; their feet had to touch the cold waters, and it was not until they were dipped into the brim, that the waters divided and the way appeared. And so our self-surrender must be right up to the edge of death itself; we must go forward until there is no way apparent, and God will not interpose until the very last hour, and then, as we march on right boldly, the sea will divide, and a way will be prepared, even in the midst of the flood, for our feet to walk upon the dry ground.

5. It must be a very thorough work.

We read – Joshua 4:10 – that "the priests stood in the midst of the Jordan, until everything was finished that the Lord commanded Joshua to speak unto the people."

The people were no doubt very anxious to go over quickly. It was an awful journey; it was a terrific pathway; it was a trying hour; but right here, in the midst of the flood, they must stand unmoved, and listen to all God had to say – how long we know not, but long enough to accomplish a thorough and everlasting work.

We are in too great a hurry to get through our transactions with God. The Holy Ghost will do thorough work if we will let Him. When God lays you low at His feet He wants you to listen to Him. There are things you can hear in the valley of the shadow of death that never can come to you again, and His word is, "Humble yourselves under the mighty hand of God that He may exalt you in due time." This is a place that you can never come to again; let nothing be wanting to its completeness. Let your heart answer back, "I will hear what God, the Lord, will speak;" and the echoes of those messages will come back to you amid the hallelujahs of His coming.

6. Again, it was an enduring act.

They brought up from the bed of Jordan memorial stones, and they planted them on the other shore as a memorial of that crossing, so that it could never be forgotten. And so, God wants us to remember this hour, and to be established in this experience forever. He wants you to be dead, and to know it, and so He uses the strongest figure of arithmetic when He says: "Reckon yourselves to be dead" – reckon by a process which admits of no evasion – "indeed unto sin but alive unto God through Jesus Christ our Lord."

III. THE GRAVE AT GILGAL.

Next, we come to the third grave. It is the grave at Gilgal, which is the place where they were to be circumcised after they had crossed the Jordan. But why is this added symbol here introduced? Is it intended to emphasize especially the death of the flesh, and its affections and passions, as one of the things we need most carefully to watch? Or has it some broader and larger significance? Undoubtedly, it does mean that we should be very sure that our self-crucifixion reaches to our natural life, and lays our tenderest affections and all our appetites and propensities at the feet of Jesus for His filling and consecration.

But it means more than this. The crossing of Jordan expresses the faith side of our dying; the circumcision at Gilgal, the experimental side. Jordan teaches us how to reckon ourselves dead, but Gilgal teaches us how to realize the dying in actual life.

Surely we all have learned the difference between these two things. There is a day in our spiritual life when we yield ourselves up unto God, and pass the sentence of death upon ourselves, and register it in heaven, and begin to "reckon ourselves dead indeed unto sin, but alive unto God." And there is another day when we step out into the battle of life, and find our old self, at the first temptation, rising up in all the strength of self-assertion, and refusing to be reckoned dead. Then it is that Gilgal comes in, and as we come face to face with the touch of God, He makes the death real. Helpless and distressed, we throw ourselves upon Him, and claim the fulfillment and realization of the great transaction which we have so sincerely entered into. Then the Holy Ghost actually touches our inmost life with the sharp knife of His power and the consuming fire of His breath, and withers the evil that we cannot touch, and fills us with the life of purity which excludes the darkness through the coming in of the light. And so, day by day, as we go through the repeated tests, we find the promise holds; the faithful love and power of God continue to meet us, the reckoning becomes a reality, and the promise tried and proved.

Now, all this is beautifully illustrated in the idea of crucifixion. Crucifixion was not an instantaneous dying, but a lingering death. And yet the victim was said to be crucified the moment he was suspended upon the cross.

It was high noon on that Friday which never shall be forgotten, when Jesus was hung by the cruel nails on Calvary's cross, but it was three o'clock in the afternoon before He died, yet from the very first moment it was said by the sacred narrative: "They crucified Him." He was regarded as crucified from that midday hour; but it was not until hours later that He breathed out His glorious spirit into His Father's arms, and went down amid the regions of the dead.

This is exactly fulfilled in the crucifixion of the believer with His Lord. There is a moment when we yield ourselves to be dead with Christ; and from that moment it is true: "I have been crucified with Christ." But after this, there come hours and days of suffering, during which we are hanging with Him upon that cross, and a thousand voices are saying to us as they said to Him: "Save thyself, and come down from the cross!"

Oh, how many do that, and forfeit all they have suffered and done! It is of these that the Apostle says: "Have ye suffered so many times in vain?" But there are others who remain unmoved and undismayed through all the severity of the test, and it is to these that the spirit comes with His love and power in the actual experience of the death.

How long those three hours represent, God only knows. Each life has its dark Friday and its dying day. The first of these is represented by the Jordan, and the second by the circumcision at Gilgal. And as "they abode at Gilgal until they were whole," so God holds us still until His testing is complete and the work is done. This must surely be the meaning of that passage in Philippians, where the Apostle prays, "That I may know Him and the power of His resurrection and the fellowship of His sufferings, being made comfortable unto His death," after which comes the great hope, "if by any means I might attain unto the resurrection from among the dead."

IV. JOSHUA'S GRAVE.

There is one more death. Even Joshua, the captain of the Lord's host, must die. The picture of his self-surrender is very striking and significant. Standing over against Jericho, perhaps at dead of night, reconnoitering the position, and thinking of the assault which he was about to make, suddenly there stood before him a man with his sword drawn in his hand. Nothing daunted, but every inch a soldier and a captain, Joshua went unto him and said, "Art thou for us or for our adversaries?" The answer came that thrilled his soul and laid him on his face before the supernatural Presence: "Nay, but as Captain of the host of the Lord am I now come." And Joshua fell on his face to the earth and said unto him: "What saith my Lord unto His servant?" And the Captain of the Lord's host said unto Joshua: "Loose thy shoes from off thy foot; for the place whereon thou standest is holy." And Joshua did so.

This was no other than the Son of God, the true Captain of the host. Joshua had supposed that he was captain, but henceforth, his sword was laid down before the Captain of the Lord's host, and Joshua, with his shoes off his feet, took a servant's place, took his orders from above and followed where the Lord should lead.

This is the secret of Christian victory; this the place where we must come before we can be overcomers. This is the meaning of that sublime announcement of the Apostle: "Thanks be unto God who always leadeth us in triumph in Christ Jesus." It is not "that causeth us to triumph." We are not the victors, but simply the followers of the great Commander, as He leads us conquering and to conquer. With such a Leader we must always be victorious. But to have such a leader, we must die to our self-sufficiency and strength. There cannot be two commanders; you and Christ cannot both rule.

How much there is among consecrated Christians and the best of God's children that needs to be laid down at His feet! How much there is in our Christian service that reflects honor upon ourselves, or springs from self-consciousness! Sometimes it throws around us such a glamor that it dazzles us with its brilliancy, and we do it for the work's sake, rather than for the Lord's sake. All this is false and wrong. To all this we must die, so that our service will not be affected by the approval of others or their neglect, by the pleasantness of the surroundings, or the self-denial it costs us. We should be like the holy angels, of whom it has been said, that if they were sent to sweep a street crossing, they would be just as willing as to minister in a palace, or lead an army into victorious battle. The holy I, the pious I, the useful I, the spiritual I, the ecclesiastical I, the I that says, "I am of Paul; I am of Apollos, and I am of Christ," – all these must cease, and Christ alone be known and glorified. Then shall our service abide the testing day; then can Christ lead us through all the land of victory and power, and then shall "our light so shine before men that they shall see our good works and glorify" – not us, but – "our Father in heaven."

CHAPTER III.

THE TWO WATCHWORDS OF VICTORY.

"Now after the death of Moses the servant of the LORD it came to pass, that the LORD spake unto Joshua the son of Nun, Moses' minister, saying, Moses my servant is dead; now therefore arise, go over this Jordan, thou, and all this people, unto the land which I do give to them, even to the children of Israel. Every place that the sole of your foot shall tread upon, that have I given unto you, as I said unto Moses. From the wilderness and this Lebanon even unto the great river, the river Euphrates, all the land of the Hittites, and unto the great sea toward the going down of the sun, shall be your coast. There shall not any man be able to stand before thee all the days of thy life: as I was with Moses, so I will be with thee: I will not fail thee, nor forsake thee. Be strong and of a good courage: for unto this people shalt thou divide for an inheritance the land, which I sware unto their fathers to give them. Only be thou strong and very courageous, that thou mayest observe to do according to all the law, which Moses my servant commanded thee: turn not from it to the right hand or to the left, that thou mayest prosper whithersoever thou goest. This book of the law shall not depart out of thy mouth; but thou shalt meditate therein day and night, that thou mayest observe to do according to all that is written therein: for then thou shalt make thy way prosperous, and then thou shalt have good success. Have not I commanded thee? Be strong and of a good courage; be not afraid, neither be thou dismayed: for the LORD thy God is with thee whithersoever thou goest." – Josh. 1:1-9.

LIKE the two wings of a bird, like the two oars of a boat, both essential to its proper movement, are the two principles of Faith and Obedience, which are ever linked together in a rightly regulated Christian life, and which are interwoven in the opening scenes of the Book of Joshua. Let us look at them separately and then jointly.

I. THE WATCHWORD OF FAITH.

The land of promise was won by faith. Every step was a step of faith; the Jordan was crossed by faith; by faith the walls of Jericho fell down, after they had been compassed seven days; by faith Rahab was saved, and perished not with them who believed not. By faith every victory was achieved in their onward progress, until at last Caleb had claimed the heights of Hebron, and Joshua had reached his inheritance at Timnath-serah. Here we have some of the features of faith most strongly emphasized.

1. We have the present tense of faith: Joshua 1:2, "The land which I *do* give to them, even the children of Israel." God here speaks in the immediate present. It is not something He is going to do, but something He does do, this moment. So faith ever speaks. So God ever gives. So He is meeting you today, in the present moment.

This is the test of faith. So long as you are waiting for a thing, hoping for it, looking for it, you are not believing. It may be hope, it may be earnest desire, but it is not faith; for "faith is the substance of things hoped for, the evidence of things not seen."

God meets us first in the future tense, as He did Abraham, Genesis 17:2, "I will make My covenant between Me and thee." But He brings us immediately, if we are willing, into the present tense; so we read in Genesis 17:4, "My covenant is with thee."

There must come a moment in your life when you really receive Christ as your Saviour, and in that moment you are saved. There must come a crisis-hour when you yield yourself to Him, and take Him as your Sanctifier, and from that moment you are sanctified.

The command in regard to believing prayer is in the present tense. "When ye pray, believe that ye receive the things that ye desire, and ye shall have them." Have we come to that moment? Have we met God in His everlasting Now?

2. We have next the perfect tense of faith. We see this in the third verse: "Every place that the sole of thy foot shall tread upon, that *have I given* thee." The present has now become the perfect tense. That which but a moment ago was the present is now the perfect tense. And so in Genesis 17:5 we find the present tense passing into the perfect, and God saying: "A father of many nations *have I made* thee." This is perfectly consistent. God cannot repeat Himself, or allow His words to be of no effect. When He speaks it is done; when He commands, it stands fast. And He is pleased to have us recognize His work as perfect, and His word as everlasting, and step out upon it in unfaltering confidence.

So we find Him speaking in His own Word, of Jesus as "the Lamb slain from the foundation of the world," although it was not actually fulfilled until the world was 4,000 years old; but His purpose and His promise were counted fulfilled, and God speaks in the language of faith and certainty.

3. We have the imperative mood of faith, verse 9: "Have I not commanded thee? Be strong and of good courage; be not afraid, neither be thou dismayed." This is the faith that falters not, fears not, refuses to be dismayed, and with defiant courage goes forth and faces every foe. It says, with Isaiah: "The Lord God will help me; therefore shall I not be confounded; therefore have I set my face like a flint, and I know that I shall not be ashamed." And with Paul: "None of these things move me." "In nothing shall I be ashamed; but always Christ shall be magnified in my body." "I know whom I have believed, and I am persuaded that He is able to keep that which I have committed to Him against that day."

Our faith must not only be real, but it must be strong; sometimes it must be audacious. The faintest fear will paralyze it. A quiver in that regimental line will bring disaster and defeat to the whole army. There must be unfaltering steadiness and bold defiance throughout. Unbelief always begins in little doubts and fears, and God reiterates the command, "Fear not, fear not, fear not." "Be careful for nothing." "Take no anxious thought for the morrow." Not with the fiery artillery of hell is our faith first assaulted, but by an army of little moths, with their soft touch and velvet wings; and soon our spiritual garment is riddled and ruined before the real fight begins. If we would win in the conflict of faith, we must stand without fear, unfaltering and unmoved, and resist in the imperative mood of victorious confidence.

4. The active voices of faith.

True faith expresses itself in action. It reaches the soles of our feet, and steps out in actual movements that prove its reality and sincerity. We read of "the steps of our father Abraham." Faith has stepping stones. So their faith expressed itself; first, in their stepping into the waters of the Jordan, and next in their circuit of Jericho for seven days.

Their faith was not only active, but persistent. They continued to go through the whole testing until it was thoroughly proved and finally triumphant. So our faith must ever step out and claim its blessing until it fully receives it. It was as the lepers *went*, that they were healed. Had they lingered pleading at the feet of Jesus, they never would have been healed; but when they moved forward in obedience to the Master's command, they found His promise awaiting them as they advanced.

It was as Naaman stepped into the Jordan at the command of Elisha, that his healing came. But he had to do it more than once; seven times had he to persevere until his faith was fully proved, and then the answer came. It is in the midst of the proving that faith often breaks down. It is easy to take one bold step, but a patient continuance in the work of faith tries the inmost soul.

Their faith had not only to encompass Jericho seven days, but on the seventh day it had to rise to a height to which it had not before attained, and with seven-fold patience and perseverance complete the circuit over and over again, until the trial was complete, and the shout of victory came at last.

It must have been very hard. To their own rational sense it must have seemed strange, and to the people of Jericho, no doubt, it looked contemptible. One can see them gathering on the walls, as, day after day, the procession was resumed, until at last it became ridiculous; and doubtless on the seventh day the circuit was scarcely noticed. But, on and on, those faithful soldiers marched, until at last, their movements became accelerated, and quicker and quicker their footsteps repeated that course until, as the sun went down, the last round was finished, the trumpets gave the signal, the shouts of the people rent the heavens, and with a resounding crash, the walls of Jericho tumbled down before the assault of victorious faith.

Again, we see faith following up God's working, in the story of Jericho. In answer to their advance and their shout of faith, the walls of faith fell down, but this would have been unavailing if they had not at once followed up God's mighty working and marched in at the open gates. And so we read that "they went every man straight before him, and they took the city." So in our lives there is ever a place for the faith which recognizes God's mighty working and advances along the lines which He has prepared.

Once more we have an illustration of faith in the saving of Rahab. We learn that this glorious principle of action is not only for the higher stages of our Christian life, but that the vilest sinner may rise through it into the place of pardon and salvation. Rahab was the vilest of the Canaanites, but that little scarlet thread which she hung from the walls of her house, that crimson sign of her trust in God and the word of His messengers, was sufficient to obliterate the stains of her whole life, and to place her in the very line of His redeemed; yes, among the very ancestors of Christ Himself.

This is the watchword by which we too must enter our land of promise. By the faith that believes and receives forgiveness and salvation, before we feel it, must we pass from condemnation into justification. By the faith that takes Christ as our sanctification, and reckons ourselves dead indeed unto sin, but alive unto God through Jesus Christ our Lord, must we cross the Jordan and take our inheritance of full salvation. By faith must we receive the Holy Ghost and recognize His indwelling, before we feel His touch; by faith must we overcome our enemies, and utter the shout of victory in the thickest of the fight; by faith we must receive the answers to our prayers and turn them into praises and thanksgivings, before we witness their fulfillment. "We that have believed do enter into rest." "Let us, therefore, fear, lest there be in any of us an evil heart of unbelief, in departing from the living God."

Let us claim the faith that receives the promise in the present tense, that confesses it in the perfect tense; that triumphs in the imperative mood, and that conjugates it through all its moods and tenses, until it can write under every promise, "Tried and proved," and over every difficulty, "More than conquerors through Him that loved us."

II. THE WATCHWORD OF OBEDIENCE.

This is just as emphatic as the other. "Only be thou strong and very courageous, that thou mayest observe to do according to all the law which Moses my servant commanded thee; turn not from it to the right hand or to the left, that thou mayest prosper whithersoever thou goest."

"This book of the law shall not depart out of thy mouth; but thou shalt meditate therein day and night, that thou mayest observe to do according to all that is written therein; for then thou shalt make thy way prosperous, and then shalt thou have good success."

Here we have the various moods and tenses of obedience.

1. It must be intelligent and diligent. "Observe to do." It is not merely the blundering and clumsy obedience of careless feet, but the earnest, thoughtful, watchful obedience of the whole mind, and soul, and heart. It takes pains to find out the will of God, as well as to do it; it heeds and hearkens, as well as runs to do His bidding. How often hearkening is emphasized in the Old Testament! "Obedience is better than sacrifice, and to hearken than the fat of rams." The obedient heart is one that listens for the whisper of His voice, watching daily at wisdom's door to know the heavenly message, and vigilantly observing that it make no mistake. Most of the failures and faults of our lives arise not from intent, but from culpable ignorance. We ought to have known better, and our ignorance will not excuse us. Therefore, a spirit of meditation upon God's law, and thorough familiarity with it, is required on the part of Joshua. Do we thus study our Bible? Do we meditate on its precepts day and night? Do we thus diligently compare our life with His Word? Do we regulate our hearts, our homes, and our conversations according to His Word? Do we deal with our friends and our foes according to the very Word of God?

A sanctified life is a life conformed to the Scriptures in every particular. It commences with our hearts; it next reaches our ears, and then it is accomplished in our feet. First, we love the Lord our God with all our heart, next we hearken to His voice, and finally, we walk in all His ways. Hence, in the anointing of the ancient priest, the thumb of the right hand was anointed as a symbol of the faith that takes God's promises; and the right ear and the right foot, as an expression of the obedience that hearkens and follows.

We need a very attentive ear and a very watchful spirit, to escape being deceived, and to avoid missing the Master's perfect will. There is no more solemn instance in all the Old Testament, than the story of the nameless prophet who came from Judah to Bethel, in the days of Jeroboam, and at God's command, boldly denounced the idolatry of Israel's king, and bore witness for Jehovah with magnificent fidelity, and at the risk of his life. Then he started home, but on his way, disobeyed Jehovah in a very small and apparently trifling thing. God had told him to go home without lingering on the way, and not to enter any man's house until he had left the accursed land. But on his way back, another prophet enticed him, by telling him that he also was a prophet, and had received a word from the Lord, bidding him to tarry for a night at his house. He listened to the insidious temptation, went home with the false prophet, and the next day, as he was pursuing his way home, a lion met him on the way and devoured him, because he had broken the command of his God.

God would thus emphasize the meaning of real obedience, and the way He regards the slightest deviation from His perfect law. And though He has in His great long suffering, often borne with many of us, none the less does He hate our negligence, and sometimes indifference; and none the less does real holiness and obedience involve such watchful and entire regard to His slightest word.

2. But our obedience must be invariable and inflexible – "turn not to the right hand or to the left." There can be no compromise about it; it is as inflexible with respect to the least as to the greatest command. The highest test of the spirit of obedience is always given in some little thing. When God hung the testing of the human race upon a single act in the garden of Eden, it was not a great act, but a simple abstinence from a single indulgence, so

slight as to be in itself unimportant; but for that very reason, the greater test of the spirit of obedience. When a thing itself is insignificant, we do it not for its own sake, or because of its intrinsic value, but because we have respect for the will of our Master. Therefore, in almost every case, the most fatal acts of disobedience are little compromises. A bold and daring act of wickedness compels us to recognize our awful position and carries with it a certain check; but a trifling compromise escapes the ordinary conscience, and leads on by imperceptible stages to the final and farthest degrees of disobedience and sin. Saul lost his kingdom, not by refusing to do what God commanded him, but by doing nearly all that he was sent to do, and simply compromising on one little detail. He went against Amalek, he took much trouble and underwent many sacrifices, perhaps risked his life in the campaign, defeated armies and destroyed cities, and thought he had done all that he had been told to do; but he simply put aside a little of the spoil for himself, and received the awful rebuke, "Obedience is better than sacrifice, and to hearken, than the fat of rams. Because thou hast rejected the word of the Lord, He also hath rejected thee from being king."

David has emphasized in the one hundred and nineteenth Psalm this essential quality of true obedience in these great words: "I esteem all thy precepts concerning *all things* to be right, and I hate every false way."

And Jesus has put it into a still more emphatic sentence in His last words to His disciples: "Ye are my friends if ye do whatsoever I command you."

As the principle of faith was illustrated in the early incidents of the Book of Joshua, by the story of Jericho, so the principle of obedience is exemplified in the failure of Achan and the defeat of Israel at Ai.

Flushed with their first victory, Israel's hosts marched against Ai, expecting an easy triumph. But they were surprised to find that their hosts were hurled back in defeat. Joshua threw himself on his face before the Lord, but God would not listen to his prayers, but commanded him immediately to arise and put away the sin which had brought dishonor to Israel and separated them from the presence and blessing of God. "Neither will I be with you any more," was the awful threatening, "unless ye put away the accursed thing from among you." How solemn the lesson! how fearful the effect of a single sin!

But there was a remedy for their disobedience; the sin was to be acknowledged, brought into the light, and put away forever; and then God said, in that wonderful message, "Fear not; see, I have given into thy hands the king of Ai, and his people, and his city, and his land."

Is there a remedy for the disobedience of the sanctified Christian? Yes! surely God is not less merciful to His dear children than He is to the ungodly world, and it is graciously true of us, His people, that "if we confess our sins, He is faithful and just to forgive our sins, and to cleanse us from all unrighteousness." The way is very simple: confess; call the evil by its right name; recognize it in God's light; do not excuse or palliate it, or call it by some complimentary term, but bring it out into the full light of God's holiness, and forever abandon it, as an accursed thing, and the blood of Jesus will not only expiate it, but will wash away its stain and cleanse you from all unrighteousness, restoring you to more than your former place in God's fellowship and favor.

We have a still further illustration in this book of Joshua of the true spirit of obedience, in the incident related in the ninth chapter, with respect to the Gibeonites. It will be remembered that these men came in disguise, pretending that they were pilgrims from a far country, and by their wiles they inveigled Joshua into a treaty with them which became a permanent snare. This illustrates the spirit of watchful obedience and hearkening to God, and the necessity of constant vigilance, if we would know His perfect will and not be deceived by the wiles of the adversary.

And so these two words – Faith and Obedience – are interwoven with the story of the first Canaan, even as they are inseparable from any true experience of our higher spiritual inheritance. Indeed, faith and obedience are the reverse sides of the same shield. When Abraham's faith is spoken of in the Epistle to the Hebrews, it is called obedience. "By faith Abraham, when he was called to go out to the place that he should have received as an inheritance, *obeyed*." And indeed, the old Saxon word believe, is just a combination of the two words – live, and by. To believe is to "live by" the thing you believe; that is, to translate it into your daily life and conduct. Hence, the Apostle speaks of those who "having put away a good conscience, have made shipwreck of their faith." You cannot obey rightly without a true faith, and you cannot keep the true faith if you cease to obey.

Let us join together the wings of faith and obedience, and so mount up into the heavenly places and press our glorious way into the heights of grace and glory.

CHAPTER IV.

THE CONFLICT AND THE CONQUEROR.

"Finally, my brethren, be strong in the Lord, and in the power of his might. Put on the whole armour of God, that ye may be able to stand against the wiles of the devil. For we wrestle not against flesh and blood, but against principalities, against powers, against the rulers of the darkness of this world, against spiritual wickedness in high places. Wherefore take unto you the whole armour of God, that ye may be able to withstand in the evil day, and having done all, to stand. Stand therefore, having your loins girt about with truth, and having on the breastplate of righteousness; And your feet shod with the preparation of the gospel of peace; Above all, taking the shield of faith, wherewith ye shall be able to quench all the fiery darts of the wicked. And take the helmet of salvation, and the sword of the Spirit, which is the word of God: Praying always with all prayer and supplication in the Spirit, and watching thereunto with all perseverance and supplication for all saints;" – Eph. 6:10-18.

THE Book of Joshua is a story of conflict and victory. Almost every chapter echoes the thought of this picture in Ephesians of our spiritual warfare with the principalities and powers in heavenly places.

I. CONQUERING BUT NOT POSSESSING.

"And to the Reubenites, and to the Gadites, and to half the tribe of Manasseh, spake Joshua, saying: Remember the word which Moses, the servant of the Lord, commanded you, saying, The Lord your God hath given you rest, and hath given you this land. Your wives, your little ones and your cattle, shall remain in the land which Moses gave you on this side Jordan; but ye shall pass before your brethren, armed, all the mighty men of valor, and help them; until the Lord have given your brethren rest, as He hath given you, and they also have possessed the land which the Lord your God giveth them; then ye shall return unto the land of your possession and enjoy it, which Moses, the Lord's servant gave you on this side Jordan toward the sunrising." – Josh. 1:12-15.

Here we have the story of the Reubenites, the Gadites, and half the tribe of Manasseh. They had chosen their inheritance on the wilderness side of Jordan, but they were required by the Lord to leave their wives and children in their inheritance, and pass on with their brethren and assist them in fighting their battles, and conquering the western tribes and nations. This they did; and not until Joshua had subdued the whole land did they return to Gilead and settle down with their families on their chosen heritage.

Now this, at first sight, looks like a brave and loyal course. They sacrificed the comforts of home. They separated from those who were dear to them. They risked their lives and exposed themselves to dangers and toils, to fight the battles of the Lord. They crossed the Jordan and fought the giants of Canaan. Are they not examples of a high and holy consecration and a most unselfish victory?

This is all true; but back of it the fact remains that they had deliberately chosen their inheritance on the other side of the Jordan, in the land that bordered on the world, and they went back to it as soon as they were through their campaign, and made it their permanent home.

They are types of a great many people who believe in the truths of a higher Christian life, who testify for them, who contend earnestly for them, who fight their battles, who help others to enter into them, who lead, perhaps, hundreds of souls into deeper blessing, who pass through, in a certain sense, the experience of Jordan, and live for a time in the Land of Promise and know much of the deeper things of God; but they do not stay there; their chosen rest is somewhere nearer the world, and they always recognize their home and resting-place as on the wilderness side.

It is possible to know all about these things in theory, it is possible to have a certain experience of them for a time, and yet to be sojourners, not residents; to be working for the truth rather than enjoying it, and living it; and to settle down at last, not, perhaps, in the world, but on its borders, and find, as these trans-Jordanic tribes did, in the end, that the world, beside which they so willingly sat down, at last sweeps over them, and finally almost blots them out of existence.

Where are we living? Where are our interests and affections invested? Where have you got your money? What is your real home and the center of your life?

It is not enough to be fighting for the truth and helping others to receive it. Are you yourself living it, and wholly committed to it? Which side of Jordan is your home?

II. FIGHTING AND NOT PREVAILING.

"Israel hath sinned, and they have also transgressed my covenant which I commanded them; for they have even taken of the accursed thing, and have also stolen, and dissembled also, and they have put it even among their own stuff. Therefore the children of Israel could not stand before their enemies, . . . because they were accursed; neither will I be with you any more, except ye destroy the accursed thing from among you." – Josh. 7:11-12.

We here see the hosts of Israel for the first time turned back before their enemies. There was no lack of faith, apparently, for their confidence was so great that they attacked Ai with a small contingent, and expected it would be an easy victory. But they were ignominiously routed and defeated. The reason was very plain: they had sinned, and sin always brings defeat and failure. Faith cannot live except in an atmosphere of purity; the slightest disobedience will wither it and leave us exposed to the successful fury of our foes. God was obliged to dishonor even His own cause, rather than countenance evil. One enemy in the camp is worse than a million in front. We must keep pure and walk in obedience, or we shall always fail. "Holding faith, and a good conscience, which some having put away (that is, a good conscience), concerning faith, have made shipwreck."

III. RISING OUT OF FAILURE AND DEFEAT.

"And the Lord said unto Joshua, Fear not, neither be thou dismayed: take all the people of war with thee, and arise, go up into Ai: see, I have given into thy hand the king of Ai, and his people, and his city, and his land." – Josh. 8:1.

Here we see the army which yesterday was flying from their pursuers, today marching forward with undismayed, victorious tread, and carrying all before them.

The secret was very simple: they had put away their sin, and God had also put it away; and now He meets them with a yet bolder assurance of victory and blessing.

There is still for us the same remedy. When sin has come between us and the Lord, there is but one thing for us to do: it must be definitely recognized and utterly put away. We must go right back to the very thing, however hard, and deal with it definitely and thoroughly, and then all the train of sins and sorrows that came with it will pass away, and God will start afresh with us, as if it had never been. The simple direction in the New Testament is, "If we confess our sins, He is faithful and just to forgive us our sins, and to cleanse us from all unrighteousness."

This one little word, "confess," is explicit and unambiguous. It does not mean merely to ignore it, or even to be sorry for it, but to recognize it, identify it, and call it by its right name.

What God wants is to bring the evil to light, strip it of its disguises, force it out of its hiding place and bring it into the light of His Holy Word, so that it can never again deceive us. And therefore, we must confess it to God, to ourselves, and, if anyone else has been wronged, to the one we have injured. Then God will immediately forgive it, cleanse it, and clear away all the avalanche that has accumulated around it.

If I have a thorn in my finger, it will fester; my hand will swell, my arm will become involved, and gradually my whole body will suffer, and I will die if the trouble continues. What am I to do? Treat the finger, the hand and the arm with lotions and plasters? No, take out the thorn. Until you do that, all the treatment is vain; but the moment you remove the irritating thorn, the trouble will cease.

Back of all your defects, temptations, and wrongs, there is one little fault in which all the trouble began. Go back at once, lay your pride in the dust; don't be afraid to confess that you have lost your sanctification. You have not lost Jesus, but you cannot touch Him again until you recognize this thing and lay it on the sin-offering. Then, in a moment, He will become your righteousness, and go on with you as before.

You may hang on to the fiction of your sanctification all you please, but ever back of it lies the fact of your unconfessed sin, which will explode all your hopes like a sunken torpedo.

A friend said publicly, a few days ago, "Almost all our troubles and spiritual difficulties would be removed if we would just call things by their right names."

There is a whole world of truth in this simple thought. God is utterly upright and honest, and we must deal honestly with Him and with ourselves, if we would "walk in the light." "If we walk in the light, as He is in the light, we have fellowship one with the other, and the blood of Jesus Christ, His Son, cleanseth us from all sin." – 1Jn. 1:7.

We need not be afraid of the light and all its disclosures, because the blood is ever there to cleanse.

Let us welcome our great High Priest, who comes to us with the lamp in one hand and the hyssop in the other, wherewith to cleanse the sin that He reveals, and to keep us by the sprinkling of His blood, so cleansed and purified that we shall not fear the light, but gladly come to it, that our "deeds may be made manifest, that they are wrought in God."

IV. THE WILES OF THE DEVIL.

Our great adversary does not usually make his attacks openly. He is a master of strategy, and his greatest art is to hide his hand, and to attack us in disguise.

His choicest argument is to try to prove to people that there is no devil.

Nothing pleases him so much as to lose his identity, and when he comes to us, persuade us that his insinuations and suggestions are the voice of God, or the thoughts of our own minds. He loves "to call evil good, and good evil." He is an adept in mixing moral principles and compromising things. He is a great diplomat, and our greatest need of a Divine equipment is that we "may be able to stand against the wiles of the devil."

We see all this very finely illustrated and typified in the conduct of the Gibeonites, in the ninth chapter of Joshua. They found they could not resist Israel in open warfare, and so they resorted to subterfuge. Disguised as travelers from a far country, arrayed in old clothes, and carrying provisions that seemed to have been brought from distant lands, they pretended that they were a company of pilgrims from afar, and before Joshua had taken time to counsel with the Lord, he was entrapped into a league with them, contrary to the Divine command, and was obliged to keep them in Israel under honorable protection, through all the coming centuries. True, they were degraded to the rank of servants, but their presence and influence were there all the same, and they became snares and sources of temptation which eventually led to loss of the national separation, and the judgments of God upon their backsliding.

Oh, how many Christians have been led into similar compromises! Some evil course has been presented to you under the guise of harmless indulgence, or possibly Divine revelation.

Some compromise with evil has been made, under the plea of doing good to some one and obtaining an influence over him for his spiritual benefit. Some business partnership has been formed which has entangled you in all your financial affairs for the rest of your life, and put your money at the disposal of the devil and the world, because you allowed yourself to be drawn into this compromise under some plausible pretext.

How many times a Christian girl has allowed herself to become attached to an ungodly man, in order to save him, and given her life to him in marriage, and the result has been that either both are lost, or she is held back and embarrassed in all the future course by his unholy influence.

The Church is full of Gibeonites today, and they are leading her into backsliding and imbecility.

What is the remedy? It is very plain. "And the men took of their victuals, and asked not counsel at the mouth of the Lord."

They are not blamed for exercising bad judgment, they are not condemned for lack of wisdom, for it was a case where their wisdom was wholly unequal to the emergency, and where they were absolutely dependent upon the will of God; but, confident in their own good sense, they did as sensible people so often do, relied upon their own judgment and made a fatal error.

Oh! how true it is that "the wayfaring man, though a fool, shall not err," but "He taketh the wise in their own craftiness."

In this heavenly life we are insufficient even to think anything as of ourselves, but we must ever depend upon the mind of Christ, and the counsel of the Holy Ghost, or we shall fall into continual error, and be involved in the most fatal mistakes.

"Trust in the Lord with all thy heart, and lean not to thine own understanding. In all thy ways acknowledge Him, and He shall direct thy steps."

"He that trusteth in his own heart is a fool, but he that putteth his trust in the Lord, he shall be safe."

V. TREADING ON CONQUERED FOES.

"Then said Joshua, Open the mouth of the cave, and bring out those five kings unto me out of the cave. And they did so, and brought forth those five kings unto him out of the cave, the king of Jerusalem, the king of Hebron, the king of Jarmouth, the king of Lachish, and the king of Eglon. And it came to pass, when they brought out those kings unto Joshua, that Joshua called for all the men of Israel, and said unto the captains of the men of war which went with him, Come near, put your feet upon the necks of these kings. And they came near, and put their feet upon the necks of them." – Josh. 10:22-25.

This is a picture of our attitude toward our great adversary. We are not equal to the conflict if we allow him to get on our level. If we meet him breast-high, we shall be struck by his dragon wing. But if we keep him under our feet, we shall be upheld.

"The very God of peace shall bruise Satan under your feet."

"Behold, I give you power to tread on serpents and scorpions, and on the whole power of the enemy."

Christ has conquered our enemies, and He brings them forth to us, and bids us put our feet where He has already put His, and we must not fear to do so. We must boldly take a stand, and we shall have victory. We must not give place to the devil.

Nothing encourages him so much as fear, and nothing dwarfs him and drives him away so quickly as audacity.

If you for a moment acknowledge his power, you give him that power. If you for a moment recognize that he is in you, you will find that he is in you. If you let the thought or consciousness of evil into your spirit, you have lost your purity. If you "reckon yourself dead indeed," you will find that you are "dead indeed." If you recognize him as in your heart, he will stay in your heart. If you put your foot upon his neck and stand in victory, shouting, "Thanks be to God, who always causeth us to triumph in Christ," you shall hold your victorious stand, and be "more than conqueror through Him who loved you."

VI. UNCOMPROMISING WAR.

"There was not a city that made peace with Israel, save the Hivites, the inhabitants of Gibeon; all other they took in battle." – Josh. 11:19.

This was a war of extermination, or should have been. These Hivites should never have been admitted to peace. They were the Gibeonites who made the forbidden league with Joshua.

There was no possible meeting ground between Israel and the Canaanites. One was the seed of Satan, the other the seed of God. And so in our spiritual warfare there is no place for compromise.

God can do more with a single, uncompromising Christian than with a whole nation of mixed people.

There is no more extraordinary spectacle than the contrast between the kingdom of Judah and the men of Babylon.

For more than six centuries God tried through Judah's kings, and priests and prophets, to magnify His name among the heathen, but they always failed Him.

There was much good in them. There was a Jehoshaphat, a Hezekiah, a Josiah, an Isaiah, a Jeremiah, a Hosea, and many a holy prophet; but there was a mixture of worldliness, idolatry and sin which always checked the perfect blessing, and qualified the best service.

Consequently, Judah failed, and at last even the temple had to fall, and the name of God was blasphemed among the heathen, and Nebuchadnezzar glorified his gods because they had triumphed over the God of Israel.

Then God rejected the nation and selected the individual.

He took out a Daniel, a Shadrach, a Meshach, an Abednego; and, first of all, he separated them from the evil of their time, and gave them a purpose and a principle which refused to compromise with anything contrary to the will of God.

The secret of their victory was all expressed in two single sentences:

"Daniel purposed in his heart that he would not defile himself with the king's meat."

These men answered: "We are not careful to answer thee in this matter, O king. If it be so, our God whom we serve is able to deliver us from the burning fiery furnace, and He will deliver us out of thy hand, O king. But if not, be it known unto thee, O king, that we will not serve thy gods, nor worship the golden image which thou hast set up."

This was the gage of battle, and the battle was short, but decisive. Such men must ever be victorious.

Before the story of their life was all told, God had humbled Babylon and Persia, and the two proudest kings of antiquity had issued a decree that there was no God like Jehovah, and even provided for the restoration of Israel and the return of the captives to Jerusalem.

Four uncompromising men were stronger than all the kings of Judah, and all the pride and power of Nebuchadnezzar and Cyrus. These are the men that God wants in these last days, wholly consecrated and utterly uncompromising men who will stand where God has placed them, and on whom heaven can wholly depend.

VII. RECOGNIZING GOD'S HAND OVER THE HAND OF OUR ENEMIES.

"For it was of the Lord to harden their hearts, that they should come against Israel in battle, that He might destroy them utterly, and that they might have no favor, but that He might destroy them, as the Lord commanded Moses." – Josh. 11:20.

It must often have seemed discouraging to Joshua and his brave followers, after each successive victory, to see still before him fortress after fortress, and foe after foe, and to find the campaign renewed again and again, until slowly the whole land was successfully subjugated. But as each enemy came with fiercest hate and strongest force, we are told that "it was of the Lord to harden their hearts that they should come against Israel in battle."

God sent each one of them in turn, – not a single one was accidental. Every one of these tests was needed, and, unconsciously to themselves, they were fulfilling the word of God, and becoming tributary to His great purpose.

There are two ways that God can use a man. One is with the intelligent and loving consent of the man, as a fellow worker with God. The other is, to be used in spite of himself, by the sovereign will of God, overruling his life in mighty power for the glory of God and the good of others.

It is a very awful thing to be used in this way; but God will use everything, even the wrath of man and the hate of Satan.

Some people are called to go as angels on missions of love; some are called to be street scavengers, sewers, or files, to keep God's people pure and sweet. If that is your business, go ahead and do it. God can use you to teach His people patience. But God have mercy on you when He is done with you!

Everything that comes in our life is permitted of God, for our complete training. Everything that reveals itself in your own heart and life is a part of God's final plan, to show you that thing, in order that you may be saved from it, be strengthened against it, and be made a better man through the discovery.

When you find anything wrong in your heart and life, rejoice that you find it. Take victory over it, and go on praising God for His faithfulness.

When you meet an enemy that is too strong for you, rejoice and fall back on God, who will give you power to come back a victor, and stronger for that temptation.

"Blessed is the man that endureth temptation, for when he is tried he shall receive the crown of life that the Lord hath promised to them that love Him."

Do not attempt to run away from your life, but let it make you run to God for more of His fullness and grace, and you will often sing,

> Happy for me was the thorn that stung,
>   And sent my heart crying to Thee;
> Thanks for the sorrow that taught me to find
>   Thy grace all-sufficient for me.

VIII. THE CAPTAIN OF OUR SALVATION.

The secret of victory is all found in the vision of the Captain.

"And it came to pass, when Joshua was by Jericho, that he lifted up his eyes and looked, and behold, there stood a man over against him with his sword drawn in his hand; and Joshua went unto him, and said unto him, Art thou for us, or for our adversaries? And he said: Nay; but as captain of the host of the Lord am I now come. And Joshua fell on his face to the earth, and did worship, and said unto him, What saith my Lord unto His servant?" – Josh. 5:13-14.

We are accustomed to think of Joshua as the type of Christ, and Moses as the type of the law. But I believe this is a mistake. Joshua is simply the pattern of a man of faith, and Christ Himself seems to be revealed, in this book, not in Joshua, but in the Captain whom Joshua met as he stood over against Jericho.

This was none other than the Son of God, our victorious Leader, who wants to bring us also into the Land of Promise, if we, like Joshua, will die to our own strength, and accept Him as our leader and our Lord.

Have we done so?

All our experiences, all our toils, all our failures are meant to teach us our utter insufficiency. It is not His help we need; it is Himself, as our All in All.

We have proved the promise, "I will strengthen thee," but that is not sufficient.

We have tested the great word, "Yea, I will help thee," but even His help has not been enough. We have come to the end of all this, and, fainting at His feet, we have sunk in utter despair.

Then it is that the greatest promise comes, "Yea, I will uphold thee with the right hand of my righteousness."

This is something more. This is His upholding altogether, when He takes us in His very arms, and carries us Himself, and we just trust and see Him triumph.

Then, indeed, we shall accept the testimony of the Apostle, "I am not sufficient to account anything as of myself, but my sufficiency is of God;" and of this greater word, "Thanks be unto God, which always leadeth us in triumph, through Jesus Christ."

CHAPTER V.

THIRTY-ONE KINGS, OR THE VICTORY OVER SELF.

"THESE are the kings of the country which Joshua and the children of Israel smote on this side Jordan on the west. . . . All the kings were thirty and one. – Josh. 12:7-24.

"Arba was a great man among the Anakims." – Josh. 14:15.

"Caleb drove out thence the three sons of Anak, Sheshai, Ahiman, and 'Talmai." – Josh. 15:14.

"For the love of Christ constraineth us; because we thus judge, that if one died for all, then were all dead: and that He died for all, that they which live should not henceforth live unto themselves, but unto Him which died for them and rose again." – 2Cor. 5:14-15.

These words describe the great conflict of the higher Christian life in the Land of Promise. This is not a conflict with the grosser forms of sin, for we leave them behind us when we cross the Jordan and come into the land of holiness, obedience, and rest.

Surely it ought to go without saying, that no consecrated Christian would dare to indulge in willful disobedience or sin. But there are other foes more subtle, and these are symbolized, we believe, by these kings with whom Joshua made war so long.

They are the various forms of self-life which, while not perhaps directly and willfully sinful, in the grosser sense, are yet as contrary to the will of God, and as necessary to be subdued and slain, before the soul can be in perfect harmony with the Divine will. They are all tyrants which, if allowed to remain, will ultimately bring us into subjection to sin and separate us from the Lord.

They belong to one family, and the progenitor of everyone of them is Arba, the father of Anak; and his firstborn son, Anak, has perpetuated his generation through many children, and the numerous offspring constitute a line of no less than thirty-one; so that there is a foe for every day in the month, in the Christian's calendar.

The name Arba means – "the strength of Baal." This represents the strength of the natural heart. Baal was the ancient Sidonian god of nature, and Arba stands for the natural heart, in all the force of its self-will and self-sufficiency.

The name of his son, Anak, signifies in Hebrew, "long-necked," and everybody knows that a long neck suggests pride and self-will; so that these two names express the character of the whole family.

The other three sons whose names are mentioned, Sheshai, Ahiman, and Talmai, carry out the family resemblance.

Sheshai means – "free," suggesting the idea of the license in which selfishness delights.

Talmai means – "bold," representing the independence of the self-life, which brooks no control.

Ahiman means – "brother of men," and expresses aptly the humanitarianism which ignores God, and would make humanity a god unto itself, expressing the self-sufficiency of the race, rather than of the individual.

Shall we look at these kings of the old Self Dynasty, and see if we can recognize any of them in our own experience?

I. SELF-WILL.

This is old Arba, the head of the dynasty. It expresses its decrees in the personal pronoun and the active verb – I will, I shall. It recognizes no king but its own imperative choice.

Arba must die before Hebron can be won by Caleb. Self-will must be slain before love can reign.

Yield yourself unto God, is the watchword at the gate of holiness and peace.

It is not only the evil will, but the self-will that must die. Things that it would be right for us to have, God cannot give us when we want them willfully, and therefore He has often to crucify us to our own will, for no other reason than to break us, and make us self-surrendered and wholly subjected to His control.

Often, therefore, in our lives, we have had to surrender something to Him which He really wished us to have; and later in our life, when we no longer wanted it because we wanted it, but because it was His will for us, He could trust us with it without harm, and it was freely given, when we could receive it no longer as a selfish idol, but as a Divine trust.

So God had to take Isaac from Abraham, and then give him back as no longer Abraham's Isaac, but God's.

The will thus surrendered becomes a stronger will, because it is henceforth not our will, but His within us; and when we choose, we choose with the strength of God, and choose forever.

Have we yielded our will and received His in return? Has the city of Arba become the city of Hebron, and the home of His love?

II. SELF-INDULGENCE.

This is the gratification of self in any of its forms. Is it wrong to eat and drink, and indulge our appetites? No, the act may not be wrong in itself, but it becomes wrong when we do it for the sake of the indulgence. I am not to eat because it gratifies me to eat; I am not to drink because I enjoy the act, but I am to eat and drink for the glory of God; that is, with the distinct thought and purpose of pleasing Him and ministering to my bodily wants that I may be strong to serve and glorify Him. It is the thought of self-gratification that defiles the act which in itself is right, but in its motive may be wholly selfish and sinful.

So the commonest acts of life are to be wholly consecrated to Him and done unto Him, and thus they become sacred and holy.

Have we learned the secret of thus living for His glory, and dying unto ourselves?

III. SELF-SEEKING

is one of the forms of self-life which must be surrendered. "Love seeketh not her own." Her object is not to accomplish some personal end, but to benefit another and to glorify God.

The great business of the people of this world is to seek their own ends, aggrandizements, honors and pleasures. But a consecrated life has but one purpose: to "seek the kingdom of God and His righteousness," and then to rest in His will, knowing that "all these things shall be added."

IV. SELF-COMPLACENCY.

This is the spirit of Anak, the long-necked one. It is the spirit of pride; the pride that takes delight in our own qualities and rests with satisfaction in ourselves.

It is very different from vanity, which seeks the approval of others. Self-complacency is so satisfied with itself that it cares little for the opinion of others, and has a lofty independence about it that even scorns their criticism and rises superior to their praise. It is a god unto itself.

It is one of the most subtle forms of self-life, and has a sort of lofty grandeur which blinds its possessor to its danger and its deep sinfulness.

V. SELF-GLORYING

is the converse of this. It seeks the praise of others, rather than its own. It may be very small in its own eyes, and for this very reason tries to shine in the eyes of others.

A lady of rank is not dependent upon her dress or her equipage for her position, but is usually very simple. It is the lack of real greatness that makes the society butterfly eager to attract attention by her gaudy display.

Self-glorying vaunts itself and inflates its little bubble because it is so small. There is no creature so diminutive in its real proportions, when really reduced to its actual dimensions, as the dude and the daughter of fashion.

The truly consecrated life wants none of this. It is conscious of its nothingness, and knows that it is dependent on God alone for all it can ever possess, and therefore it covers its face with the veil of His loveliness, and robes itself in His own righteousness, and then hides in His bosom, saying, "Not I, but Christ that liveth in me."

VI. SELF-CONFIDENCE.

This is a form of self-life which relies upon its own wisdom, strength and righteousness. It is Simon Peter, saying, "Though all men shall deny thee, yet will not I."

This is your man of strong common sense and self-reliance. He believes in his own opinion. He relies upon his own judgment. He laughs at the people who talk about Divine guidance and the Spirit's leadings.

This must die before we can become established in the strength of Christ. Therefore, the strongest natures have often to fail in order to bring them to the end of self, and lead them, like Peter, to lean on God, and like Jacob, with wounded thigh, to go forth depending henceforth on the strength of God.

Closely allied to this is

VII. SELF-CONSCIOUSNESS.

This is the self that is always thinking of itself and covered with its own shadow.

Every act and look and word is studied. Every feeling and inward state is morbidly photographed upon the inward senses.

Sometimes we become conscious of our own physical organism. We watch our breath, our pulses, our temperature, and our physical state. We carry about with us continually a morbid consciousness of our functions and conditions. All the simplicity is taken away. We are bound to ourselves like a man with his hand on his own collar, trying to pull himself along.

This is a dreadful bondage. God wants us to have the freedom of a simple child, that acts without thinking from spontaneous impulses and with a beautiful liberty. He does not want us to see the shining of our faces, to be conscious of our holy acts, or to make a note of every sacrifice and service; but He would have us, when He comes at the last, to say, "I was an hungered and ye gave me meat; I was thirsty, and ye gave me drink;" to be so self-forgetful that we shall answer back, "When saw we thee an hungered and fed thee, or thirsty, and gave thee drink?"

How shall we get out of this wretched self-consciousness?

Only by getting into a higher consciousness, even the presence of our Lord, and a purpose and object beyond ourselves, to live for God and others, and realize that He is living for us, and living in us, in those sweet, spontaneous impulses, that are the true springs of action.

An exaggerated form of self-consciousness is

VIII. SELF-IMPORTANCE.

This is very offensive and yet very common. Some people carry it in their very gait and bearing, as they walk along the street, and almost tempt one to step up to them and ask the question which it is said Sydney Smith used occasionally to ask of people whom he saw on the street, "Excuse me, sir, but may I ask if you are anybody in particular?"

This is not the usual accompaniment of true greatness, but it is very common in very small men and women, who make up for their lack of real weight by an immense amount of self-assertion and swaggering assumption.

This is very offensive to a true Christian taste.

Holy modesty will show itself in the very bearing.

True humility consists not so much in thinking meanly of ourselves, as in not thinking of ourselves at all. And the ripe head of wheat always hangs down in proportion to its weight.

Closely allied to this is

IX. SELF-DEPRECIATION.

This is just as bad as the other. Some people are egregiously conscious of their own shortcoming and inability. It keeps them from useful service, and is always thrusting its littleness and nothingness upon every situation.

If it sees its name in print, it is afraid of being puffed up. If asked to be seated on the platform, it will blush and shrink, and hide away. If called upon to do some service, it will refuse on the ground of inability. This is all self.

A truly-surrendered heart hasn't got any name to see in print, any person to be conscious of any power to serve. Its name has been given to Christ, and if He wants it used, let Him have it, and blaze it before the universe in fame or infamy. It hasn't any ability to work, and if Christ wants to send it, He must equip it and supply it with all necessary resources.

Therefore, it goes unquestioning, und fully assured, because all its strength must come from God.

X. SELF-VINDICATION.

This is the self that stands for its own rights and avenges its wrongs. It is quick to detect an injury or an offense, and to express its sense of it in some marked and unmistakable way.

It believes in receiving the respect and consideration due to it in all cases, and while it asks nothing beyond, yet it insists upon all its rights.

It is not egregious in its own conceit. It does not demand applause beyond its merits, but it asks proper consideration, and is going to have it.

Now, this is a very respectable, but a very real form of selfishness. It is directly contrary to the spirit of Christianity and the Lord Jesus Christ.

The very idea of His incarnation was the renunciation of all His rights. Being in the form of God, He was entitled to be equal with God, but we are told He did not count this a prize, but "He emptied Himself and made Himself of no reputation."

If God wants to bring you here, it is very easy for Him to empty you, and make you of no reputation, and there will be lots of people who will be ready to help Him do it. But it is very lovely to do this ourselves, as Jesus did, and not wait to have it done for us.

The very essence of Christ's humiliation was that He gave up all His heavenly rights, and when He came down to earth He gave up all His earthly rights, and made it the business of His life to let go, until there was nothing left to give up, but even His very life was yielded.

You have not begun to deal with the question of self-surrender until it reaches your dearest rights, and you let them go into His hand as a glorious deposit; and every time you do so, He puts it down in your bank account, and when the interest has all accumulated, O! how He will pay you back, – much of it in this world, but how much more in the day of eternal recompense!

I solemnly believe that most of the blessings that have been given to me in my life and ministry have come because of the evil things people have said of me, and because God made me willing to allow them to do it.

"Let Shimei curse; it may be the Lord will requite you good for his cursing this day."

is one of the most painful forms of selfishness.

One day, in India, I picked up a beautiful little vine that was spreading over the ground. I thought how lovely it would be to press it in my notebook. But by the time I had taken it up it disappeared, and there was nothing left in my hand but a long string on which the leaves had been. It was as stiff and hard as a leafless stem, and I said, “Why, where has my plant gone?” I looked on the ground, and the other leaves were spreading over the grass as before, but I could see no trace of the one I supposed I had dropped.

I looked at the little dry stem in my hand again, and I found it was the same little branch I had picked from the ground, but its leaves had all folded up as firm and dry as if it had been struck by an autumn blast. And when I touched the other leaves on the ground, they disappeared in the same way. Then I said, “Why, it is a sensitive plant!”

I thought of people I had seen who had been all bright and radiant for a time, but something touched them that was offensive, uncongenial, or humbling, and they suddenly disappeared and shrank into such hard, dry, leafless sticks that there was no point of contact with them. They seemed to have become all at once like Egyptian mummies, ready for a glass case. What is the matter! Self!

“Great peace have they that love thy law, and nothing shall offend them.” The Lord bring and keep us there!

There is a place where we can be, or rather where we can cease to be; and Christ become instead of me. And of that place it is true, “He that was begotten of God keepeth him, and that wicked one toucheth him not.”

XII. SELF-SEEING.

There are some people who always see things from their own side. How does this affect *me*?

You see your own side of it, but if you would wait and see your brother's side, if you would be willing to believe that there is another side, you, yourself, would be saved from a thousand stings and others from a thousand misunderstandings.

"Look not every man on his own things, but every man also on the things of others." Put yourself in your brother's place. Take into consideration his circumstances, his views. Think how you would act if you felt as he feels, saw with his eyes, were placed as he is placed. You will be surprised to see how differently you will look at things. And yet this is only one of the first things in the holy art of self-forgetfulness.

XIII. INTROSPECTION.

Our morbid and excessive self-examination is one of the forms of self-life that causes much pain and works much injury in our Christian life.

There is a right, but there is a wrong, self-examination. God alone can truly search us. We are very apt, when we attempt it ourselves, to get poisoned with the effluvia of the sepulcher into which we penetrate. Even Paul said, "Yea, I judge not mine own self, but He that judgeth me is the Lord."

Let us commit our own way unto Him, and honestly say, "Search me, O God, and know my heart; try me and know my thoughts, and see if there be any wicked way in me, and lead me in the way everlasting."

Thus let us walk in Him, trust Him to show us all we need to see, and then believe, "if in anything we be otherwise minded, God will reveal even this unto us."

XIV. SELF-LOVE

is the root of all these forms of the self-life. It is a heart centered upon itself, and so long as this is the case, every affection and every power of our being is turned inward and self-ward, and the whole character distorted by the false adjustment of our nature; just as much as our eye would be if it were ever turning inward upon itself, rather than outward upon the objective world which it was made to perceive.

God, who is the type of all true being, is essentially love, and lives not for Himself, but for others, and when we become self-centered, we are the opposite of God, and really assume His Throne, and become gods unto ourselves.

It is the ruin and perversion of a soul to love and live for itself.

XV. SELFISH AFFECTIONS

are the natural fruit of self-life.

We love our own friends and families and the people who minister to our pleasure; and even those we love, we love not so much for the blessing that we can be to them, as for the pleasure that they minister to us.

Love that terminates on ourselves is selfish and degrading. The love that seeks another's blessing is elevating and Divine.

XVI. SELFISH MOTIVES

may enter into the highest acts and mar and pervert them to their inmost core.

It is not only what we say and do, but why. God sees the very thought and purpose, and He judges the act by its intent.

The natural heart cannot do a good thing without some selfish object which perverts and destroys its purity.

XVII. SELFISH DESIRES

are always springing up in the old natural heart, and even if they never reach fruition, or ever become choices, acts or facts, we want to be free from the very wish, and have God so give us our desires that they shall spring from Him, and be prompted by His love.

The spirit of covetousness is just a selfish desire, and God has pronounced it idolatry, and most dreadful sin.

XVIII. SELFISH CHOICES

are still more serious, for the will is the spring of human actions, and determines all our words and deeds.

We want a rightly directed will, which chooses not its own gratification, but because of "Him who worketh in us to will and to do of His good pleasure."

XIX. SELFISH PLEASURES.

There are two kinds of enjoyment: one, which we seek for its own sake, and this is selfishness; the other is the pleasure that comes to us from doing good, and because we are in harmony with God and with our own being, which is the truest enjoyment.

Selfish pleasure, the desire that seeks its own, and terminates on itself, is earth-born, transitory and wrong.

XX. SELFISH POSSESSIONS.

The worldling seeks to gain the world, and calls his possessions his own. The true child of God has nothing for himself, but holds all as a sacred trust for God. "Neither said any of them that aught of the things that they possessed was their own."

The true Christian conception of property is stewardship; the holding of the gifts of God for His service, and subject to His direction, and for His glory.

This is the sovereign remedy for avarice and the grasping spirit of the world, and we are never consecrated until all is laid, absolutely and forever, at His feet, and held there, subject constantly to His will.

XXI. SELFISH FEARS AND CARES.

Nearly all of our cares and anxiety spring from pure selfishness.

If we were wholly yielded to God, and recognized our life in its every moment as absolutely His, we would have no anxiety, but would regard ourselves as His property and under His safe and constant protection. The Lord has said, "Ye cannot serve God and Mammon," and has added, with strange logical suggestiveness, "Therefore, I say unto you, take no anxious care for the morrow."

That little word, "therefore," discovers the link between Mammon worship and anxious care.

XXII. SELFISH SORROWS.

Many of our griefs and heartbreaks spring from the purest selfishness, wounded pride, ambition, self-love, or the loss of something which we should not have called our own.

The death of self blots out a universe of wretchedness and brings a heaven of joy.

XXIII. SELFISH SACRIFICES AND SELF-DENIALS

are as real as they are paradoxical.

A man "may give all his goods to feed the poor, and his body to be burned, and have not love." He may do it all for the gratification of his vanity or the display of his orthodoxy, and the propagation of his own beliefs and opinions.

Simon Stylites, after sitting a quarter of a century on the top of a pillar, and living on roots and pauper pittances, was, perhaps, the most egregious embodiment of self-righteousness and self-consciousness in the whole world. He had denied himself to gratify himself, to exalt himself, and to save himself. It was simply the old stream of his life turned into a new channel.

And so there may be

XXIV. SELFISH VIRTUE AND MORALITY.

The Pharisees were virtuous, but their virtue was a selfish cloak, intended for display, and therefore worthless, or worse. It was simply an advertisement, and its motive destroyed its value.

The lady who walks the street with her skirts held carefully away from the touch of her fallen sister may be an icicle of selfish propriety; while her poor sister, with all her faults, may have a generous heart, and may even be sinning from some motive of mistaken love, and sacrificing herself for another. And while this does not palliate her sin, it may make her a nobler character than even the virtuous one who scorns her.

And so there is a

XXV. SELF-RIGHTEOUSNESS

which would even seek to justify itself before God by its own religious works, and thus forfeit His righteousness and salvation. For it is not of our sins alone, but even of our righteousness, that He has said, they are "as filthy rags," and they must be laid down, and we, as helpless, worthless sinners accept the righteousness of Christ for our justification before God.

We may have

XXVI. SELFISH SANCTITY AND SANCTIFICATION,

and be so absorbed in our religious experience that our eye will be taken off Jesus and centered upon ourselves, and thus we shall become offensive exhibitions of religious self-consciousness, and our very good be marred by its indirection and introversion.

True sanctification forgets itself and lives in constant dependence upon the Lord Jesus as its Righteousness and All-sufficiency.

So we may have

XXVII. SELFISH CHARITIES AND SELFISH GIFTS.

The largest generosity and the most munificent offerings of money may be only an advertisement of ourselves, and prompted by some motive which terminates on our own interest or honor.

Some people give liberally, and then hamper their gifts with so many conditions, and get themselves so wrought into the administration of their beneficence, that all its disinterestedness is lost, and it looks like the gratification of their own higher pleasure.

XXVIII. OUR CHRISTIAN WORK MAY BE SELFISH.

We may preach because of the intellectual pleasure it gives us.

We may work for the church because we like the church, the minister, or the people.

We may engage in a benevolent or Christian profession because it enables us to make a comfortable livelihood, and gives us congenial employment.

Or we may do our religious work on selfish principles, and from religious selfishness.

The Church of God today is blighted by the selfishness of her evangelistic work. She is spending seven hundred times as much for her own people as she does upon the heathen world, and the spirit of religious selfishness runs through all her plans.

XXIX. SELFISH PRAYERS.

There is nothing that sounds so selfish as the prayers of many Christians.

They travel in a circle about the size of their own body and soul, their family, and perhaps their own particular church, and the suffering household of faith and the perishing world are scarcely ever touched by their sympathies or their intercessions.

The highest prayer is the prayer of unselfish love, and as we learn to pray for others, and to carry the dying world upon our hearts, we shall find ourselves enriched in return, a thousand fold, and prove, indeed, that "it is more blessed to give than to receive."

XXX. SELFISH HOPES.

The future of many persons is as selfish as their present. They live in the dreams of coming joys and triumphs, and their vision is all earth-bound, and often, alas! as baseless as the fading cloud-land that floats upon the summer sky.

The true Hope of the Gospel swallows up all these selfish visions and earthly hopes. Looking for that blessed Hope and the glorious appearing of our Lord and Saviour Jesus Christ, we hold all other prospects subordinate and subject to that supreme prospect. Even the old hope of heaven that was sometimes a selfish weariness, and a longing to be at rest, has been exchanged for that high and glorious looking for His coming that lifts us out of ourselves into the greater blessing it is to bring to millions, and nerves us to the highest and noblest efforts to work for the hastening of the coming glory and the preparation of the world to meet Him. God alone can give this new and heaven-born hope, which is as Divine as it is lofty and inspiring.

XXXI. OUR LIFE.

Our very life must be held not as a selfish possession, but as a sacred trust.

"Neither count I my life dear unto myself," is the true spirit of consecration; "but that I may finish my course with joy, and the ministry which I have received of the Lord Jesus Christ."

That is the meaning of life, and the only object for which it should be cherished.

So we find the same Apostle saying, "For me to live is Christ, and to die is gain;" and he adds, "Therefore, I know that I shall continue with you all for the furtherance of your faith."

The unselfish life is a safe life, and it is immortal till its great purpose shall be fulfilled.

CONCLUSION.

How shall we overcome these giant Anakims? How shall we win the victory over self? How shall we possess Hebron, the city of love?

1. We must definitely and thoroughly enter into the meaning of that mighty word, "Ye are not your own." We must surrender ourselves so utterly that we can never own ourselves again.

We must hand over self and all its rights in an eternal covenant, and give God the absolute right to own us, control us, and possess us forever.

And we must abide in this attitude, and never recall that irrevocable surrender.

2. We must let God make this real in detail, as each day brings its tests and conflicts, and each of these thirty-one kings comes face to face before us. That which we did in the general must be fulfilled in the particular, and, step-by-step, we must be established in the full experience of self-renunciation and entire consecration.

As each of these issues meets us, God is asking us the question, "Are you your own, or are you mine?" And as we stand true to our covenant, He will make it real.

We must choose that each new Agag shall die, and God will make the death effectual the moment we sign the death warrant.

3. We must receive the great antidote to self – the love of Christ.

We have seen the power of love in a human life transforming a selfish girl, living for the pleasures of society and the gratification of her own self-love, into a patient, self-sacrificing wife and mother, willing to endure any privation and go any length for the man she loved with all her heart.

In a far higher sense the love of Christ, and that alone, can slay the strength of self-love, and enable us to say, "The love of Christ constraineth me; for I thus judge that if One died for all then all died; and He died for all, that they which live should not henceforth live unto themselves, but unto Him who died for them and rose again."

4. Finally, we need not only the love of Christ, but the Christ Himself.

It is not a principle, nor an emotion, nor a motive, that is to transform our life and conquer these determined foes, but it is a living Person.

Christ will put His own heart into us, and so live in us, and we so live in His life, love in His love, and think, speak and act in Him, in all we do, that it shall be "not I, but Christ that liveth in me."

So let us receive Him, the Antidote of self, the Lord of love, the Conqueror of the heart.

There is a foe whose hidden power
  The Christian well may fear,
More subtle far than inbred sin
  And to the heart more dear.
It is the power of selfishness,
  It is the wllful I,
And e'er my Lord can live in me
  My very self must die.

There is, like Anak's sons of old,
  A race of giants still,
Self-glorying, self-confidence,
  Self-seeking aud self-will.
Still must these haughty Anakim,

By Caleb's sword be slain,
E'er Hebron's heights of heavenly love
Our conquering feet can gain.

O save me from self-will, dear Lord,
Which claims Thy sacred Throne;
O let my will be lost in Thine,
And let Thy will be done.
O keep me from self-confidence,
And self-sufficiency;
Let me exchange my strength for Thine,
And lean alone on Thee.

O save me from self-seeking, Lord,
Let me not be my own,
A living sacrifice I come, –
Lord, keep me Thine alone;
From proud vain-glory save me, Lord,
From pride of praise and fame;
To Christ be all the honor given,
The glory to His Name.

O Jesus, slay the self in me,
By Thy consuming breath;
Show me Thy heart, Thy wounds, Thy shame,
And love my soul to death.
When the Shekinah flame came down,
E'en Moses could not stay;
So let Thy glory fill me now,
And self forever slay.

O Jesus, come and dwell in me,
Walk in my steps each day,
Live in my life, love in my love,
And speak in all I say;
Think in my thoughts, let all my acts
Thy very actions be,
So shall it be no longer I,
But Christ that lives in me.

CHAPTER VI.

POSSESSING THE INHERITANCE.

"THE Lord said unto Joshua, Thou art old, and stricken in years, and there remaineth yet very much land to be possessed." – Josh. 13:1.

"How long are ye slack to go to possess the land which the Lord God of your fathers hath given you?" – Josh. 18:3.

We have looked at the conquest of the land and the kings who disputed its ownership. This is over now, and the occupation of the conquered territory next engages the attention of the great leader. This is quite different from its subjugation.

It is one thing to fight a decisive battle and disperse the opposing forces of a hostile province. It is another thing to settle down to the employments of peace, and cultivate the conquered territory, covering it with peaceful homes and fruitful fields, and developing its resources.

This was the next business of the conquerors of Canaan, and in this we find a strange and long delay. For a considerable period after the conquest of Canaan, we find no less than seven of the great tribes still lingering around the tabernacle at Shiloh, and failing to go forward to claim their respective inheritances, so that God had to reprove them for their negligence and delay, and Joshua had to send forth a special commission to divide the land and apportion it to the tribes that had not yet received their inheritance.

This is all applicable to our spiritual inheritance. There is much more for us than the conflict with temptation and sin. There are positive advances in the Christian life into which God is calling us as well as them, and it is to be feared that a much larger proportion of the spiritual Israel has failed to enter into its inheritance than even the seven tribes who lingered at Shiloh.

God is obliged, after eighteen centuries, to send forth His messengers to plead with His negligent and faithless people to take the blessings which He has, at such a tremendous cost, provided and prepared.

He is pleading with us, as He did with them, and saying, "How long are ye slack to go to possess all the land which the Lord your God hath given you?" There are not, perhaps, ten Christians in a hundred who even claim to have accepted all the fullness of the Gospel of Christ; and the people of God as utterly fail to enter into their inheritance of service in the evangelization of the world. In every direction, there remaineth yet very much land to be possessed.

Let us survey this unoccupied territory, and listen to the challenge which is speaking to us from heaven, to arise and occupy it.

I. WHAT IS MEANT BY POSSESSING THE LAND?

It is much more than conquering the land. It is one thing to break down the walls of Jericho; it is another thing to enter in and possess the city.

It is one thing to fight a great, decisive battle with temptation; it is another thing to go on to perfection, and add to our faith, knowledge, temperance, godliness, brotherly kindness, charity, and all the fruits of the Spirit.

Every word is extremely suggestive. The first thought suggested is, appropriating as our own the inheritance. It is one thing to understand the promises, to desire the experience, to purpose obeying the commands. It is another to put our own name in all, and claim for ourselves the things promised and commanded. The personal pronouns, my and mine, make all the difference in the world.

The second thought suggested by the expression is the actual experience of the thing that we have claimed, – the entering upon it and living it out.

The immigrant may go to the land office and put in his name and application for a free grant on the Western Reserve, but that is not enough. It cannot become his property until he settles down upon it, builds a house and lives in it, and begins to cultivate the estate. Then he is the real possessor, and his title cannot be alienated.

This is what God requires us to do. First, by faith, to appropriate the inheritance promised, and then, by actual experience, to settle down upon the promise and take it into our lives.

There is something very real in this idea of appropriating for ourselves a distinct Christian experience. Most people are trying to live somebody else's life. But God has an inheritance for each of us, – unique, distinct, and personal. He wants us to appropriate it, understand it, catch the vision of it, claim it for ourselves, and realize it in our actual life.

The great majority of people are made up of patchwork. They take a rag from one, a piece from another, and they stitch them on as best they can, until they become like a patchwork quilt, and it is little wonder if sometimes it is a "crazy quilt."

God wants you to be yourself, in Him. He has a pattern for you that He has for nobody else, and if you will let Him, He will weave it into your life, and work it out in all its unique and beautiful design.

Is not this the meaning of this remarkable, and oft misapplied verse, "Work out your own salvation with fear and trembling, for it is God that worketh in you to will and to do of His good pleasure?"

This does not mean that we are to earn salvation by our works, for before the works begin, we are assumed to have the salvation, and to have made it "our own." Then, when it is our own, when we have claimed and appropriated it, we are to work it out, – develop it; we are to enter into it in all its fullness, work it out as the weaver works out the pattern of his web; work it out as the artist works out the design on his canvas; work it out as the sculptor works out the figure in his marble; work it out as the oak tree is worked out of the acorn, and work it out "with fear and trembling," with a sense of the tremendous responsibility, the infinite trust, the mighty possibilities, and the Divine Worker who is working in you, and pressing you on to apprehend all that for which you are apprehended in Christ Jesus.

II. THE UNOCCUPIED LAND.

"There remaineth very much land to be possessed."

1. There is much unoccupied territory in the Word of God. There are promises that we have not yet made our own. There are conceptions of truth that we have not yet grasped with our minds, or translated into our lives. There are commandments whose finer shades of sacred duty we have not yet conceived, far less fulfilled. There are fields of truth into which the Holy Teacher and Comforter is waiting to lead us. There are many things which He would say to us, but we cannot bear them now. But if we will follow on, we will find that

He who so wondrously hath taught,
  Yet more will make us know;
He who so wondrously hath wrought,
  Yet greater things will show.

2. There is much territory in the land of Christian living to be possessed. The things we know, have we fully believed? The things we believe, have we fully realized? The things we realize, have we fully proved?

We have learned some lessons of love, but have we the love that "beareth all things," that "never faileth?" We have learned to suffer long, but have we learned to "suffer long," and yet be "kind?" And have we come into “all patience and long suffering with joyfulness?” We have received the white robes, but have we also put on the wedding robes? We have been made holy, but have we received “the beauty of holiness” and the finer touches of His polishing and perfecting hand?

We have known something of the joy of the Lord, but have we learned to “count it all joy when we fall into divers temptations,” and to “glory in tribulation also?”

We have learned something of answered prayer, but have we come into the life of prayer, the prayer of the Holy Ghost, and the higher prayer of self-forgetfulness?

We have submitted to the will of God, and chosen it, but have we come to delight in it? and not only to delight in it, but to prove what is that good, and holy, and acceptable, and perfect will of God?

3. In the realm of Christian work there remaineth yet very much land to be possessed. What infinite varieties of holy service there are for the consecrated and obedient servant!

Most of us can remember how, within a short lifetime, Christian work has grown in its various phases and opportunities.

Fifty years ago, there was usually but one worker in an ordinary congregation – the preacher. His business was to work, and the others were simply worked upon.

After a little while, the Sunday school was added to the machinery of the ordinary church, and there was more work to be done and more workers were required. So the circle increased, until there were, perhaps, a dozen workers in the church.

In the past quarter of a century, how many new forms of Christian work have arisen – rescue missions, work for the fallen and the suffering, calling out all the varieties of talent and capacity in the church of Christ, and all the gifts of the Holy Ghost – so that today there are ten people working in every thoroughly awakened church, for one a quarter of a century ago.

But this is only the beginning. And how has this come about? Simply because some of God's children, who were walking with Him, and waiting upon Him, caught the vision of His higher will, received His commission to go out in some new field, obeyed, and were used to originate some new department of service for God.

But the day is coming when all this will be multiplied an hundred fold, and when it will scarcely be respectable for anyone to be a member of a Christian congregation, for any considerable period, unless he can point to precious souls whom he has led to Christ; and the very least that Christ has suggested as the test of discipleship and the measure of fruitfulness, is thirty fold.

God is waiting for workers to whom He can commit greater trusts than anything that we have seen. As the century hastens to its close, everything is moving on accelerated time, and God is going to multiply the agencies for Christian work in a manner that we can scarcely realize. If we are willing to open our ears to His voice, He will speak to us, and send us, and we shall wonder at the ways in which He will own and multiply our efforts, if made in the Holy Ghost.

Beloved, "lift up your eyes, for the fields are white already to the harvest," and ask the Lord to show you His highest thought and will for your precious life.

III. THE CAUSES OF FAILURE IN ENTERING INTO OUR FULL INHERITANCE.

"How long are ye slack to go to possess all the land?" This little word "slack," expresses the secret of all the failure. It is a very difficult word to translate, but many of us will doubtless recognize some of its applications to our own souls.

1. It denotes indolence. There is no meaner vice in the world than laziness. Most people would be ashamed to claim it as a relation; but the fact is, more people are suffering from it than would be ready to own it.

It is the cause of most of the failures in secular life. God hates it and always blesses the diligent in natural ways.

"Seest thou a man diligent in his business? He shall stand before kings," God has said. "He shall not stand before common men." Even if a man is wrong in many things, God will recompense him in natural things, as far as He can.

Many are kept back from spiritual progress by a spirit of indolence and unwillingness to put forth any real spiritual effort. It is so much easier to be content with things as they are, and take the easy way.

One of our missionaries in Peking told me of a Chinese beggar, for whom she got a good situation, but he only kept it two or three days, and then was back on the "Beggar's Bridge" once more. When she asked him why he had given up his job, he said, "Well, the truth is, I can stand almost anything; I can bear to be cold and hungry, to be beaten and kicked, to be poor and homeless, but I cannot bear to be tired."

A good many people are like him. It is true of spiritual, as well as natural things, that "the hand of the diligent maketh rich." We cannot reach the highest place in heavenly things, unless, like the great spiritual athlete of whom we read in the Epistle to the Philippians, we "reach forth unto those things which are before, and press toward the mark for the prize of the high calling of God in Christ Jesus."

2. Indifference.

Many persons are kept back from the highest blessing by spiritual indifference. They have no intense or holy ambition or desire for the highest things. They are content to be saved any way, and the prizes of the high calling have no attraction for their hearts. Like Esau, they despise their birthright, and do not think it worth the trouble or the cost. They that would enter into that rest must "labor to enter in," and kindle with the holy intensity that "counts all things but loss for the excellency of the knowledge of Christ Jesus the Lord."

God will never give His prizes to an indifferent heart. He wants them to be prized above all cost, and sought above all treasures.

3. Self-complacency.

This keeps many back. They are quite satisfied with what they have attained. They have received enough blessing to assuage a guilty conscience, and heal the fear of future punishment. And, perhaps, they have gone further, and had some experience in the past on which they are continually lingering, which effectually displaces all true and honest hunger of the heart for the larger life that God can only give to self-emptied souls.

"Blessed are they that hunger and thirst after righteousness, for they shall be filled."

"Because thou sayest, I am rich and increased in goods, and have need of nothing, and knowest not that thou art wretched, and poor, and miserable, and blind, and naked.

4. The life of ease and pleasure.

There is nothing that so relaxes the cords of spiritual earnestness as the life of the world. Men who contend for earthly prizes have to forego the pleasures of earthly indulgence.

The trainer for an athletic contest denies himself every gratification that could relax his vigor or weaken his physical energy. Much more must they who strive for an incorruptible crown keep under their body and bring it into subjection.

The cost of holiness is too great for the lover of this present evil world. Many of you, dear friends, who read these lines, are hindered in your holy ambitions and heavenly aspirations because there is some selfish thing in your life which has shorn you of your strength, even as Delilah robbed the mighty Samson of his Nazarite separation, and brought him to disgrace and ruin by the fascination of earthly pleasure.

5. The influence of others has much to do with slackening and relaxing the holy purposes of many hearts.

There is nothing so depressing as the tendency of some persons to look at things on the average. They say: "Why should I be better than my neighbors? Why should I claim more than my father ever knew? Thousands of good people are content to go on in the old way, and they are all going to heaven; why should not I be content to be as good as they?"

And so, measuring themselves by themselves, and comparing themselves among themselves, they rise no higher than the human standard, and comfort themselves by the average Christian and the average measure of the Gospel, and are slack to go up to possess all the land which the Lord our God hath given them.

Beloved, "Let God be true, and every man a liar." You cannot afford to come short of anything which God has prepared for you at such large cost. There is not a promise in His Word, not a command in His precepts, which is not essential to you for your complete Christian life.

If you miss any part of His will, you shall be an eternal loser, and your future will be defective to just that extent. God's faithful people in every age have had to be in the minority. The man who goes with the crowd is invariably wrong.

God is calling you to step out and stand alone, and, putting your fingers in your ears, to press forward in the narrow way, calling, "Life, life, eternal life!"

6. Unbelief keeps many slack. They say, "It is of no use for me to attempt this higher life." Like Israel at Kadesh-Barnea, they admit that "the land is a good one, but the enemies are so great and we so little, we shall never be able to enter in." But as old Caleb answered, "If the Lord our God be with us, we shall drive them out, as the Lord hath said."

Faith in the promises of God and in the power of the Holy Ghost will nerve the feeble arm, steady the relaxed spirit, and make us more than conquerors over every obstacle and adversary.

7. Lack of courage slackens holy energy and ambition. Some people are moral cowards. They are afraid of self-denial, singularity, criticism, conflict and spiritual hardship. Only spiritual heroes can win the inheritance. Cowards will always fail. God is willing and able to give us true courage, if we will dare to stand where He bids us.

Beloved, let us face the difficulties and the enemies. Let us set our face like a flint. Let us take His own Divine courage, and let us go up at once and possess all the land which the Lord our God hath given us.

8. The figure suggests lack of power.

Slackness expresses feebleness. This well characterizes the spiritual condition of the great majority of Christians. They are like a bow so relaxed that the bow-string has no spring, the arrow no momentum. The life that should be an example of the Omnipotence of God, and show the credentials of holy energy and Divine efficiency, is, in most cases, such a poor, flabby, limp, powerless form, that the men of the world despise it, and feel that they are better off without it.

9. The lack of persistence is implied in the figure of slackness. There are some bows that retain their spring for a short time, but the wood is inferior, and after a few hours the spring becomes relaxed.

So many start out for the heavenly inheritance with high ambitions and hopes, but they have no real perseverance. The fair promise of their beginning soon becomes "like the morning cloud and the early dew."

We are made partakers of Christ if we hold our confidence steadfast unto the end. There can be no allowance anywhere for ease, indulgence, or laxity. It is a life-long way, and every step we must stand with girded loins, forgetting the things that are behind, reaching forth to the things that are before, press forward to the mark of the prize of our high calling in Christ Jesus.

IV. HOW LONG?

This is a solemn and tender appeal to us to act promptly, and obey, without a moment's delay, the impulses of the Holy Spirit. If we are not prepared to go forward today, how can we be better prepared tomorrow? If we are disposed to take the easy way this morning, we will be just as likely to do it the next morning.

Besides, time is passing by, and that which is more important, opportunity, is slipping away. There are crisis hours in life, when everything concentrates at a solemn focus, and if the decision is not made then, it may never be made.

There is something very pathetic in the words, "Thou art old and stricken in age, and there remaineth yet very much land to be possessed."

There is a spiritual age that comes to people, and comes sometimes before their life-work is fulfilled. We have all seen people young in years, but old in heart, their pulses benumbed, their spiritual forces paralyzed by disobedience to the voice of the Holy Ghost.

There is such a thing as losing the spring of life, the high and heavenly inspiration that comes from the breath of God, and makes sacrifice and toil luxurious delights.

There is a heavenly glow, there is a Divine enthusiasm, which comes from the continual presence of Christ within us, and the sweet voice of His approval; and if these are lost, life is drudgery indeed. Every toil will be a task, and every trial a crushing weight of unutterable woe.

And all this comes from disobedience. The Holy Spirit leads us up to the great decisive hour, and then presses us forward to the right decision. If we hesitate, if we shrink, if we refuse, there comes a time when that Presence is withdrawn, and the heart sinks back into a strange heaviness, and life has lost its glow. Temptations overcome us; trials discourage us; joy and gladness leave us; and gradually we sink back into premature old age, and yet we know not what is the matter, and perhaps never fully realize where the fatal error was committed.

Oh! what is so sad as to see gray hairs on the hearts of people, and they know it not; to see the loss of spiritual freshness, buoyancy and power gradually creeping over the life that once was all aglow, and to know that another soul has looked back on the way, and another crown has been lost by slackness!

Beloved, do not disobey the voice of God. Cherish the inspirations of the Holy Ghost, and follow on after the hand that is beckoning you to higher things. Lose not a moment; meet every question of God today; or tomorrow you may find your self unprepared for further advances. If you once begin to lose time on this heavenly highway, you may never make it up again.

There are some railway trains whose schedule time is arranged at the highest possible maximum, – there is no room to make up a lost hour. If the train is late at this station, it will be late at the next, and come in late at the end. If it were a freight train, or an accommodation train, it might make up what was lost; but the great Limited Express has no room for the recovery of loss.

Beloved, you and I have taken our passage to the heavenly land on God's great Limited Express, and we cannot afford to lose a moment on the way. Let us be true to our high calling, and let us begin today to press forward, that we may apprehend all that for which we have been apprehended of Christ Jesus.

CHAPTER VII.

THE INHERITANCE OF LOVE.

"HEBRON, therefore, became the inheritance of Caleb, the son of Jephunneh, the Kenezite, unto this day, because that he wholly followed the Lord God of Israel." – Josh. 14:14.

The City of Hebron is still one of the most interesting and delightful places in Palestine. It is a highly elevated spot, overlooking a wide extent of country, and even amid the desolations of Palestine it is still a scene of surpassing beauty, fertility and luxuriance.

The country is covered with vineyards and plantations. The grapes of Eschol still grow in the valleys, and the rains and water springs are returning in something like their former fullness.

One cannot wonder that Caleb should set his heart upon this choice inheritance and claim it as his own.

The incident of this chapter is one of the most stirring in the Book of Joshua. Caleb was one of the faithful spies who returned from the survey of the land at Kadesh, and, unlike the rest of his brethren, he encouraged the people to go up and claim their inheritance. But they refused, and for forty years he waited until that unbelieving generation had passed away. And now, for more than four years, he had stood shoulder to shoulder with his comrades in the conquest of the land and the securing of their various inheritances, until at last the kings were all subdued and the land divided by lot. Then he comes forward and claims his own inheritance, and justly receives it.

The whole scene is full of spiritual meaning, and vividly sets forth the higher inheritance which faith may claim from the greater Commander in the better Land of Promise.

I.

Hebron represents a special inheritance; something more than the ordinary lot of the tribes. Caleb's act expressed a holy ambition which is worthy of our imitation.

God is pleased to have us claim all there is for us in His great redemption. The Master was not angry with James and John when they wanted more than their brethren. The prophet of old was angry with Israel's king when he was willing to take so little, and reproved him that he had not struck five or six times with the arrows of faith upon the ground.

There is more for each of us than an ordinary Christian experience. There is much more than just being saved and sanctified. God has choice possessions for choice spirits, and He lets each one of us decide for ourselves how much we shall have.

He is always watching with loving jealousy to see how earnest our spirit is, and how much of our high calling in Christ Jesus we will claim.

II.

Hebron represents not only a higher inheritance, but the very highest. It was the choicest spot in all the land. Caleb wanted it just because it was the best, and Anak held it for the very same reason. God has for each of us a good, a better, or a best. The great majority are languidly content to have the good, a minority choose the better, and one out of myriads occasionally claims the best. But it has been truly said: "The better is the greatest enemy to the best." If we rise a little higher than the average we are apt to rest there in self-complacency, and so miss the highest calling.

Caleb would take nothing less than God's best, and he got it. God wants us to be content with nothing but His highest thought, and to "press forward into all the good pleasure of His goodness" and "the good and acceptable and perfect will of God."

III.

Hebron represents a very hard-won victory. It was not only the highest, but the hardest choice. It is ever true that God's highest gifts are the most costly.

In natural things, value is expressed by rarity and cost. Pearls do not grow on the trees. Sovereigns do not fall like snowflakes. The laurel of fame does not hang on every branch along the way. Success is not a capricious accident.

All these things are the recompense of labor, sacrifice, self-denial, and often great suffering. And so the highest spiritual things are costly things, and involve intense labor and self-denial.

Satan does not dispute our way over the plains of average blessing, but when we ascend to higher altitudes we find his principalities and powers disputing our advance, and they are thickest at the end.

The devil is too shrewd to waste his ammunition on ordinary, average things. The reason that Arba, the greatest of the Anakims, chose Hebron was because it was the choicest place in Palestine.

The reason why the best things in your life cost you such great temptations and pressures is because such mighty and unspeakable blessings lie behind the breastworks of your foe, for you if you will only dare to claim your inheritance.

If you are to reach the heights of holiness, you will have, like Habakkuk, to have "hind's feet," and learn to "walk on your high places." If you are to come into the more delicate shades of Christian experience, you shall have to know the heaviest touches of the adversary's hand.

If you are to sit with Christ upon His throne, you must go with Him through His Gethsemane. Christ is not holding you back from the highest places at His side, but He is asking you, as He did His disciples of old, "Can ye drink of my cup? Can ye be baptized with my baptism?"

Caleb understood all this when he asked for Hebron, and the reason he wanted it was because "the Anakims were there, and the cities were great and strong."

Christ is still looking for men and women of the heroic type, those who will bear the hardest things, and fear not the cost of the highest things in His Kingdom.

Once in my life, when almost tempted to discouragement by the temptations and pressures around me, my eye fell on this line in an old book: "The best evidence that you are in God's will is the devil's growl." And so I thanked the devil for his growl, and found that the reason he was there in force was because there was a Hebron just beyond.

IV.

Hebron represents the victory of waiting faith. The promise claimed at Hebron had been given forty years before. It was the realization of a lifelong vision. It was the fulfillment of a long deferred hope.

God's richest blessings often require not only sacrifice, suffering and hard conflict, but long delay and patient waiting. But the blessing grows with the delay. The interest gathers with the extended time, and God's ratio is always compound interest.

It is very blessed to receive, in the early morning of life, some precious promise, and then stand, as the years go by, and wait for God to fulfill it, undiscouraged by the lapse of time, but knowing that "a thousand years with God are as one day, and one day as a thousand years."

So God gave all His ancient people the early promise and the waiting years. And oh, how His heart looks down with delight as His children hold fast, amid all the testings, knowing that "if it tarry it will surely come, and will not tarry too long."

Thus, and thus alone, are the strongest things matured. The bass-wood tree can grow in a decade, but the mighty oak that lasts for centuries, takes many years to mature. So God is teaching us to reach our highest blessings. Let us hold fast to all His promises. Let us learn to wait for the best wine at the last.

I am sorry for the man who has got all his blessings, and has no unanswered prayers, and no reserve of faith and hope beyond the present hour. Like the painter who wept when he had reached his ideal, because he could never rise beyond the present, so the heart loses its spring when it reaches its full desire.

The Holy Ghost is always pressing us forward in holy aspiration and infinite outreaching after greater things, that He may lure us on by the hopes He sets before us.

Let us store the heavens with these waiting prayers, and let life's perspective be crowned, height above height, with our unrealized blessings; and we shall praise Him as much for what He has not yet given us as for the blessings we have received, and often sing with one of the sweetest spirits of our century:

"A sweet new song is in my mouth,
To long-loved music set;
Glory to God for all the grace
I have not tasted yet."

V.

Hebron represents specially the inheritance of love and holy friendship. It was the city of Abraham, the friend of God, and its name to the present day is "The Friend." It is the type of love, the highest heritage of Christian faith and experience.

I do not speak of love in its ordinary, natural meaning, as a human instinct, but of the love which is the grace and gift of Christ; and I think that Hebron represents not the commoner phases of Christian love, but the choice and finer shades which the Holy Spirit has to give to those who will "come up higher."

We know the Lord Jesus had some disciples who came nearer to His heart than others; and love has still its inner chambers and finer shades. Hebron seems to express these heights of love and heavenly fellowship.

There is "the love that casteth out fear;" the perfect confidence in the Father which has no cloud; a fellowship which is eternal and unbroken, and covered with His mighty oath. "I have sworn that I will never be wroth with thee, nor rebuke thee." Do we not want this mountaintop of love?

Then there is the love of Christ shed abroad in our hearts, that is the very heart of Christ in us. I cannot sing the song,

> Give me a heart like Thine,
> Help me to love like Thee,

because I am not able to resemble Christ. I must have Christ Himself to live in me. This is my highest Hebron, that "As He is, so also are we, in this world." "That the love wherewith thou hast loved me may be in them, and I in them."

Again, there is what we have sometimes called the love-life of the Lord; the blessed tender relationship in which we call Him Ishi and He calls us beloved; where we are betrothed unto our Lord and He becomes the Bridegroom of the heart, quickening all our being with a touch so real, and so infinitely holy, that it is preeminently true of this as of everything else,

"The love of Jesus, what it is,
None but His loved ones know."

Do we not want to dwell on this high place of love?

Then there is the love that adjusts all our natural and spiritual relationships, and enables us to love each one in Christ, not with an earthly, sentimental love, a selfish love that often hurts what it would bless, but just as Christ loves each one with a perfect, righteous, unselfish love and simplicity.

How our hearts often ache because they are unadjusted! How bone fails to fit bone, in the body of Christ, and joint to fit into its socket, until the whole frame is distorted and diseased!

But Christ has a love for each of us which is stronger than our natural affection, and infinitely sweeter, quieter, more unselfish and blessed than any earthly love.

Some of you would die for your friend today, through your passionate devotion; but tomorrow, if he should slight your corpse, you would instantly rise from the dead to pour upon him your angry recrimination. That is not the Christ-love. It is peaceful and everlasting.

Some of you will fasten on the fault of another until you become blinded to his better qualities and forget his real goodness.

The Christ-love can see the error, but it can see also the other side, and can cover the error with the faith and hope that will claim from Christ its healing, and see him only in the light of Christ's own perfect love and grace.

The Christ-love has no respect for persons. It loves most dearly those whom God has fitly framed into the nearest place, but it loves each in his or her place, simply, wholly, unselfishly, with Christ's own thought and blessing.

The sun looks into the little daisy and gives it all the light the daisy can hold. The same sun looks into the great bosom of the summer lake and gives it a larger, richer glory, because the lake can hold more and reflect back the sun and the glory.

And so the love of God meets each person that comes in contact with your life, and touches each according to the adjustment of God's providence and the principles of His Word.

This Christ-love can love even the unworthy for its own sake and not for theirs. It loves not for the worth of the object, but, like the sunshine, it covers the meanest thing with its own glory, "and loves the loveliness itself hath given."

Are not these some Hebron heights we long to climb, where it would be sweet to dwell above the clouds of our murky skies and malarial plains?

And so we might speak of Hebron as the type of fellowship, as the name expresses. There are heights of fellowship with God into which we need to rise. Do you not want to know the prayer of the Holy Ghost in all its mighty possibilities? Do you not want to know the prayer of faith in God in all its limitless forces? Do you not want to know the prayer without ceasing, and the abiding communion where the curtains are never closed and the Presence is never withdrawn?

Do you not want to know the communion of wordless fellowship which waits upon the Lord, which brings in His very life and fullness, which breathes His breath and lies upon His bosom in perfect rest, without a murmuring wave upon the peaceful shore?

Do you not want the sympathetic intuition that catches the very thought of God, that meets the Spirit's finest shade, that understands the Master's will, that responds to the still, small voice, and reaches out into the very mind of God?

Are these the things that weary you and oppress you and have no charm for you? Or does your spirit cry, "Oh, thou whom my soul loveth, tell me where thou feedest, where thou makest thy flock to rest at noon?"

I'm leaning close to Jesus' breast;
  So close that I can hear
The softest whisper of His love
  In fellowship most dear;
And feel that His almighty hand
  Is with me in this hostile land.

And then this brings the fellowship of others just as close and holy. In this secret place of the Most High, God brings to us the most sacred companionships of love, leads us into their inner lives, lays upon us their needs, and makes it a luxury to pray for them, uses us to carry their work and share in their sorrows, and begins even here the holy fellowships of the world above.

There are none so near to us as those that are far away, across wide seas and distant continents.

There are cables underlying
  Every ocean wide;
Cords of love and prayer are stronger
  Than the Atlantic's tide:

These are some of Hebron's Heights. Beloved, shall we claim them and dwell there with Caleb, in the summer-land of life?

VI.

Hebron was the city of Abraham and of David. As the city of Abraham, it represents the covenant right of all the children of faith. It is our right to have these highest blessings.

There is nothing within the limits of the promises of God, or the possibilities of faith and love which we are not entitled to claim through the everlasting covenant, if we will but dare to appropriate it and enter in.

And so David was crowned at Hebron before he reigned at Jerusalem. So Hebron is a royal city, and so the place of love is always the place of kingliness. If we would rule in human hearts, and influence human destinies, we must have the heart of love. As I watch people in the work of God, I always see the loving heart go out in advance, and just as certainly the souls that have not won the highest victories of love, notwithstanding the most brilliant gifts, will become disqualified for the highest service.

If God is to make you a king, and crown you for the highest place in His work, you must get settled at Hebron, and begin your kingdom there, in the place of perfect love. Sensitiveness, selfishness, irritability, censoriousness, lack of sympathy, gentleness, and infinite compassion, will bar you from the highest work and the grandest compensations.

VII.

Hebron represents the victory of faith. How did Caleb win this mighty citadel? Listen. "If the Lord be with me, I shall be able to drive them out, as the Lord said."

It was all of faith. And so every victory must be one of faith. When Jesus told the disciples of the vast requirements of love for the erring, requiring forgiveness even unto seventy times seven, they might well have cried, "Lord, increase our love!" but their Spirit-prompted prayer was wiser than this. It was "Lord, increase our faith!" They were right, and Jesus well said in reply, "If ye had faith like a grain of mustard seed, ye could say to this mountain, be ye removed and cast into the sea, and it should be done."

The mightiest mountain of unbelief and alienation will yield to one germ of Divine love. We cannot grow into faith; it is not a plant indigenous to the soil of earth, but it must be claimed in the name of Jesus, on the ground of the covenant, through the Holy Spirit, as the direct obtainment of His grace.

And if today you have seen any lack of love in your heart and life, you have but to appropriate it according to your covenant right, to put down your name there, and then to put down your foot upon it and believing that you do receive it, step out into the testing of that love, insisting upon it as your right, and it will come into your life through His faithful and all-sufficient grace.

VIII.

Once more, Hebron represents the recompense of obedience. Hebron became the inheritance of Caleb "because he wholly followed the Lord his God."

Human love gives its rewards capriciously. That mother will hug her child almost to death this moment, and an hour hence may beat it almost to death.

But God loves on principle, and His caresses are always given for something. It is when we obey Him, when we please Him, when we stand fast in some place of testing, when we sacrifice some selfish thing at His bidding, – it is then that we hear the sweet words, "Well done, good and faithful servant, enter thou into the joy of thy Lord."

Like a loving mother, He takes up His child in His tender embrace, and lavishes upon him the fullness of His affection. It was when Abraham had proved his fidelity by the sacrifice of his son that God met him with that sweet testimony, "Now I know that thou lovest Me, because thou hast not withheld thy son, thine only son, from Me."

This is what Jesus means in these wonderful words: "He that hath My commandments and keepeth them, he it is that loveth Me, and he that loveth Me shall be loved of My Father, and I will love him and manifest Myself unto him."

This is something more than He says to the ordinary Christian. This is His special love for the always obedient heart. And so struck were the disciples with it that they asked Him again concerning it, and He repeated the same promise in still stronger language: "If a man love Me he will keep My words, and My Father will love him, and we will come unto him and make our abode with him."

This is the pathway to Hebron. Shall we walk obediently in it, and so enter into all the joy of our Lord?

And now, in conclusion, God has been calling us in these lessons to the highest things. Do we realize that in these waiting years Caleb had accomplished much more than an ordinary life already? He had reached nearly a century of years. He had seen two generations pass away. He had been a slave amid the brick-fields of Egypt. He had crossed the Red Sea, had stood under Sinai's awful cloud, had crossed the borders of Canaan, and stood on Hebron's Heights nearly half a century before, and had afterwards traversed the whole round of the wilderness, without once turning from his God, following like a faithful dog, as his name signifies, and obeying all the will of his Master.

And now he had gone through the whole campaign of the conquest of Canaan, had marched around Jericho and entered through the breaches of its walls, had triumphed at Bethhoron, and walked through the length and the breadth of the land; and as his gray hair streamed in the wind that day, a man of nearly a century old, almost anyone would have said he, at least, might well deserve to claim a release from work and toil and enter the richest inheritance his Commander could give him. But we find him instead just stepping out on the threshold of his greatest life work, attempting the mightiest achievement of his career, and, like a young man of twenty-one, begging for the privilege of fighting the hardest battles that remained and conquering the mightiest giants of the Anakims.

Glorious Caleb! Inspiring leader! Bright example! Speak to the men and women that have been sanctified and called to meet the mighty opportunities of these momentous days.

O, as we stand on the threshold of the coming kingdom and await the first beams of the Millennial dawn, Lord, send us out to higher, Diviner, victorious achievements of faith and love than we have yet experienced, for the glory of our Master's name. Amen.

CHAPTER VIII.

KIRJATH-SEPHER, OR THE MIND OF CHRIST.

"AND Caleb said, He that smiteth Kirjath-sepher, and taketh it, to him will I give Achsah my daughter to wife. And Othniel the son of Kenaz, the brother of Caleb, took it; and he gave him Achsah his daughter to wife. And it came to pass, as she came unto him, that she moved him to ask of her father a field: and she lighted off her ass; and Caleb said unto her, What wouldest thou? Who answered, give me a blessing; for thou hast given me a south land; give me also springs of water. And he gave her the upper springs, and the nether springs." – Josh. 15:16-19.

The conquest of Hebron by Caleb was followed a few days afterwards by the capture of Kirjath-sepher, also known as Debir. For its capture Caleb offered as a prize the hand of his daughter Achsah; and Othniel, Caleb's own nephew, took up the challenge and won both the city and the maiden.

She brought her husband not only her fair self, but a still richer dowry from her father, who gave her, at her request, not only the splendid inheritance looking toward the south, but also the upper and the nether springs.

All this is full of holy suggestiveness and sacred teaching in connection with our higher inheritance in Christ.

I. KIRJATH-SEPHER.

Kirjath-sepher and Debir suggest the victory of faith over the natural mind and the wisdom of the world. Kirjath-sepher means "the city of the oracle, or the book," and Debir means "the speaker."

One is the fitting symbol of the natural mind, and the other of its most powerful instrument and expression, the tongue, and both together represent the hardest victory of the spiritual life, the conquest of our thoughts and our words.

Human nature is three-fold, and consists of the spirit, soul and body. We have not only a spiritual nature, but we have an intellectual being, the seat of reason, mind and intelligence.

This has been blighted by the fall, and requires to be renewed through the blood and Spirit of Christ just as much as any other part of our being.

Our mind influences our whole character and life. "As a man thinketh in his heart, so is he," and intelligence without character is the most dangerous of created powers. Satan himself is just a great unholy intelligence. In one of the versions of the Bible his name is translated "the knowing one."

He is a being of transcendent brightness, but utterly without any right principle, his whole moral and spiritual being perverted and corrupted. Like the serpent – his Scriptural image – his life is all centered in his head. You cannot kill a serpent until you strike its head. You may bruise its whole body, but if you leave the head intact it still lives. Hence, the first promise of redemption was, "Thou shalt bruise his head."

He came to our first parents' intelligence. There was one tree in the garden that was prohibited to them. Everything else that could constitute happiness was theirs. All possible delights were given to them without stint. But there was one little bit of knowledge they must not claim; one single tree whose fruit they must not taste; one secret that must remain unknown, and it was with this that he tempted them, and with this that he destroyed them.

He lured them on to enter the forbidden precincts. He attracted them by the dazzling promise of Divine wisdom. He covered the forbidden prize with the glamour of his false light until everything else seemed eclipsed by its delusive brightness, and they reached forward over the precipice to grasp it, and when they had claimed it they found it was but an empty bubble; but it had cost them an eternity of ruin for all their race.

And so still the tree of forbidden knowledge is the mystery with which he lures men and women on until they venture beyond God's holy prohibitions and sink into the depths of ruin.

Temptations still assail us chiefly through our thoughts. In speaking of the depths of corruption in the days of Noah, God said, "Every imagination of the thoughts of the heart is only evil continually." It is through imagination that sin approaches. Floating like a beautiful vision through the mind, the evil thought at first seems harmless, but if entertained and allowed to lodge, it becomes the seed that springs up into a living plant of unholy desire, which quickly bursts into blossoms of unwholesome fragrance, and if they are permitted to fertilize and linger, the fruit of evil choice, sinful yielding and actual transgression follows with awful certainty and rapidity.

We must meet temptation, therefore, in our thoughts. We are so constituted that if we dwell on an evil thought it creates its own character within our spirit. The man of old who looked on the Gorgon's head was instantly turned into stone, and the soul that complacently and willingly indulges the thought of evil absorbs the evil into his own nature.

Walk down the street and let your eyes be fixed for a moment on a picture of obscenity, and you will immediately find your whole soul clouded by spiritual darkness and defilement, and although your spirit may revolt from it, still you will be conscious of a horrible fascination, and if you allow it to linger it will overpower your better feelings and change your nature into that of another man. Even your very body will be affected, and you will be conscious of being benumbed with the draught from the fountains of the pit.

The inventive genius of modern literature has given us the picture of a man who, by a certain draught, could be changed from one man into another of higher, nobler character, but would immediately fall back from the nobler man into the lower ideal the moment he thought of it, feared it and recognized it. There is a strange truth here. The consciousness of evil creates evil, the thought of good becomes the fertile soil of good.

Christian Science, which is itself one of Satan's false and unholy thoughts, has one truth in it, as all lies have, and that truth is that the thought of evil creates evil, and the thought of good has a tendency to produce good.

Not only do we need to correct our thoughts, but we must go farther and actually crucify the old natural mind and receive an entirely new mind in Christ. The sanctification of the spirit is not the improvement of the old natural spirit, but the renouncing of it and the receiving of God's Holy Spirit instead. So the sanctification of our mind must be just as radical. We must recognize that our natural mind is wrong, and must be laid wholly down, and we receive the mind of Christ instead, to think in us God's thoughts after God. So that our first experience is not the correcting of our thoughts, but the entire surrender of our mental being to the Lord Jesus Christ, to be crucified with Him.

The Apostle has said that the wisdom of this world is entirely wrong in its principles and nature. His language is exceedingly strong. He says, "The world by wisdom knew not God." Its *very wisdom* kept it from knowing God. "If any man would be wise, let him become a fool that he may be wise, for the wisdom of the world is foolishness with God."

"David says, "I hate thoughts;" not only vain thoughts, but all thoughts that are human. This is the source of all our unbelief, our anxious care, our doubts and fears, our envies, jealousies, irritations, seditions, strifes, controversies – all have their seat in the strong intellectual life of the human heart; the willfulness of our opinions and the entertaining of thoughts, questionings, evil surmisings and imaginings that disquiet and defile the soul. From all these Christ wants to save us, to give us the mind "stayed on Him," "the peace of God that passeth all understanding," and garrisons the thought and the heart through Christ Jesus; the heart so subdued that every evil imagination is cast down, and every high thing that exalteth itself brought low, and every thought brought into captivity to the obedience of Christ.

In the picture given of the works of the flesh, in Galatians, seditions, strifes and controversies are spoken of in the same category as adulteries, fornications and uncleanness. All these things are just as unholy in God's sight as the things that we call immoral.

Thus, Kirjath-sepher not only represents the mental source of evil thought, but the outward expression of it, the tongue. The control of the tongue, James says, is the rarest form of practical righteousness, and he adds that he who wins this victory will have little trouble in living a triumphant life in every other direction. "If any man offend not in word, the same also is a perfect man, and able also to bridle the whole body."

The awful evils of the tongue are well described by the same Apostle in language of terrible strength. "And the tongue is a fire, a world of iniquity; so is the tongue among our members, that it defileth the whole body, and setteth on fire the course of nature; and it is set on fire of hell."

This is the Kirjath-sepher and the Debir that the Lord Jesus Christ is calling on us to smite and take. When we win this citadel of Canaan, we receive in Christ a Divine inheritance in the very thing that we have surrendered. Instead of our own mind, we have the mind of Christ. Instead of our foolish and restless thoughts, we have the thoughts of God. Instead of our vain imaginings, we have the vision of His light and glory. Instead of our limited knowledge, the eyes of our understanding are enlightened, and we are able to know the "hope of our calling and the exceeding greatness of His power to usward."

Instead of the profoundest thoughts of man, we are led into "the deep things of God." "For eye hath not seen nor ear heard, nor hath it entered into the heart of man to conceive the things that God hath prepared for them that love Him. But God hath revealed them unto us by His Spirit, for the Spirit searcheth all things, yea, the deep things of God."

God will open His glorious Word to us, and give the revelation and illumination of the Holy Ghost, and "our eyes shall see the King in His beauty and the land of far distances."

The tongue that has learned to be silent for self and Satan will become the instrument of God's messages and the channel of His glorious power.

The very symbol of the Holy Ghost at Pentecost was a cloven tongue. The very member He wants to use most is our voice and our power of utterance, but He will not use it until He has its absolute control and He can stamp it with His own signature and monogram, as His exclusive property and His own living voice.

Beloved, is not this a glorious possibility? Is not this a choice possession? Shall we go up and smite Kirjath-sepher and take it, to be henceforth owned and occupied by the Holy Ghost, to the Glory of God alone?

It will be noticed that Kirjath-sepher comes after Hebron. It is love first, and then light. It is only as we learn the love-life of the Lord, and get out of self and all its sensitiveness, that we can do rightly, speak rightly, think rightly, and know rightly.

We want to get the seat of life centered not in the brain, but in the heart and spirit; in love, and not in truth. Then we shall understand the meaning of – "Speaking the truth in love, we grow up into Him in all things, who is the Head, even Christ."

is the type of the secret victory over the natural mind. The word Othniel means the lion of God, or "the force of God," as Dr. Young translates it. He represents the power of the Lord Jesus Christ and the Holy Ghost in a courageous spirit.

Nothing less than Omnipotent power can overcome the pride and strength of the carnal mind. It needs the very "force of God." "The tongue can no man tame; it is an unruly evil, full of deadly poison." "The carnal mind is enmity against God, for it is not subject to the law of God, neither indeed can be."

It is a wild and desperate rebel; your own resolution never can control it. But if we will be brave enough to choose to die to it Christ is able to subdue it. "For the weapons of our warfare are not carnal, but mighty through God to the pulling down of strongholds, casting down imaginations and every high thing that exalteth itself against God, and bringing every thought into captivity to the obedience of Christ."

We are so glad that God put that word "mighty" there. Every one who has tried to still the overactive brain; to subdue the flood of thought; to drive out the burning image from the imagination; to cleanse the foul picture from the chambers of the heart; to think calmly; or, better, cease thinking altogether, knows how useless the endeavor in the strength of the human will.

But there is a voice that can say to the wildest tempest of the heart and brain: "Peace, be still;" and lo! there is a great calm! There is a power that can keep every thought, like handmaids and servants, waiting outside the inner chamber to come at call, a troupe of obedient servants, not a horde of wild disturbers; waiting for the call of will and conscience, and utterly controlled by the voice of the Holy Ghost.

Oh; this indeed is peace! Happy are they who know it! Thank God, it waits for all who are willing to yield themselves in complete surrender to the mind of Christ and the thoughts of God.

III. ACHSAH,

or abounding grace for victorious souls.

Othniel's victory was accepted as the price of Caleb's daughter, the fair Achsah, whose name signifies – grace, and who may be regarded as the type of the special grace which Christ will give to victorious souls, and especially to those who have overcome the carnal mind.

There is a grace that saves the sinful soul, but there is a deeper, richer grace that sanctifies and fills it with all the fullness of God.

"We have access by faith into this grace wherein we stand." "God is able to make all grace abound toward you, so that ye, always having all sufficiency in all things, may abound unto every good work." "They who have received abundance of grace shall reign in life by One, which is Jesus Christ." "Out of His fullness have we received grace for grace," the grace that meets the need of every moment, and supplies the lack of grace in us for every emergency.

Do we need the grace of faith, of love, of patience? There is grace for this, grace to supply it in abundance; so that we shall be patient in His patience, gentle in His gentleness, strong in His strength, and loving in His love.

This is the grace that Jesus has to give the souls that have become victorious over their own self-will and self-sufficiency, and are content to take Him as their strength and wisdom.

Achsah moved her husband to ask great things of her father. And so the grace of God moves us to the highest, mightiest prayers and to take the riches of Divine grace and blessing.

Achsah, it would seem, moved Othniel to ask even more than Othniel asked for himself. We find her going to her father with a large prayer for him and for herself. And so grace asks for us even more than we ask for ourselves.

She brought her husband a rich inheritance, the south land, lying toward the warm sunshine, and then she claimed for herself and him, an added and a double blessing.

It is very beautiful to see her alighting off her ass, before she approaches her father with her great request. Grace stoops to plead, and the lower it goes, the more it can ask and receive. Abraham got on his face when he asked the everlasting covenant from Jehovah. The Syrophenician woman rose to the very highest faith in the New Testament from the deepest humiliation, accepting even the terrible word the Master spoke about her sin, and willing to count herself "a dog," yet claiming and receiving all the fullness of His infinite grace.

And so grace can stoop to the very depths of self-abasement, and yet rise to the heights of glory to claim all the fullness of God.

What she asked her father for was springs, and this grace always has for thirsting hearts. The life of works is a life of constant labor and painful effort, and the life of grace is a perpetual spring of spontaneous fullness and freedom.

It is so delightful to live and work for God from impulses that carry us beyond ourselves. There is a place in the mid-stream of human life where the current sweeps us along in the infinite fullness of God. But there is a place where we have to contend with eddies and cross-currents, to row and struggle against the stream and to press our way through the greatest difficulties.

Oh, it is so blessed to be carried on the current of His love and fullness and say continually, with an overflowing heart: "All my springs are in Thee."

Achsah asked for springs, and her father gave her more than she asked; "he gave her the upper and the nether springs."

This beautiful figure tells us that the glorious fullness of the grace of God sweeps the whole circle of our being, and gives "promise both of the life that now is, and also of that which is to come."

There are upper springs, – springs of faith, that keep us trusting in the face of every discouragement; springs of prayer, that come from the promptings of the Holy Ghost, and carry our petitions straight to the throne, with a consciousness of acceptance; springs of love that leap up to God, and enable us to say: "The love of God constraineth me;" springs of joy that burst from the eternal hills, a joy so unspeakable that it is full of glory; springs of hope that reach out to the yet unseen and invisible, anticipating all that shall yet be revealed in our future inheritance; springs of power, that make our service a delight, our testimony a great overflow from a heart that cannot be silent, because it is so full. These are some of the upper springs.

But there are nether springs which we value even more. There are springs that flow in the low places of life, in the hard places, in the desert places, in the lone places, in the *common places* which seem farthest removed from all that is sacred and Divine.

How blessed it is to drink from the springs of health, and find our strength renewed day by day, and the life of God flowing into even our physical organs and functions!

How delightful it is to have His gladness in the low places of sorrow, and to be able to "glory even in tribulation also."

How precious the springs that flow into the places of temptation, for there is nothing in life so trying as the touch of Satan's hand and the breath of the destroyer.

Oh, how sweet it is even there to find that the light is as deep as the shadow, and heaven is nearest when we are hard by the gates of hell, so that we can "count it all joy when we fall into divers temptations," and say, "Blessed is the man that endureth temptation, for when he is tried he shall receive the crown of life, that the Lord hath promised to them that love Him."

There are springs that flow amid the places of toil and secular business. It is possible to be filled amid the common things of life with the conscious presence of God. It is possible to work in the shop and the kitchen with a zest as sweet as that which inspires the preacher in his sublimest flights of thought, the singer in her highest notes of devotion, the saint in his most blessed moments of communion.

God loves to cheer those that toil in lowly places, and we can hear the sweet bells of the high priest's garments within the veil and the echoes of the harps of God even amid the din of the busy streets and the rattle and roar of the ten thousand hammers and the whirling wheels of the factory.

The heart that has its spring within can be happy anywhere. The soul that is set to heavenly music can never be out of tune. The light that is kindled from above can shine in darkness, though "the darkness comprehendeth it not."

Beloved, God has for us these springs, and we need them every day. Let us drink of the living waters. Nay, let us receive them into our very hearts, so that we shall carry the fountain with us wherever we go, that it may be true of us as He said of old, "Whosoever drinketh of the water that I shall give him shall never thirst, but the water that I shall give him shall be in him a well of water springing up into everlasting life."

CHAPTER IX.

THE DISCIPLINE OF HARD PLACES.

"AND Joshua answered them, If thou be a great people, then get thee up to the wood country, and cut down for thyself there in the land of the Perizzites and of the giants, if Mount Ephraim be too narrow for thee." – Josh. 17:15.

This chapter gives us three instructive lessons on the meaning of hard places and the discipline they should bring us.

I.

The case of the daughters of Zelophehad, verses 3, 4: "But Zelophehad, the son of Hepher, the son of Gilead, the son of Machir, the son of Manasseh, had no sons, but daughters; and these are the names of his daughters: Mahlah, and Noah, Hoglah, Milcah, and Tirzah.

"And they came before Eleazar the priest, and before Joshua, the son of Nun, and before the princes, saying, The Lord commanded Moses to give us an inheritance among our brethren. Therefore, according to the command of the Lord he gave them an inheritance among the brethren of their father."

Half a century before, Moses had made special provision for the daughters of the tribes inheriting their portion, under certain circumstances equally with their brethren, when there was danger of their patrimony being alienated to another tribe, through intermarriage. The five daughters of Zelophehad came to Joshua and claimed their inheritance, in accordance with this provision of the Mosaic statute, and they received it at the hand of the great leader.

This is a fine example of faith triumphing over difficulties and claiming its promised rights. This was the faith of Ruth, the Moabitess. She had found, through her mother's teachings, that there was an ancient provision of the Mosaic law entitling her to claim the protection of Boaz, as her nearest of kin; and although it cost her the sacrifice of her sensitiveness, and the risk even of her reputation, yet this daughter of faith dared to go forward and claim her rights, and place herself at the feet of Boaz.

The consequence was that she became one of the honored line of the Saviour's ancestry and the aristocracy of the kingdom of God.

So God has given to us redemption rights in His covenants of promise, and it is the part of faith to press through every difficulty, and, claiming our full inheritance, we shall receive it.

This is the ground on which we claim our temporal blessings, our physical healing, and ten thousand things which so many allow to go by default. They are ours by right of promise, and there is no generosity in giving them away, or letting them be lost, for they have already cost our Saviour His precious blood, and the only recompense He asks is that we claim them and enjoy them. Let us press forward and claim all our great bequest.

There is a special suggestion in this passage of the rights of woman under the gospel. We little realize, in western lands, how much Christianity has done for our sisters, and how high and glorious the equal place of honor and privilege which Christ has given to every daughter of faith.

Has woman a right to speak in the Church of God? Certainly, if she has anything worth saying, and if she is living what she says.

We believe she has no right to exercise the special ministry given to man as the ruler and pastor of the Church of God. But the New Testament Scriptures have given her undoubted freedom to the ministry of testimony to the gospel of Christ, both in public and private, provided she does it in the modest way becoming to her holy womanhood.

These five dear girls in ancient Canaan were pioneers of the great army of brave and holy women whom Christ is sending forth today to minister to Him in the fields of Christian service, both at home and abroad.

Their names are suggestive of the highest womanly qualities.

Mahlah means melody or song. She represents the spirit of praise, which should always go in front of Christian life and spiritual movement.

Noah means rest, and implies that spirit of gentleness, stillness and peace which is woman's peculiar adorning, even "the ornament of a meek and quiet spirit, which, in the sight of God, is of great price."

Hoglah, the third, means festival, and fittingly expresses the spirit of joy which is the strength of every Christian life, and peculiarly the fruit of woman's sweet ministry. Every true Christian woman should be a joy-bringer, and make life a festival of gladness wherever she goes.

Milcah means counsel, and suggests the spirit of wisdom, propriety, and good sense, without which all other womanly qualities fail of their object.

The true woman never speaks an indiscreet word, or does a thing which is out of place, but moves with such a sense of propriety and the fitness of things, such true instincts of rightness, tact and holy wisdom, that she is a sort of balance-wheel in the mechanism of life. The picture of Solomon in his ideal woman is sweetly fulfilled in her, "She openeth her mouth in wisdom, and in her tongue is the law of kindness." Some of our sisters, I am sure, know women who do not meet this ideal.

Beloved, shall you be a true Milcah, and claim as your inheritance the mind of Christ and the wisdom which is from above, which is "first pure, then peaceful, easy to be entreated, full of mercy and good fruits, without partiality and without hypocrisy?"

Tirzah, the last of these five blessed women, means benevolent, and represents the spirit of unselfishness, without which no woman can be true to her mission, or anything but a disappointment to herself and everybody else.

Selfishness is bad in anybody, but it is intolerable in a woman, for it is a perversion of the center of her being, and the primary object of her existence – love. If woman is not love, she is a fallen angel and a melancholy wreck.

Dear sisters, shall you ask the Lord to give you, as your inheritance among the daughters of Zelophehad, this glorious life of praise, of peace, of joy, of wisdom, and of heavenly love?

II.

We have next an example of slothfulness and sinfulness, compromising with difficulty and yielding to defeat. We read in the twelfth verse that "the children of Manasseh could not drive out the inhabitants of those cities, but the Canaanites would dwell in that land."

This seems very strange. They could do much harder things. They could cross the Jordan at flood-tide. They could break down the walls of Jericho before the trumpet blast of faith. They could conquer thirty-one kings in five years, and subdue all the strongholds of Canaan. They could conquer Kirjath-sepher, drive out Arba and Anak, and the giant races; and yet they could not dispossess a few Canaanite hordes in the small towns and villages of their inheritance.

This is passing strange. Alas! the secret is revealed in the next verse, and it is a very humbling one: "Yet it came to pass, when the children of Israel were waxen strong, that they put the Canaanites to tribute, but did not utterly drive them out."

Ah! that is the secret; there was some tribute in the question! There was some advantage to be gained by compromise. There was some loss or pain to be incurred by a brave, determined effort. And so they gave the Canaanites the right of way, with the understanding that they should pay for it. And they fancied for a while that they had made a good bargain.

But the day came when the Canaanites put them to tribute, crushed them beneath their feet, and placed them in an intolerable bondage, so that the Israelites became the slaves of them they had conquered. And not only so, but they were led into terrible sins which brought upon them the displeasure and judgments of God, through the allurements and temptations of the tribes which they had tolerated.

This is just what Satan is doing today. He is getting people to compromise, for the sake of some benefit. God is trying to raise up a few uncompromising men. Half a dozen such men in Babylon were sufficient to shake the whole Babylonian Empire. One such man in Persia was stronger than Haman and all his plotting. And today, a handful of whole-hearted, uncompromising Christians would do more to revolutionize society arid evangelize the world than ten millions of half-hearted professors.

We learn from this chapter the real nature of our inability. The children of Manasseh could not drive out the Canaanites because they *would* not. Inability is usually unwillingness. Christ summed it all up when He said: "Ye will not come to me, that ye might have life." It is true there is a place which says: "No man can come to me, except the Father which hath sent me, draw him." But we must not forget it is added, "Every man, therefore, that hath heard, and hath learned of the Father, cometh unto me."

The Father is always teaching, and those who are willing to learn will find no difficulty in coming. The unwilling heart does not want to learn, and is unable, because unwilling.

Any soul that will choose to come to Christ will find Christ there to enable him to come.

Any Christian who desires to take any advance step in the spiritual life has but to choose to take this step, and Christ will enable him to do so.

God will give you just as much as you really choose to take, and He will not only do this, but He will also "work in you to will and to do of His good pleasure."

If you really want to choose the right and holy, God will enable you to do so.

There is a beautiful expression in the story of Nehemiah, full of encouragement to timid hearts: "Thy servants, who desire to fear Thy name." Nehemiah was a little afraid to say he feared the Lord's name, but he could honestly say that he desired to fear it, and God accepted that choice, and enabled him to make it.

Our gracious and all-sufficient Saviour asks no more of us than we are really able to give. He puts His grace within reach of every human being, and if you will take it you can, and He will do the rest. The chariot of grace is passing by, and He is saying, in the language of one of old, "Is thy heart right with my heart, as my heart is with thy heart? Come into my chariot." And He will carry you in the chariot of His grace above all your trials, conflicts and difficulties, and make you more than conqueror, through His all-sufficient grace.

III.

In the closing incident we have a picture of the way to reach the highest things. The children of Ephraim came to Joshua with a special request for a double inheritance.

Their plea was that they were a great people, and that the Lord had blessed them hitherto. Their request was that they should receive part of the fertile valleys adjoining them, and held by the native tribes; and it seems to be implied that they expected their brethren to help them to drive them out. It really amounted to a request that they might receive a larger share from the inheritance of their brethren, and the help of the other tribes to win this inheritance.

Joshua's reply is full of keen sarcasm and shrewd wisdom. He does not deny their claim; he does not discourage their ambition. He says, "Thou art a great people, and hast great power," and then he bids them go and prove their greatness by doing something great, and thus conquering the enemy over against them.

The mountain, he adds, is there, with its powerful Canaanites and its chariots of iron, and they can have no grander opportunity than to conquer these hordes, and they can have just as much as they can take and prove their right to by valorous conquest.

They seem to have disliked his sarcastic and practical message, and they came back the second time. But he only sharpened his caustic words a little more, and repeated his former challenge – that if they were as great as they claimed to be, they must prove it by some great achievement, and they could have all they could conquer.

They seem to have dropped out of the drama at this period; and, as we learn from a former verse, that they could not drive out the people of the land, but the Canaanites should dwell in the land, we have reason to fear that the greatness of Ephraim faded away "like the morning cloud and the early dew."

But the words remain for us, and a grander inheritance still awaits every brave heart that is willing to take up the challenge and climb the mountain heights of hardship and opposition.

There are several things in the plea of the Ephraimites that are fitted to fill us with humiliation. The first is, their consciousness of their own greatness. This is very humbling and discouraging. "We are a great people!" It is a good deal better to have somebody else say this than to say it ourselves.

We are all in danger of getting self-conscious. It is not only a blemish upon a noble character, but it is a source of great weakness. In conscious nothingness alone lies our strength and security evermore.

The next serious criticism is the reference to their claim for superior blessing. "The Lord hath blessed me hitherto." Well, He has blessed other people, too and if He has blessed you more than others, it is only a stronger reason why you should do more than others, and it gives you no claim for a special possession or an easy inheritance won for you by others.

A true servant – like the Seraphim – hides his feet as well as his face with his wings, and presses forward to the things that are yet undone.

The third fault of the Ephraimites was that they looked for others to help them. They wanted somebody to give them an inheritance, and Joshua told them they could have it for the taking.

How much would any of us amount to if we were separated from the people that surround us and uphold us, and, stripped of our props, were sent out to stand alone?

Take you out of this assembly, with its hallowed associations, and send you out to stand alone with God in some lone field, at home or abroad, and how much faith and courage would you have left?

These are tests that have to come to us sooner or later. Every one must learn to lean upon God, and then God can trust him with human surroundings and supports, without the danger of his leaning upon an arm of flesh.

Ephraim wanted other people to conquer his inheritance for him, and there are lots of people today willing to accept the prizes of grace if somebody will give them without effort. They will allow the Lord to heal them if somebody will pray it into them and believe for them.

They want to have sanctification and the baptism of the Holy Ghost, but they want to get it from somebody's hands or prayers. They are willing to work for Christ, but they want someone to prepare the work for them, and give it to them, like a piece of machinery, all wound up and ready to go.

Put them into the pulpit, with a nice congregation, choir and salary, and they will go with considerable regularity for awhile.

Start them in some routine of Christian work, and buoy them up with sympathy, appreciation, encouragement and praise, and they will do nicely.

But send them out to the regions beyond; set them down, like Paul and Silas in the prison of Philippi; plant them in a wilderness of isolation and desolation, and they will shrink into nothing, and wither like a fading flower.

There are people who are as tall as church spires now, who will scarcely be fit for doorsteps in the temple yonder. Thank God that He does send us out alone sometimes, and prove how much of Himself we really possess.

But there are, on the other hand, some very cheering things in this message.

The first is that God is not displeased with our holy ambition, and does not discourage our high aspirations. If we want a larger work, God will give it to us. We may step out into the regions beyond, and conquer as much territory as we dare. There is nothing to hinder any ambitious Christian starting out tomorrow and starting a mission in Central China that will be as much blessed as the China Inland Mission, if he dare to take it from the Lord.

There is nothing to hinder any earnest Christian, who has the call, from starting a work in the slums that will be as fruitful as the Water Street Mission. That began with nothing, and you can begin with just as much capital if you take the Lord for it.

When James and John came to Christ with their mother, asking Him to give them the best place in the kingdom, He did not refuse their request, but told them it would be given to them if they could do His work, drink of His cup, and be baptized with His baptism.

Do we want the competition? The greatest things are always hedged about by the hardest things, and we, too, shall find the mountains, the forests, the Canaanites, and the chariots of iron, as well as the Ephraimites.

Hardship is the price of coronation. Triumphal arches are not woven out of rose blossoms and silken cords, but of hard blows and bloody scars.

The very hardships that you are enduring in your life today are given by the Master for the explicit purpose of enabling you to win your crown. Do not wait for some ideal situation, some romantic difficulty, some far-away emergency; but rise to meet the actual conditions which the providence of God has placed around you today.

Your crown of glory lies imbedded in the very heart of those things – those hardships and trials that are pressing you this very hour, week and month of your life.

The hardest things are not those that the world knows of. Down in your secret soul, unseen and unknown by any but Jesus, there is a little trial that you would not dare to mention, that is harder for you to bear than martyrdom. There, beloved, lies your crown. God help you to overcome, and some time to wear it!

Oh, how the days are telling as they pass by! The Spirit is testing us and trying our fitness for something beyond.

Each one of us is conscious, as we meet people, of measuring them mentally and physically, and determining their character and weight, and what they are fit for. And how disappointed we are when those whom we have trusted do not come up to our standard for them, and we feel that they are not fitted for the place we had given them in our thought! And how pleased we are when they do come somewhere near our ideal of them!

Beloved, this may help you to understand how God is watching you from the heights above, not with the eye of a critic, but as a loving Master, and when we rise to His standard how His arms will enfold us! How He will press us to His bosom, and rejoice as He can say: "Well done, good and faithful servant, enter thou into the joy of thy Lord." "Sit down with me upon my throne, even as I have overcome, and am set down with my Father upon His throne!"

God grant we may all press forward to the high places He has prepared for us, and meet the moments that come as witnesses that shall come back some day to testify either for or against us in the great day of eternal recompense!

CHAPTER X.

TIMNATH-SERAH; OR, THE CITY OF THE SUN.

"WHEN they had made an end of dividing the land for inheritance by their coasts the children of Israel gave an inheritance to Joshua, the son of Nun, among them: According to the word of the Lord, they gave him the city which he asked, even Timnath-serah in Mount Ephraim; and he built the city, and dwelt therein." – Josh. 19:49-50.

This was the last of the special inheritances in the Land of Promise. Joshua, the unselfish leader, left his own inheritance until the last, and even then it was his people who gave to him his portion, and he accepted it only when they pressed it upon him. It is no wonder that it was the highest and best of all the choice possessions of the land.

Its name is suggestive of its value and significance. Timnath-serah in Mount Ephraim means the city of the sun, and it speaks to us of the highest and best possibilities of our own Christian life.

1. The city of the sun is a place of delightful happiness, for the sun is the type of the Lord Himself, our light and our salvation, and "in His presence there is fullness of joy, and at His right hand there are pleasures forevermore. "Blessed is the people that know the joyful sound;" they shall walk, O Lord, in the light of Thy countenance, in Thy name shall they rejoice all the day, and in Thy righteousness shall they be exalted."

The figure speaks of gladness and sunshine. Are we living there?

There is no better way for us to glorify Him than to be happy in Him, and "rejoice before Him all our days." This will be a witness to the world that they cannot resist, and it will give a strength and energy to our own life and service which cannot be exaggerated.

Oh! ye downcast souls, ye children of anxious care and gloom, come up into the city of the sun and dwell in the light of the Lord! There is a heaven below in which victorious souls may dwell before they reach the heaven above.

2. The city of the sun is a place of abundant and glorious grace, for "the Lord God is a sun and shield; the Lord will give grace and glory, and no good thing will be withheld from them that walk uprightly."

Its inhabitants have the immunities and privileges of heavenly citizens, and dwell continually in the presence of their King, and all the riches of His grace are their free inheritance.

He gives them not only His grace, but His glory, and withholds from them no good thing. They have His resources for all their undertakings, and out of His fullness do they receive even grace for grace.

Beloved, are we dwelling in this city of the sun? Have we received this abundance of grace, and are we reigning in the light and joy of Jesus Christ? Can you say with a glad and rejoicing heart, "My God shall supply all my need according to His riches and glory by Christ Jesus," and "Surely goodness and mercy shall follow me all the days of my life, and I shall dwell in the house of the Lord forever!"

3. The city of the sun is the place of Christ's manifested presence. In the fourteenth chapter of John, Jesus said to His disciples, "He that hath My commandments and keepeth them is he that loveth Me, and he that loveth Me shall be loved of My Father, and I will love him and will manifest Myself unto him."

This word "manifest" in the original involves the figure of the brightest sunlight, and it literally means the outshining of the sun, and expresses the glory of Christ's inward revelation of Himself to the trusting and obedient heart.

Brighter than the noonday sun, more real than the effulgence of the orb of day, is the light with which Christ makes Himself known, ofttimes, in the inner sanctuary of the consecrated soul.

It was foreshadowed in the Shekinah glory, that lit up, in ancient times, the Holy of Holies and hovered above the mercy-seat. Speaking of it, the apostle says: "God, who commanded the light to shine out of darkness, hath shined in our hearts to give the light of the knowledge of the glory of God in the face of Jesus Christ."

The Holy Spirit is spoken of as "shedding abroad," or shining abroad, the love of God in our hearts. Do you know the vision of His glorious face? Have you seen Him in the revelation of His inward glory, "whose countenance is as the sun shining in his strength," and of whom you can truly say, "He is chief among ten thousand, yea, He is altogether lovely?"

4. The city of the sun is a place of light and guidance. For again the Master has said: "I am the light of the world; he that followeth Me shall not walk in darkness, but shall have the light of life." The light of life is the light that shines upon our daily life.

There is a place where we may walk continually in the light of the Lord, and receive habitually the guidance that will guard us from serious error, and keep us in the light of God.

There is a way of coming to God occasionally for direction in great crises, and then doing the best you can on ordinary occasions. But it is possible to have our whole life so possessed by the Holy Ghost that our very thoughts and intuitions will come to us in quietness and simplicity, with the consciousness that they have been touched by His thought and illumined by His light, that we are walking continually with our Father, and receiving constantly the testimony that we please God.

This is a very beautiful freedom which He has promised to the meek and consecrated spirit. "I will instruct thee and teach thee in the way thou shouldst go. I will guide thee with Mine eye." "Thine ear shall hear a word behind thee saying, This is the way, walk ye in it, when ye turn to the right hand or to the left."

Beloved, are you dwelling in this city of light, walking continually under His directing eye, and with the consciousness of being in His blessed light?

5. The city of the sun is a place of quickening life and power. The sun is the source of life and force. As he ascends the higher meridian of spring and summer, how the pulses of nature revive, until every tree and plant is throbbing with new vitality, and all the forces of nature are stimulated and vivified!

How easily yonder sun holds this world and all the train of planets and satellites in their circling orbits, without a quiver of restlessness or a flutter of decaying strength! How mighty the force of gravitation that sweeps from yonder ball of fire and holds the solar system in harmonious activity!

Christ is our sun and source of life and power, and as we dwell in His presence we are quickened into resurrection life and animated with His own almighty power.

The joy of the Lord is our strength, and they who dwell above the clouds and mists of earth's lower planes know "the exceeding greatness of His power to usward who believe," and are used by His Spirit as the instruments and vessels of His mighty plans.

Are we dwelling in this city of life and working in His All-Sufficiency?

6. The city of the sun is a place of warmth and love. It is a summer clime, where the frosts and chills of selfishness and bitterness never come, where the warm atmosphere of God's everlasting love melts every ice bond, dissolves the wintry chains, and brings all hearts into the family relationships of the heavenly world, and

we are “one, even as the Father is in the Son and the Son in the Father,” and, fitly framed together, the whole building groweth into a holy temple in the Lord.

We cannot know anything about love unless we dwell in God and God in us. All true love must come from Him, and as we live in the light of His presence and the warm atmosphere of His fellowship, we shall love even as He loves, and we shall reflect on others the radiance which is shining in our hearts from His.

7. The city of the sun is a place of Divine Healing.

Let us listen again to His own words: “Unto you that fear My name shall the Sun of Righteousness arise, with healing in His wings, and ye shall go forth and grow like calves of the stall.”

In the natural world sunlight is essential to health, and darkness and shadow create a congenial atmosphere of disease. Good light and pure air are agencies of health.

Still more is the life and joy of the Lord essential to spiritual healthfulness. The light of Christ is the true source of physical strength, and the joy of the Lord is the best of all medicines. The inflowing and indwelling of the Holy Ghost brings quickening strength to every fiber of our being.

If you would rise above the depressing influence of climate, contagion and natural infirmity, build your house in Timnath-serah, and dwell continually in the loving presence and cloudless communion of the Holy Ghost.

8. The city of the sun is a place of cloudless and unbroken communion.

There is a place in Northern Europe which they call “The Land of the Midnight Sun.” There, as the months pass by, the sun completes his circle above the horizon, and it is one continual, cloudless day.

There is such a land in our higher inheritance of grace. There is a promise which we may prove and claim even in this life. “Thy sun shall no more go down, neither shall thy moon withdraw itself, for the Lord shall be thy everlasting light and the days of thy mourning shall be ended."

There are human friendships, especially those that are very intimate, whose exquisite delight is this, that they have never been clouded, and that these friends could not even imagine the shadow of a cloud passing over them. The very thought that you could be alienated from your friend would at once place that friendship on a different plane and make it common.

It is its exquisite prerogative that you cannot even conceive of its being clouded by a doubt or a breach of confidence.

And there is a friendship with Christ so exquisite and true that it not only has no severance or interruption, but we cannot even conceive of any breach of suspension.

In its very nature, the love is everlasting, infinite, unconditional, and capable of no separation. He has given to us His eternal oath: "I have sworn that I will never be wroth with thee, nor rebuke thee." And you would as soon think of blaspheming Him to His face as of even imagining the shadow of a doubt of His perfect and everlasting love.

Beloved, have you come into this high place of unclouded light and love? Have you tasted the exquisiteness of that communion which you know will never be interrupted? It is for you. This is the city "where they go no more out, and where they have no need of the sun, for the Lord God giveth them light, and the Lamb is the Light thereof."

II. HOW DO WE GET TO THIS CITY?

1. We get there through Jesus Christ, the only Mediator. There are two sides to a mountain. One is precipitous and dangerous. If you attempt to ascend you will be hurled from dizzy heights and slippery places to awful chasms, or wrapped in veils of impenetrable mist, through which you cannot find your way.

But there is another way, up a gentle incline, where a pathway has been prepared, and you can safely reach the loftiest heights.

And so there is a way by which we cannot find God – the way of mere research, human wisdom or moral righteousness. In vain have the ages sought to find the seat of His gracious presence, and gaze upon His countenance in light and love.

It is like ascending Sinai through the thick darkness and the angry fire.

But there is a way which Jesus has prepared, and of which He says: "I am the way; no man cometh unto the Father but by Me. No man hath seen God at any time, but the Only Begotten Son, who is in the bosom of the Father, He hath declared Him." Not only *was* He in the bosom of the Father but He *is* in the bosom, and when we come into His bosom we are in the Father's bosom, too. It is like the ascent of the ancient Mount, when Moses took the elders of Israel up to meet God, and they carried in their hands the atoning blood; and as they went up into that glorious Presence-Chamber, we are told with exceeding beauty, "They did eat and drink, and they saw God, and there was under His feet, as it were, the paved work of a sapphire stone, and, as it were, the body of heaven in His clearness."

This is the way to Timnath-serah. "Having boldness to enter into the holiest by the blood of Jesus, by a new and living way which He hath consecrated for us through the veil, that is His face, let us draw near;" and we shall find ourselves in the city of the sun.

2. Let us build there. Joshua not only chose Timnath-serah, but he ascended to the mountain-height, and he built the city. Now there are a good many ways to build a city, especially with reference to the sun. We can build so as to shut out all the warmth, or we can turn its face toward the sunshine and open all the windows to the light. Some people seem to be constituted so as to catch

every shadow and cloud that comes, and some seem to focalize every ray of sunshine at their own door.

Were I building a city of the sun, I should make all the gates of praise and the walls salvation. The houses should be of transparent glass, that the sun might shine through them every day, and the outlook for every window should be toward the sun-rising.

There is a story of an Oriental king who worshipped the sun, and he wanted to build a temple to him. He sent for three architects and asked each to give him a model of the temple. After many days they returned to submit their models.

The first prepared a temple of stone, beautifully carved. The king admired it and called for the second. His was of pure gold, and the walls were polished and burnished until they reflected the sun from every side. The king was delighted with it, and the architect thought he had won the prize. But the third brought his little model, and, lo! it was all of glass, so that the sun could come in every side and fill it spontaneously with his light and glory.

"Ah," said the king, "this is the true temple of the sun; this is his own fitting shrine, letting him into every chamber, and having no glory but his own perfect light."

Beloved, shall we be such temples of the Sun of Righteousness, open to Him in every avenue of our being, and filled in the inmost part with His glorious light and presence? He will come wherever there is an opening to receive Him.

3. But Joshua not only built there but dwelt there. He did not visit Timnath-serah occasionally to get mountain views from the sunlit hills, but he made it his abiding home.

Are we dwelling in Timnath-serah? Are we abiding in the light and love of God? Have we come to that settled place where "the sun no more goes down, and the Lord becomes our everlasting light?"

And now there are two more words that tell us how we may obtain this blessed portion.

The first is, Joshua received this inheritance "According to the commandment of the Lord." God provided it for him in His word, and so He has provided it for each of us. It is not only God's promise, but His command for us, that we shall rise to the fullness of His blessing.

"Let us therefore fear, lest, a promise being left us of entering into His rest, any of you should seem to come short of it."

But there is another word. We are told that Joshua also asked it. God gave it and Joshua asked it; and we shall receive what we ask for, and take.

There are many things in the commands of God for you, which are missing by simple default. "Ye have not because ye ask not."

How sorry you would be if you found, after spending a lifetime of poverty and toil, a will had been left by a friend providing you with affluence and wealth, and you had simply neglected to prove it and claim it!

Your bountiful Father has left you a city of glory and joy. Do not let it be lost through your default, but claim your inheritance, enter upon it, build it and occupy it, and you, too, shall be able to sing,

"I am dwelling on the mountains,
Where the golden sunlight gleams,
O'er a land whose wondrous beauty
Far exceeds my fondest dreams;
Where the air is pure, ethereal,
Laden with the breath of flowers,
They are blooming by the fountains,
'Neath the amaranthine bowers.

Is not this the Land of Beulah,
Blessed, blessed Land of Light,
Where the flowers bloom forever
And the Sun is always bright?"

CHAPTER XI.

THE CITIES OF REFUGE; OR THE SINNER'S INHERITANCE.

"Who have fled for refuge to lay hold upon the hope set before us." – Heb. 6:18; Josh. chapter 20.

THIS chapter describes the arrangements in ancient Israel for the protection of persons accused of murder or manslaughter. It was no unusual thing in ancient times to provide asylums for such persons.

It is said that the city of Rome was ordinarily peopled by refugees from all countries, who were promised immunity by Romulus, and who came to the asylum established for them, and afterward became citizens of Rome.

The arrangements made by God through Moses and Joshua were of a much wiser and more righteous character. It is very significant that God should so emphasize His care for the sinner in this book, which is so specially devoted to typify the principles of the higher Christian life.

At the very threshold of the land we meet Rahab, of Jericho, a woman representing the very worst class of society, and we find her not only saved, by the grace of God, but introduced into the ancestral line of David and of Christ Himself, and one of the mothers of the royal family of the eternal ages. And here at the close of the Book, in the most careful provision which Jehovah made for the protection of the manslayer, we see a very emphatic hint of God's gracious care for the sinful and the lost.

Surely, it is meant to teach us that the higher we rise in the experience of God's grace, the lower we will stoop in the exercise of His mercy toward the fallen, and the more will we labor and care for the recovery of the lost.

Let us never get so sanctified that we shall be out of reach of poor sinners, or lose our sympathy for them, and theirs for us. The nearer we come to our Master, the more frequently will we be found by His side in the company of publicans and sinners.

I should greatly suspect my sanctification if it led me to lose my interest in the salvation of men, and my love for the souls of the lost and the unworthy. Thank God that in these days the men and women that are going deepest into the slums and searching farthest for the sheep that have gone astray, are those who believe in the fullness of Christ, and live in His abiding fellowship, and in all the higher things which we have been studying in this wondrous Book!

In this connection it is very noteworthy that all the cities of refuge were placed under the care of the Levites, and, in fact, were Levitical cities.

The Levites, as we know, were the types of the highest consecration; and the lesson is, that God has given the sinful world in trust to His true Levites, and as His consecrated people fulfill the mission of the Levites they will be found seeking and saving the souls that have gone astray.

I.

In the ancient cities of refuge there is a beautiful type of God's provision in the Gospel for the salvation of men.

1. It was a legal and Divine provision.

It was guarded and sanctioned by Divine enactment, and it was as secure as the will and power of God could make it.

If the law of the land stands behind you, you are stronger in your humble home, with a simple thread to hold the door, than you would be in a fortified castle, if you were contrary to the law.

Entrenched behind the right, you can fold your arms and defy all the power of man to disturb you. But against the law, and in a position of wrong, you may be barricaded and defended by walls of adamant and bastions of steel; but the law will break through your defenses, drag you from your hiding-place, and consign you to the dungeon of a criminal in spite of all your fancied security.

The protection which God gave to the ancient manslayer was a legal and Divine protection. Asylums were provided under special laws, to which he might flee and defy the avenger to touch him. Within that sacred enclosure it would be a crime to shed his blood, and every law and power in the land were bound to protect him.

And so the salvation which God offers to the sinner is not a mere adventitious escape from punishment, but a security so Divinely arranged, so justly secured, so eternally guaranteed, that "we might have strong consolation, who have fled for refuge, to lay hold upon the hope set before us."

If you accept the Gospel of Jesus Christ, you will have all the power of God back of you to defend you; all the will of God on your side; all the justice and righteousness of God pledged to your defense, as well as all the infinite love and mercy of God to welcome and bless you.

It is not a mere caprice of conditional clemency, which He may change at will, but an everlasting protection, based upon the principles of right, and immovable as the throne of God.

Every debt is not merely forgiven, but paid absolutely and forever by a just equivalent fully accepted by the offended party. The atonement of Jesus Christ has met every requirement of justice, and it would be wrong on the part of God to punish one who has availed himself of this Divine provision. Therefore, we are told that "if we confess our sins, He is *faithful and just* to forgive us our sins, and to cleanse us from all unrighteousness."

He is bound by the very attributes of justice to save the soul that accepts the atonement of Jesus, and His word is pledged as one that cannot lie, to save and keep the trusting heart.

Oh, sinner, if you come within this enclosure you are as safe as though you were in heaven! That word – "Him that cometh unto Me, I will in no wise cast out," will be a wall of adamant against your guilty conscience, and all your foes. That mighty promise – "I give unto them eternal life, and they shall never perish, neither shall any pluck them out of My hand," will hold you as "an anchor both sure and steadfast, and which entereth into that within the vail."

2. The city of refuge was a just and righteous provision.

It was not indiscriminate immunity from punishment for all classes of criminals, but it was a place of safety for the man who had accidentally, or without intent of evil, taken the life of his neighbor, and he was sheltered and guarded until his case could be investigated, and if he were found to be innocent of any intent of evil, he was allowed to remain in safety in this refuge until the death of the high priest.

And so the Gospel of Jesus Christ is not a premium on vice, or an excuse for license. It does not say to a man, "commit all the sin you please, and you shall have plenary indulgence." But it is God's provision for men who sincerely desire to be delivered from sin, and be right with God and man.

If you really want to be saved and cleansed, and to live a right and a true life, and will honestly choose it, the blood of Christ and the grace of the Holy Spirit will instantly and fully save you, no matter who you are, or what you have been or done.

But if you do not want to do right, if your intention is to commit sin; if your purpose is to do evil, and you only want the Gospel to shelter you in it, you shall find it the most terrible place beneath the heavens for a false heart to stand. No man dare trifle with the precious blood of Christ.

It says to the sinner: "Neither do I condemn thee;" but it says just as solemnly, "Go, and sin no more." "There is forgiveness with God," not that He may be trifled with, but "that He may be feared."

3. The man-slayer abode in the city of refuge until after the death of the high priest; then he was free to return to his home.

This very significantly points to the death of Jesus Christ, as the ground of our deliverance from guilt and sin, and our acceptance into the favor of God and the liberty of His sons.

More specifically it points, perhaps, to the difference between the Old Testament saints and those under the Gospel. Under the Old Testament, the sins of believers were forgiven, and they were accepted into the favor of God, in anticipation of the redemption which was to be accomplished in the future, but they did not enter into heaven, but were held up to the Ascension of Christ, under a certain reserve, in Hades, or Paradise. But after Christ's resurrection they ascended with Him into heaven, and now, the souls of believers at their death immediately pass into His glory, and enjoy the fullness of the purchase of His blood, as those of the past dispensation did not.

Therefore, we find "David gathered to his fathers," but Stephen "beholding the heavens opened, and Jesus Christ standing on the right hand of God," as he enters His immediate presence.

Lazarus is carried, not into the bosom of Jesus, but "into Abraham's bosom," with the Old Testament saints. But Paul expects to "be with Christ, and the spirits of just men made perfect."

The death and resurrection of Jesus Christ have discharged us from every claim, and given to us the glorious liberty of the sons of God in this world, and the heirs of His glory in the world to come.

4. The ancient cities of refuge were accessible from all places, and to all classes. There were no less than six of them distributed throughout the land; three of them on the west side of the Jordan, about equal distances apart, and three on the east side; and none farther than a day's run from any point in the land.

The roads that led to them were always kept in good repair, at the expense of the government. The way was always open, both day and night, for any fugitive that should fly to the asylum. The gates of the city were continually open, and persons there to welcome the fugitive the moment he might arrive, and to provide him with every necessary of life. No one was allowed to obstruct his progress on his journey. Everybody made way for him, and there was no possibility of mistaking the way, for at every crossing, and often along the way, were mile posts and inscriptions, pointing in the right direction, and the word "Refuge" written on each post, so that he could read even while he ran. This is the meaning of that expression: "He that runneth may read."

So the way to Christ and the salvation of the Gospel is just as open and just as plain. Christ is accessible to every sinner that wants Him, and the gates of mercy are never farther than a day's run – nay, a moment's look – from the most hopeless heart.

The way of salvation is so plain that it is impossible for an honest inquirer to mistake it. There may be differences of opinion about doctrines. There may be variations about Sanctification, Healing, the Lord's Coming, and the doctrines of theology, but they are all one about the way of salvation.

In the missions and in the inquiry meeting, there is but one Gospel and one salvation; and you could never find out, if you tried, what church that Christian worker belongs to, when he is pointing souls to Christ. Praise God for the simplicity of the Gospel.

No man need ever be lost through ambiguity or uncertainty about this. God has left the highway always open; the gates are never closed; and He wants us to keep all obstacles out of the way of the sinner, and speed him on his way to the hope set before him. Oh come and enter in!

5. The fugitive was perfectly safe in the city of refuge, and all his wants were supplied at the public expense. There was not even a weapon of war to be found within its gates, and there was no lack of anything which he needed for his comfort or maintenance.

And so with the provisions of the Gospel. We are eternally secure and amply supplied. "We have access by faith into this grace wherein we stand." God has provided in Christ for the supply of all our needs. There is grace for our daily cleansing and constant keeping, and our God has declared that He will supply all our needs "according to His riches in glory by Christ Jesus;" and of "His fullness, we have received even grace for grace."

6. There were two things which the man-slayer must do, and which the sinner must also do. The first was – to fly, and never to stop until he got within the precincts of the refuge. The second was – to stay, and never venture beyond those precincts until he was publicly released.

And so for us there is a refuge, there is salvation, there is abundant grace; but we must fly to it. We must claim it. We must take it, or we shall perish.

There is no safety on the way. There is no safety – almost there. The man-slayer could have perished even on the very steps of its portals. And so we must not linger or delay a moment until we have crossed its threshold and are safe within its doors.

God's words are awfully urgent. "Flee from the wrath to come." "Lay hold on eternal life." "Tarry not in all the plain." "Behold *now* is the accepted time; *now* is the day of salvation."

Outside of Christ, everything in heaven and earth is against the sinner. Destruction pursues him in every breath, element and force about him. His only safety is to *fly* to Christ without a moment's delay, and then when you enter that sacred refuge, stay there.

There was a small circle around its walls within which the inmates could have freedom, and it was large enough to give them all the freedom they needed; but beyond that there was no safety.

And so God has circumscribed our refuge. Within its precincts, within the Holy Bible, we are absolutely safe; but beyond His Word there is danger, and there may be destruction. Let us abide in Him and under His commandments, and we shall be safe and happy in His infinite protection and everlasting love.

II.

The ancient cities of refuge also set forth the *fullness of* Christ's salvation for the sinner.

It is not enough to be merely saved. God has a boundless progression of blessing through which He wants to lead us, and as we press forward into the fullness of Christ, we are not only safe and secure, but we are guarded from falling, and led on to all the heights of His grace and glory.

A wise Christian worker will never be content with simply leading a soul to Christ, and will never rest until he has introduced him to the fullness of His grace, the baptism of His Spirit, and the blessings of a consecrated life.

All this is finely set forth in the ancient cities of refuge. There were six of them, and their names are significant of the fullness of Christ.

The first was Kedesh, in the northwest, signifying righteousness. The second was Shechem, in Central Palestine, west of the Jordan. This name signifies a shoulder, and will stand for strength. The third was Hebron, in Southwestern Palestine; and this, we know, means friendship and love. On the other side of the

Jordan was Bezer, signifying security. Next is Ramoth, which means heights. And Golan, the last, means a circle, and of course signifies the everlasting things.

Now, these six names, with their beautiful significance, furnish a glorious progression in the blessings of the Gospel and the grace of God.

The first thing Christ brings to us is righteousness, making us right with God, right with our own selves, and right with everybody else. This is Kedesh.

Next, He gives us His strength to keep us and help us, carrying us upon His shoulders, helping us in our helplessness, and bearing our burdens, and us as well. This is Shechem.

The next is Hebron, where He brings us into the experience of His love, and unfolds to us the fullness of His grace and the love-life of the Lord, filling us with His love for others, and binding us to Himself, forever.

Then we come to Bezer, the place of stablishing, settling, and security, where we are confirmed in our faith and hope, and stablished in our life and love immovably.

Now we are ready to make a further advance, and so we come to Ramoth, and all the heights of His grace and glory; the resurrection and ascension life of Christ; the place where we dwell on high, and seek the things that are above, and look on all things from the heaven-side and the throne-life.

And, finally, the series closes with Golan, the circle that never ends; the way everlasting; where we have the faith that falters not, the love that changes not, the peace that abides, the health that is Divine, the joy that remains in us – in short, the indwelling Christ, who is in us, "the same yesterday, today and forever;" an experience in which we anticipate even now, the glory which is to come, and enjoy a foretaste of what awaits us in its fullness at His blessed coming.

Beloved, have we come along the whole of this glorious progression? Have we His righteousness, His strength, His love, His security, His heights of grace and glory, and do we know His everlasting way?

If not, the doors are all open. Perhaps you have entered Kedesh, but you may enter Shechem, too, and Hebron waits to welcome you, and Bezer to stablish you, and Ramoth to exalt you, and Golan to bring you into the life eternal in which we may live, even before we reach eternity. Oh, let us enter and dwell there.

There safe shall we abide,
  There sweet shall be our rest;
And, every longing satisfied,
  With full salvation blest.

CHAPTER XII.

THE INHERITANCE OF THE LEVITES, OR, ALL IN GOD AND GOD IN ALL.

"I beseech you, therefore, brethren, by the mercies of God, that ye present your bodies a living sacrifice, holy, acceptable unto God, which is your reasonable service." – Rom. 12:1.

THE twenty-first chapter of Joshua gives us an account of the inheritance of the Levites. They were the official tribe in ancient Israel, and entrusted with all the services of the sanctuary, the work of education, and the religious culture of all the tribes.

They were the types of Christian service, and represented the principles of true consecration.

I.

They represented the principle of redemption as the basis of consecration.

In the eighth chapter of Numbers and the seventeenth and eighteenth verses, we read, "For all the first-born of the children of Israel are Mine, both man and beast; on the day that I smote every first-born in the land of Egypt I sanctified them for Myself. And I have taken the Levites for all the first-born of the children of Israel."

They were thus substituted for the first-born who had been doomed to death, and saved by the blood of the Paschal lamb. The Levites stood for these, and thus represented the idea of redemption. They were as men who had been bought with a price and whose lives were not their own. But God did not require their death, but took their life instead.

Our service as consecrated Christians and our consecration should likewise spring from the redemption of Christ's blood. This is the basis which the Apostle presents as the ground of our surrender to God. "Ye are not your own, for ye are bought with a price," therefore, glorify God with your body, which is God's.

There is no credit or merit in our consecrating ourselves to God, because we already belong to Him and have no right to retain ourselves. It is sacrilege and dishonesty. He has purchased every power of our being and every possibility of our existence, and when we yield ourselves to Him, we simply recognize the fact that we are already His, and that He has a right to all that we can give or be.

"When ye have done all, say we are unprofitable servants, for we have done what was our duty to do." Let no man think, therefore, that because he has made a complete surrender of himself to God, he has put God in any sense in his debt, or has aught whereof to glory. He has simply paid his honest debts and taken his true place in the Divine economy, that is all. And he may well say with David, "Who am I, and what is my people, that we should be able to offer so willingly after this sort? For all things come of Thee, and of Thine own have we given Thee."

II.

The Levites represented the principle of separation as the element of consecration.

We read again in Numbers 8:14, "Thou shalt separate the Levites from among the children of Israel; and the Levites shall be Mine."

Our consecration separates us from the world and sin, and brings us out from our natural life to be exclusively the Lord's. Therefore, we read in the twelfth chapter of Romans, immediately after the command, to present our bodies a living sacrifice, "Be not conformed to this world: but be ye transformed by the renewing of your mind, that ye may prove what is that good, and acceptable, and perfect will of God."

It is not merely an outward separation, but a separation which transforms us by the renewing of our mind, and gives us a new spirit and a disposition which separates itself from evil, by natural detachment.

The Pharisees separated themselves outwardly from sinners, but in spirit they were identical. Christ Jesus mingled with sinners, but in spirit, He was as distinct from them as light from darkness, and oil from water.

The little plant may grow out of a manure heap, and be surrounded by filth, and covered very often with the floating dust that is borne upon the breeze, but its white roots are separated from the unclean soil, and its leaves and flowers have no affinity with the dust that settles upon them; and after a shower of summer rain they throw off every particle of defilement, and look up, as fresh and spotless as before, for their intrinsic nature cannot have any part with these defiling things.

This is the separation which Christ requires and which He gives. There is no merit in my staying from the theatre if I want to go. There is no value in my abstaining from the foolish novel or the intoxicating cup, if I am all the time wishing I could have them. My heart is there, and my soul is defiled by the desire for evil things. It is not the world that stains us, but the love of the world. The true Levite is separated from the desire for earthly things, and even if he could, he would not have the forbidden pleasures which others prize.

III.

The Levites represented the principle of dedication, as the essence of consecration.

The Levites were presented to the Lord by Moses as a living sacrifice. "Thou shalt set the Levites before Aaron and before his sons, and offer them for an offering unto the Lord. Thou shalt cleanse them, and offer them for an offering. For they are wholly given unto Me, from among them the children of Israel," Numbers 8:13, 15-16.

And again, Numbers 3:6, 13, "Bring the tribe of Levi near, and present them before Aaron the priest, that they may minister unto him. Mine shall they be. I am the Lord."

And so it is required of us, as God's spiritual Levites, that we shall present our bodies a living sacrifice. We are already the Lord's by right of purchase, but now we must acknowledge that right and make a personal surrender, and when we do this He is pleased to accept it from us. It should be unconditional, unreserved and irrevocable, giving Him the right to own us and control us as He shall see best, and renouncing the right to self-control and self-ownership forever. And not only so, but we must do it gladly, and without regret or apprehension.

What would you think of a girl who was shrinking and hesitating whether to commit her life to the man she loves, and saying: "How can I leave my mother and go with this man?" If she loves him, she is only too glad to go with him. She loves to put herself entirely under his control, and trust all her happiness to his keeping, for she knows that he will only seek her good, and she feels safer in his hands than in her own, if he really has her affection.

And so God requires of us not only perfect surrender, but joyful surrender. If we hold anything back in our spirit, He will not accept us. He does not need us. He could create a million souls in a minute that would serve Him better. He only takes us because of what He can do for us. He only wants us unreservedly, so that He can be able more fully to bless us, and true consecration counts it an honor and a privilege to be able to give all and receive all in return.

It is because He wants to do so much for us that He demands the absolute control of all our being, as the foster-parent who adopts a child insists on having it take his name, and give him its full control, because he wants to make it the heir to his fortune.

So God demands that we shall be His, and His alone, and then He gives us as whole-heartedly as He expects us to give to Him.

Have we accepted this claim? Have we responded to His call? Have we made this unreserved, unconditional surrender?

Have we presented our bodies a living sacrifice, our reasonable service?

IV.

The Levites represented service, as the fruit of consecration.

The ministry of the Levites is thus described: "I have given the Levites as a gift to Aaron and to his sons from among the children of Israel, to do the service of the children of Israel in the tabernacle of the congregation."

They were divided into several families; the sons of Gershon, Kohath and Merari.

The Gershonites had charge of the tabernacle, the tent, the covering, the hangings, the curtains and the cords.

The Kohathites had a still more sacred ministry; they had charge of the ark, and the table, and the candlestick, and the altars and the vessels of the sanctuary, the most sacred things.

The Merarites had charge of the boards of the tabernacle and the bars, the pillars, the sockets and the vessels thereof.

These ancient Levites set up the tabernacle, took it down, carried it from place to place and guarded it and waited upon the priests in their ministry.

Later they were the teachers of the people, and looked after all the educational and social work of the tribes, and especially had charge of the cities of refuge and the reception and protection of the man-slayer that fled from the avenger.

Thus they represented our Christian service in all its varieties as we are called to build up the spiritual house of the Lord, and to carry forward His Kingdom in all places and among all nations, bearing the burdens of His sanctuary and ministering in sacred things.

The high inscription on the crest of many a noble family consists of the two words, "I serve." No nobler dignity can be conferred on a man than to make him a servant. The minister of the Gospel is just a servant, and this is the true meaning of the word.

James and Paul loved to call themselves "the servants of the Lord, and your servants, for Jesus' sake." Moses and Joshua were servants in the Lord's house, and David "served his generation by the will of God."

The general commanding the army is but the servant of his country and his sovereign. The statesman bears the insignia of public service. The Lord Jesus Himself loved to say, "I am among you as he that doth serve;" and God is ever ministering to the whole creation.

We are called to be the servants of God, and our ministry is to set up the true sanctuary, and to wait at the unseen altar whose incense reaches within the veil. In the ages to come, we shall have still higher service. The present is but an apprenticeship for the more glorious future, and God is but schooling us for higher and nobler employments in the new earth and new heaven that are to come.

This is the purpose of our consecration, that God may use us, and that we may be a blessing. It never was intended that one tribe out of twelve should do all the service of the house of God. They were but types of all the rest, and today, under the Gospel, we should be all Levites. "He hath made us kings and priests unto God." There are no proxies in this army, and no substitutes accepted in this draft, but each must take his place, and God expects service and fruit from every follower of

Christ. "Herein is my Father glorified," He has said to every one of us, "that ye bear much fruit. So shall ye be" – wonderful disciples? No; but shall be "My disciples." We have no reason to consider ourselves His disciples, unless we are bearing "much fruit."

There are great varieties in the service of God. A few are called – like the Kohathites – to enter the sanctuary, and bear the more sacred vessels of the Lord, to take the holy ark, and touch the sacred symbols of the mystic Cherubim. Theirs is the ministry of prevailing prayer, and theirs is to hear the secret of the Lord, to know His highest thought, and catch the very whisper of His will.

Others are called to bear the boards and the rougher and heavier burdens. But to all it is enough to know that they are bearing the burdens of the sanctuary, and ministering to Him upon whom the angels wait, and at whose bidding the heavens hasten to obey.

"Having then gifts differing according to the grace that is given to us, whether prophecy, let us prophesy according to the proportion of faith; or ministry, let us wait on our ministering; or he that teacheth, on teaching; or he that exhorteth, on exhortation; he that giveth, let him do it with simplicity; he that ruleth, with diligence; he that soweth mercy, with cheerfulness."

V.

The Levites represented the principle of practical service in all the ordinary walks of life.

They were not shut up in Jerusalem in the tabernacle, but we find them distributed throughout every portion of the land, for the obvious purpose of diffusing the principles which they represented among all sections of the people.

Beautifully, this represents the application of the principles of consecration to all the ordinary occupations and walks of life. God does not want consecration bound up with our prayer book, folded away in our Bagster

Bible, left in our pew between Sabbaths, or brought out for an airing at the weekly prayer-meeting. He does not want our religious phrases and tones for holy days and special times. He wants every place sacred, every time Sabbatic, and everything inscribed "Holiness to the Lord."

He wants us to sit at our dinner table, and eat and drink to the glory of God, to talk with our families in simple happy fellowship, having our speech always "seasoned with salt."

He wants all our life to be as holy as our communion services, and even our buying and selling to be like a sacrament of sweetness and sanctity.

In the coming age, every pot will be inscribed with "Holiness to the Lord," every cooking utensil will cook for Christ, and even the bells on the horses will chime out Glory to Immanuel's name.

I heard the other day, of a company of Christians who came together for a season of waiting upon the Lord, in which they would not allow any of the party to talk on any ordinary subject, or go out to purchase any article in the stores, or to engage in any business which could be avoided. Every moment was supposed to be set apart for some sacred exercise. I thought I would like to take my little grandson in among them and give him a new top to spin to teach them the sanctity of simplicity and childlikeness.

This is essentially the idea of monasticism, and it is unwholesome. It is just as holy to laugh as to cry, and to use your handsaw as your prayer-book.

We can bring Christ into common things as fully as into what we call religious services. Indeed, it is the highest and hardest application of Divine grace, to bring it down to the ordinary matters of life, and therefore God is far more honored in this than even in things that are more specially sacred.

Therefore, in this wonderful chapter of Romans which is the manual of practical consecration, just after the passage that speaks of ministering in sacred things, the apostle comes at once to the common, social and secular affairs into which we are to bring our consecration principles, we read: "Be kindly affectioned one to another with brotherly love; in honor preferring one another; not slothful in business; fervent in spirit; serving the Lord."

God wants the Levites scattered all over the cities of Israel. He wants your workshop, factory, kitchen, nursery, editor's room, and printing office, as much as your pulpit and closet. He wants you to be just as holy at high noon on Monday or Wednesday, as in the sanctuary on Sabbath morning, and to have your consecration as much in Wall Street's whirlpool of trade and business, as in the Cathedral aisle or the quiet closet.

May God give to us this holy priesthood, and make us the light of the world and the salt of the earth!

VI.

The Levites represented the principle of finding all our resources in God Himself.

In the thirteenth chapter and thirty-third verse of Joshua we read: "Unto the tribe of Levi, Moses gave not any inheritance; the Lord God of Israel was their inheritance, as He said unto them."

This is very significant. God gave the land to the other tribes but he gave Himself to the Levites. There is such a thing in Christian life as having an inheritance from the Lord, and there is such a thing as having the Lord Himself for our inheritance.

Some people get a sanctification from the Lord which is of much value, but which is variable, and often impermanent. Others have learned the higher lesson of taking the Lord Himself to be their keeper and their sanctity, and abiding in Him they are kept above the vicissitudes of their own states and feelings.

Some get from the Lord large measures of joy and blessing, and times of refreshing from His presence that are very gracious.

Others, again, learn to take the Lord Himself as their joy; and then it is true, as He promised: "That My joy shall remain in you and that your joy might be full."

Some people are content to have peace with God, but others have taken "the peace of God that passeth all understanding, to keep the hearts and minds through Christ Jesus."

Some have faith *in* God, while others have the faith *of* God. Some have many touches of healing from God, others, again, have learned to live in the very health of God Himself, and to say: "We which live are always delivered unto death for Jesus' sake, that the life of Jesus might be manifested in our mortal flesh."

Some are always wanting to be strengthened and helped by the Lord, others have learned to take the Lord Himself as their strength, and to find His strength made perfect in their weakness.

Some are trying to serve God, and to use His Holy Spirit as their helper and strength for service. Others have so yielded themselves up to God that He just uses them, and they are the channels and vessels of His life and strength.

Such a life leads us constantly to the end of ourselves, and as we grow less He increases and becomes our all in all. True Levitical service is to be lost in God, and find in Him our wisdom, our faith, our love, our power, our peace, our joy, our portion, and our all.

Such a life lifts us above surrounding circumstances, and even inner states, and connects us with the Infinite Source of all supplies, the heart of God Himself, and we are like the old Norwegian knight, who drank from a horn that was never dry, because a little tube connected it with the river, and as fast as he drank it kept full from its unfailing source. Happy they who can sing:

I have come to the Fountain of life,
  A fountain that never is dry;
  A life that never can die;
And I drink of the boundless supply
  In God, my Fountain of life.

VII.

The Levites represented the principle of finding God in all. We read in one place that they had no inheritance, and yet we read in the twenty-first chapter of Joshua, that God gave them the choice cities among all the twelve tribes. They gave up all, and they received more than any of the tribes.

Ephraim had but one inheritance, Judah had but one; but Levi had the choice cities in every one of Israel's estates. This is very wonderful and instructive. The tribe that let all go, and chose God alone, received in return the fairest cities in every corner of the land. Hebron, in the tribe of Judah; Gibeon and Anathoth, in Benjamin; Shechem and Bethhoron, in the tribe of Ephraim; Aijalon, in Dan; Taanach and Golan in Manasseh; Kishon and Jarmuth in Issachar; Rehob in distant Asher, Kedesh out of Naphtali, Jokneam and Kartah in Zebulun, Bezer and Kedemoth in Reuben, Ramoth, Heshbon, Mahanaim and Jazer in Gad, and many others in the north and the south, the east and the west – forty-eight in all – of the choicest cities of the land, including all the cities of refuge, were given to the tribe of Levi. Who will say that they lost by giving up all for God?

Yes, Lot can have his choice. Take the best, Lot, even all the valley of the Jordan. But wait! "Lift up now thine eyes, Abraham, and look from the place where thou art northward and southward; look to all the valley of the Jordan, too, Lot's chosen inheritance. Abraham, it shall all be thine. All the land which thou seest, to thee will I give it." Because you gave it up for God, you shall have it back in God, and more.

Ah, friends, it is a great thing to learn to take God first, and then He can afford to give us everything else, without the fear of its hurting us.

As long as you want anything very much, especially more than you want God, it is an idol. But when you become satisfied with God, everything else so loses its charm that He can give it to you without harm, and then you can take just as much as you choose, and use it for His glory.

There is no harm whatever in having money, houses, lands, friends and dearest children, if you do not value these things for themselves.

If you have been separated from them in spirit, and become satisfied with God Himself, then they will become to you channels to be filled with God to bring Him nearer to you. Then every little lamb around your household will be a tender cord to bind you to the Shepherd's heart. Then every affection will be a little golden cup filled with the wine of His love. Then every bank stock and investment will be but a channel through which you can pour out His beneficence and extend His gifts.

The day is coming, when God will "add all these things unto you," and you shall have the riches of the universe at your feet, and perhaps be able to create a world, in the power of Christ; but you would not exchange for all the glory of your kingdom, one throb of His loving heart or one glance of His countenance.

Yes, "all things are yours, whether Paul, or Apollos, or Cephas, or the world, or life, or death, or things present, or things to come," on one condition – not that Christ is yours, but that you first belong to Him. "Ye are Christ's and Christ is God's.

Beloved, shall we learn the two-fold lesson, and ask God to translate it into every moment of the coming days and years; first, to have ALL IN GOD and then to have GOD IN ALL!

CHAPTER XIII.

THE TRANS-JORDANIC TRIBES.

"Therefore, judge nothing before the time until the Lord come, who both will bring to light the hidden things of darkness, and will make manifest the counsels of the hearts; and then shall every man have praise of God." – 1Cor. 4:5.

JOSHUA 22:1-34. This chapter adds a very striking picture to the incidents which have preceded in the conquest of the land of promise and the division of Israel's inheritance.

We have already referred to the inheritance of the two and a half tribes on the east side of Jordan, and to the mistake that they made in choosing their portion on the world-side of the land of promise. In this, undoubtedly, were types of those who make a similar mistake in the present day, in choosing their portion too near the edge of the world.

At the same time, there are such beautiful lessons connected with their example, that we cannot but rejoice at the compensations which the sacred story has placed over against their error.

If they did not have the highest inheritance in the land, they had the spirit of the land in themselves, at least, and in the beautiful disposition of which this chapter is such a fine example.

I.

We see in them an example of the most unselfish service and sacrifice.

They had just spent seven years in helping their brethren of the other tribes to pursue their inheritance on the west side of Jordan. Indeed, they had gone before them in the hardest places and the hottest battles, and had been the real pioneers in all these long campaigns.

The command has been, "Ye shall pass before your brethren, armed, all the mightiest men of valor, and help them until the Lord hath given your brethren rest as He hath given thee, and they also have possessed the land which the Lord thy God giveth thee. Then shall ye return unto the land of your possession and enjoy it."

They had faithfully obeyed this command, and kept themselves.

They had fought the battles of their brethren and won for them their heritages of blessing. They had marched around Jericho, stormed the heights of Beth-heron, pursued in the long day at Gibeon, triumphed by the waters of Merom, and been valiant and true until all the thirty-one kings had been subdued, and the whole land had been won for the Lord of Israel.

It was entirely disinterested; not one stroke had they done for themselves. There is no nobler example in all the book of Joshua than their high and unselfish devotion. This is the noblest quality and the rarest among Christian workers.

How pathetically the apostle Paul exclaims, "I have no man like-minded who will care for your state, for all care for their own, not the things that are Jesus Christ's!"

The world instinctively does homage to unselfish love. A little fellow was boasting the other day about his wages. "I get two dollars a week," he said, "and I run errands. My father works in the factory and he gets two dollars a day. My brother works in the office, and he gets five dollars a week, and mother, she gets up in the morning about five o'clock, makes the fire, gets the breakfast for father and us, and does the work of the house all day, gets our supper at night, and after we go to bed, she does the darning, mends our clothes and fixes up things generally."

"Yes, and what does mother get?" "Oh – mother – well – why – she does not get anything. She does all the jobs of the house, but you know there is no money in it."

It was a boy's thoughtless testimony to the noblest heroism of common life. Hundreds of such heroines are suffering and toiling unmarked and unhonored.

But this is true of Him who came not to be ministered unto, but to minister, and to give His life as a ransom for many, and of whom it has been said that "when He was reviled, He reviled not again; when He suffered He threatened not; but committed Himself to Him that judgeth righteously." Therefore, "whosoever will be great among you, shall be your minister; and whosoever of you will be the chiefest, shall be servant of all."

II.

The day of recompense comes at last to the unselfish worker.

These brave men at length received their rich reward. The long weary marches were over at last, and as they stood before their commander, it repaid them for all, to hear him say, "Ye have kept all that Moses, the servant of the Lord, commanded you, and ye have obeyed my voice in all that I commanded you. Ye have not left your brethren these many days unto this day, but have kept the charge of the commandment of the Lord your God, and now the Lord your God hath given rest unto your brethren, as He promised them. Therefore now return ye, and get you unto your tents, and unto the land of your possession." And then he added, "Return with much riches unto your tents, and with very much cattle, with silver, and with gold, and with brass, and with iron, and with very much raiment. Divide the spoil of your enemies with your brethren."

It was reward enough to have the "Well done" of the captain, but there was much more. There was the rich inheritance, the ample spoil, and the glad homecoming to the children, wives and friends so dearly loved.

Then as we hear the "Well done" of our faithful Master, we shall not regret one tear or toil, but many would give the whole world for the privilege of going back once more to win the crown by earthly sacrifice and service.

But it is not only at the end of life that this glad recompense awaits the faithful servant, but even here God has His compensations and rewards for the self-denying and the pure-hearted.

There is a day of toil and sacrifice, and waiting, and there is a day when the harvest is gathered in, and we bring our sheaves with rejoicing and wonder at the full reversions that have followed the years of tearful sowing, and what seemed hopeless waiting.

But even in the days of recompense we must not forget the old spirit of self-denying love. As they came to their inheritance, they were to divide the spoil with their brethren. There is to be no selfish hoarding. They are still to live the same life of love, even in their inheritance and home.

There are Christian workers who begin in the spirit of self-denial and win their success by sacrifice and noble heroism, and then, later in life, when their work is crowned with success, they fall into the snare of selfishness and ease, and allow the very reward, which God gave them, to benumb their holy energies, and turn aside the edge of their consecration and power.

It requires much more grace to know how to abound than to know how to be abased. Even when we reach our millennial glory it is not to be a selfish life. The highest aspiration of a noble spirit is to rise to a higher service in the life beyond, of unceasing ministries. This is the life of God, and it is the only heaven that God can give.

III.

We see in these two tribes and a half, a beautiful example of putting God first before their own inheritance.

When they reached the fords of the Jordan, they paused awhile before turning to their home, and built a great altar there as a tower of witness and an altar of worship. They feared that in coming days their children would forget the service of the true God, and might let their isolation on the further side of Jordan separate them from the common faith. Therefore, to keep in remembrance, and to bind their children to the same faith and worship, they reared this altar of witness.

It would have been natural for them to have hastened home. Long years had passed since they had looked in the faces of those they loved. Throbbing hearts were drawing them to their loved ones, but they paused, and remembered God first, and set up this memorial that coming generations might remember His name and maintain His honor and worship.

This is, indeed, a bright and beautiful example. This is the true secret of all blessing and happiness. God first, should be the watchword and keynote of every plan, and purpose, and enterprise, in the consecrated life. Then He will delight in all our service and blessing, and will love to think of us as generously as we have thought of Him.

IV.

And now we see a very beautiful act misunderstood and misjudged.

We read with astonishment that "when the children of Israel heard of it, the whole congregation of the children of Israel gathered themselves together at Shiloh, to go up to war against them." They seem at once to have begun to think they knew all about it. It was an act of treason and rebellion, and that it must be promptly and severely put down.

Very fortunately, they sent a delegation before proceeding to actual hostilities, to charge them with their crime, and at once began to upbraid them for their trespass.

"Thus saith the whole congregation of the Lord, What trespass is this that ye have committed against the God of Israel, to turn away this day from following the Lord, in that ye have builded you an altar, that ye might rebel this day against the Lord?

Is the iniquity of Peor too little for us, from which we are not cleansed until this day, although there was a plague in the congregation of the Lord.

But that ye must turn away this day from following the Lord? and it will be, seeing ye rebel today against the Lord, that tomorrow He will be wroth with the whole congregation of Israel.

Notwithstanding, if the land of your possession be unclean, then pass ye over unto the land of the possession of the Lord, wherein the Lord's tabernacle dwelleth, and take possession among us; but rebel not against the Lord, nor rebel against us, in building you an altar besides the altar of the Lord our God.

Did not Achan, the son of Zerah, commit a trespass in the accursed thing, and wrath fell on all the congregation of Israel, and that man perished not alone in his iniquity?"

This is truly very humbling, and very much like the rest of us. How often we have passed these hasty judgments upon our brethren! How many have been alienated for years by some rash conclusion, and found at last that they had misunderstood the friend and misjudged the act which, if they had only understood, they would have honored its motives and spirits, and recognized it as worthy of all praise.

Therefore, the Master has said: "Judge nothing before the time, until the Lord come," and then He will not only look at the act, but "He will bring to light the hidden things of darkness and make manifest the counsels of the heart, and then shall every man praise God." All that can be recognized He will cherish, and all that He can forget, He will love to leave in oblivion.

V.

We see, at the same time, a beautiful example of meekness on the part of the Reubenites and their brethren. They did not fire up and resent the cruel misjudgment. They did not retaliate with vindictive words and bitter strife, but they meekly and gently assured their brethren of their innocency and honest intent, and their loyal devotion to the common faith and the sacred altar of the Lord, in the tabernacle.

How much grace it requires to bear a misunderstanding rightly, and to receive an unkind judgment in holy sweetness! Nothing tests a Christian character more than to have some evil thing said about you. This is the file that soon proves whether we are electro-plate or solid gold. If we could only know the blessings that lie hidden in our wrongs, we would say, like David, when Shimei cursed him, let him curse; "it may be the Lord will requite me good for his cursing this day."

Some people get easily turned aside from the grandeur of their life-work by pursuing their own grievances and enemies, until their life gets turned into one little petty whirl of warfare. It is like a nest of hornets. You may disperse the hornets, but you will probably get terribly stung, and get nothing for your pains, for even their honey is not worth the search.

Wiser and happier they who, like old Nehemiah, say to all the Sanballats, "I am doing a good work, so that I cannot come down; why should the work cease, whilst I leave it and come down to you?"

The gentleness and meekness of the Reubenites and their brethren averted a great catastrophe, and turned a curse into a blessing. So, "a soft answer ever turneth away wrath," and a spirit of gentleness will avert many a sorrow.

May God give us more of His Spirit, who, when reviled, reviled not again; when He suffered, He threatened not; but committed Himself to Him that judgeth righteously.

VI.

We see a very beautiful example of a misunderstanding healed, and a curse turned into a blessing.

Instead of a fratricidal war, there is reconciliation and love, and they joyfully exclaim: "This day we perceive that the Lord is among us, because ye have not committed this trespass against the Lord."

There is no greater evidence of the presence of the Lord in His people than the spirit of love, and there is no sweeter testimony to God and His glorious grace than the reconciliation of strife and the healing of mutual wrongs.

"Behold, how good a thing it is, and how pleasant, for brethren to dwell together in unity; for there the Lord commandeth a blessing, even life forevermore.

When the Lord wants to make an everlasting sign that shall not be cut off, this is the way He does it: "Instead of the thorn, shall come up the fir-tree; and instead of the brier, shall come up the myrtle-tree."

God's sweetest memorial is the transformed thorn, and the thistle blooming with flowers of peace and sweetness, where once grew recriminations and maledictions.

Beloved, God is waiting to make just such memorials in your life, out of the things that are hurting you most today. Take the grievances, the separations, the strained friendships, and the broken ties which have been the sorrow and heartbreak of your life, and let God heal them, and give you grace to make you right with all with whom you may be wrong, and you will wonder at the joy and blessing that will come out of the things that have caused you nothing but regret and pain.

"Blessed are the peacemakers, for they shall be called the children of God." The everlasting employment of our blessed Redeemer is to reconcile the guilty and the estranged from God, and the highest and most Christ-like work that we can do is, to be like Him in this regard.

Shall we go forth to dry the tears of a sorrowing world, to heal the broken-hearted, to bind up the wounds of human lives, and to unite heart to heart, and earth to heaven?

CHAPTER XIV.

WARNINGS AND COUNSELS.

Joshua 22.

THIS chapter contains the parting charges of Joshua to Israel and Shechem. He reviews the faithfulness of God, and all His gracious promises and leadings, and then solemnly pledges them to fidelity to Him and His holy covenant. And when they respond to his appeal and promise to serve the Lord with faithfulness, he reminds them that they are unable to serve Him in their own strength, and then reiterates his own determination for him and his household to serve the Lord, whatsoever others may do.

The chapter closes with a very humbling statement that the children of Israel served the Lord faithfully during all the days of Joshua and the elders who survived him, and the generation that had known the works of the Lord in Canaan, but we learn from the later book of Judges, that before the third generation they were sunk in apostasy and captivity, and the glory of their early victories had been exchanged for a declension and degradation far more terrible than the story of Israel's wanderings for forty years in the wilderness.

For us there is the solemn lesson that, notwithstanding all the promises of the Gospel and the abundant grace of Christ, there is need of the humblest vigilance and the closest abiding, even in the highest places of our Christian life. The greater the height, the greater the fall, and the deeper the degradation.

Israel's wanderings in the wilderness after they came out of Egypt only lasted forty years, but Israel's declension and degradation, under the Judges, lasted over four hundred years.

For an ordinary Christian to go back from God is a very serious thing; but for one who has known Him in all the fullness of His grace, to turn aside from the higher pathway of a life of consecration, is a far more serious and dangerous thing; and the Word of God is full of the most faithful and solemn warnings and admonitions to even those who have entered into the fullness of Jesus, to watch and stand fast, lest, being led away by the error of the wicked, they fall from their own steadfastness.

While on the one hand, we have the most gracious promises of our Father keeping us, yet at the same time, we have the most faithful warnings to abide and obey.

The echoes of this chapter ring through all the New Testament, and especially those chapters that speak of our higher Christian life. When John tells us, "The anointing ye have received of Him abideth in you," he also adds, "And now, little children, abide in Him, that, when He shall appear, we may have confidence, and not be ashamed before Him at His coming." While Paul says: "I know in whom I have believed, and am persuaded that He is able to keep that which I have committed to Him against that day;" yet he also adds, "That good thing which was committed unto thee keep by the Holy Ghost which dwelleth in us." While in one breath, the Spirit says, "There hath no temptation befallen you, but such as is common to man; but God is faithful, who will not suffer you to be tempted beyond that ye are able, but will with the temptation also make a way to escape, that ye may be able to bear it," and he also adds, "Wherefore, let him that thinketh he standeth take heed lest he fall."

God's Word is not a cast-iron system of theology, proclaiming infallible security for any man, irrespective of his own attitude, but it is the wise and loving touch of a mother's hand, on the side of our spiritual life that needs adjustment, whether it be encouragement to lift us up, or admonition and warning to hold us back from presumption and disobedience.

It would have been as cruel and unwise to encourage David, in the time of his disobedience, as to have discouraged Simon Peter, when his heart was breaking with remorse and sorrow.

The one needed stern rebuke, to let him see his sin, and the other needed hope and comfort, to reveal to him his Saviour's mercy.

Therefore, let us not think it strange, if at one time we hear the Holy Scriptures saying: "They shall never perish, neither shall any pluck them out of my hand;" and at another time, "If a man abide not in me, he is cast forth as a branch that is withered."

The very warning is designed to prevent the peril to which it refers.

What were some of the causes of Israel's declension?

1. The first was, perhaps, their undue dependence upon Joshua and the fathers who had brought them into the land. "They served the Lord during the days of Joshua and the elders that survived him and who had seen the works of the Lord," but when they had passed away, and they were thrown upon their own strength, resources and character, they did not have those elements of stability, principle and permanence, which were sufficient to preserve them from the unholy influence of the surrounding nations, and so they gradually sank back again into heathenism.

There are many persons whose religious character is a reflection of the influence of others. Like young Josiah, who served the Lord during the days of Jehoiada, his adopted father, and turned back to evil when he was gone, so these persons manifest much sympathetic goodness under the influence of favorite teachers and high examples, and in seasons of deep religious excitement, they may even seem to pass through an experience of great spiritual life, exhibiting many of its emotions and some of its fruits, but when these influences are withdrawn, it becomes evident that there was no real conviction of purpose and will, and no radical transformation of character.

The test will come to all such souls, and it will find these favorable influences withdrawn, and these helpful surroundings changed, and they will be compelled to fall back on their own resources and their own direct knowledge of God and His sustaining grace. And when longer pressed forward by stronger spirits and upheld by helpful hands, but met by opposition, misunderstanding, uncongenial associations, and, perhaps, direct persecution, they will soon find whether their purpose is rooted in God, and their spirit united to the living Christ and abiding in Him as the source of their strength and service.

If this, indeed, be so, they will continue even in isolation and opposition, and Jeremiah's picture of the man "whose hope the Lord is" shall be gloriously fulfilled in them. "He shall be as a tree planted by the waters, and that spreadeth out her roots by the river, and shall not see when heat cometh, but her leaf shall be green; and shall not be careful in the year of drought, neither shall cease from yielding fruit."

The secret of Joshua's victory was that he had long before this learned to stand alone. To him the day had come, more than half a century before, when the unfaithful spies and the whole congregation turned against him, refusing to follow him, and even threatening to destroy him, while he and his faithful companion stood fast to their principles at Kadesh-barnea. His purpose was not affected by the failure of the multitude to follow him. It was not much more affected by the enthusiasm of the second generation to enter with him the land of promise. And even now, as he stood on the height and glorious elevation of an accomplished and victorious life, he was still as ready as ever to stand alone, and his lofty independence expresses itself in the heroic words: "Choose ye this day whom ye will serve, but as for me and my house, we will serve the Lord."

This must ever be the secret of steadfastness in the consecrated life. You must know the truth of the Lord for yourself, and commit yourself to it and to Him, even if you have to stand alone. You must be so persuaded of it that you cannot surrender it even if you die, and you must know the Lord so definitely for yourself, and not for another, that even if all the Christians in the world should fail, and all your friends forsake you, you must still stand and exclaim, "Here I stand; I can do no other, so help me God."

Stronger than all the power of Babylon is the spirit of the men who stand in the fiery furnace, and say, "We are not careful to answer thee in this matter, O king, If it be so, our God is able to deliver us out of the fiery furnace, and He will deliver us out of thy hand, O king; but if not, be it known unto thee that we will not serve thy gods nor worship the golden image which thou hast set up."

2. The second cause of Israel's declension was their failure to do thorough work, especially in separating from and exterminating their enemies. We read in the beginning of the Book of Judges of many of the tribes of Canaan, whom they should have thoroughly subjugated, that the children of Judah could not drive out of the valley, chapter 1:19; and that the children of Benjamin did not drive out the Jebusites that inhabited Jerusalem, chapter 1:21; nor did Manasseh drive out the inhabitants of Beth-shean and her towns, but the Canaanites would dwell in the land; verse 27; nor did Ephraim drive out the Canaanites in Gezer, but the Canaanites dwelt in Gezer among them, and so of many of the other tribes. Not only so, but Israel, in some cases, put the Canaanites to tribute, chapter 1:28-30; making it even a profitable business, and a source of income to have them remain, when the Lord had commanded their utter extermination.

And still worse, we find them even entering into forbidden alliances with them, and also intermarrying among their sons and daughters, chapter 3:5-6. God's command to them had been, "Thou shalt make no covenant with the inhabitants of this land, thou shalt throw down their altars; thou shalt smite them and utterly destroy them; thou shalt make no covenant with them, nor show mercy unto them, nor shalt thou make marriages with them; thy daughter thou shalt not give unto his son, nor his daughter shalt thou take unto thy son."

But here we read, "the children dwelt among the Canaanites, Hittites, Amorites, Perizzites, Hivites, and Jebusites; and they took their daughters to be their wives; and they gave their daughters to their sons, and they served their gods." Israel had become content with the victories which had subdued their more formidable foes, and given them the chief strongholds of the land, but in a thousand little places the enemy still lurked and lingered, and gradually became tolerated. The danger of their continuance did not seem very great, and the trouble and cost of their extermination seemed greater than the courage and patience of Israel. Thus they were suffered to remain, half conquered, and for the time, wholly subordinate. In a little while it became a source of profit to collect tribute from these bold giants, and so, many of them were made tributary to Israel, contrary to the Divine command.

A little later, relations of friendship and fellowship began to be established, and before long, they were intermarrying with the tribes of Israel and raising a mongrel race in which the true seed would soon be wholly extinguished; and to crown all, they naturally began to serve the idols of their heathen friends, and to mingle in all the abominations of their unholy religion; thus becoming in the end, really apostate from the worship of the true God altogether.

This is the sad story of the development of evil in many a life, which once seemed wholly consecrated. Little sins are left unsubdued. Like Saul they destroy the Amalekites, but they spare Agag, their king, for some good purpose, as they suppose, and keep the best of the spoil with the idea that they are going to sacrifice it unto the Lord. They have not the courage to deal bravely and firmly with evil. After awhile they begin to turn it to profitable account and tolerate certain forms of sin and worldliness because of advantage. Their business interests would be ruined by too rigid a conscientiousness, for some of their investments are not wholly separated from forbidden associations; the profits, at least will be divided with the Lord, and the end will sanctify the means. A thousand specious and plausible excuses are made for things that ought to be thoroughly put aside and which, like the Canaanites, they put under tribute, and try to justify because of some advantage that can be brought out of them.

By and by, the social element is introduced. Families that were separated from unholy friendships and ungodly alliances, become mixed with the world in the social reception, the promiscuous dance, or perhaps, in the milder form of the church entertainment. If the old people still retain their separation, yet they let their sons and daughters mingle with the Canaanites, and they do not shrink from even permitting the marriage of a Christian girl with the godless man, or receiving into this consecrated home, as the bride of a son, devoted in infancy to God, some bright and fascinating daughter of fashion, who soon succeeds in subverting all the separation to God that has been left, until it is not far now to the last step of the worship of idolatry, the unrestrained career of worldly amusement, covetousness which is idolatry, and the carnival of godless selfishness and pleasure.

Dr. Livingstone tells of a singular creature which he found in Africa, called the ant-lion. It attacked and destroyed the strongest victims by a masterpiece of strategy. Excavating a little pit in the form of an inverted cone, running to a point at the bottom, it sits down at the base of its little pitfall and waits for some unsuspecting beetle or insect to tread too near the edge of the crumbling sand. The unhappy victim at last approaches, and perhaps prompted by curiosity, looks over the edge of this strange excavation, and lo! in a moment he has lost his balance and rolls down the side of the little pit where the ant-lion waits for his prey.

Not, however, directly and instantly does the destroyer attack his victim; this might be too unequal a contest for the little strategist, but he suddenly opens his sharp little mouth, formed like a pair of powerful scissors, and with one quick movement he cuts off a limb from the unsuspecting victim and then disappears out of sight. Slowly the mutilated creature recovers itself, and climbs up the slippery side of the pit; but just as he reaches the summit his footing slips again and he tumbles once more into the jaws of the little monster. Another quick movement and another limb is gone; and again the wounded insect gathers up his remaining strength and makes another ascent of the side of this death trap, but the result is the same as before; again he sinks to receive a fresh blow, and the process is repeated until at length he is so dismembered that he has not strength enough even to attempt to escape, but sinks, a bleeding, suffering mass, into the hands of his enemy who devours at leisure the antagonist that he would not have dared to approach directly.

This, alas! is the story of many a defeated and ruined life. Some little adversary that was not even dreaded, has been the final destroyer, not only by one bold attack, but by a thousand little wounds that, at last, have left the victim helpless to resist or to return.

Saul's career is a sad example of a noble beginning, ending in mournful disaster; and the saddest part of it is the very smallness of the cause where the pathway of declension and ruin began. It was simply in this very thing of refusing to deal firmly with the enemies of God. The reason of his failure was because of his deeper fear to deal firmly with the sin and self-will of his own heart.

Saul's failure to slay Agag and his soft dealings with the Amalekite chief, were but the outward type of his tolerance of a greater giant in his own heart, even his own self-will, and the spirit of disobedience which, Samuel tells him, was expressed by his conduct in this case, and was the ground of his rejection and the secret of his final ruin. But not all at once did Saul go down; for nearly ten years did he still sit upon Israel's throne and work out the dreadful proceeds of sin's development, leading from step to step, until at last a branded murderer, a slave of blind and furious passion, and an awful instrument of Satan's very possession, he closes his wretched life in tragedy almost as dark as the story of Judas.

Oh! let us beware how we tolerate a single sin, how we leave an enemy in the land, how we make terms with any forbidden thing, how to enter into alliance with the world, or let its spirit touch our fondest affections. "We cannot serve God and mammon." We cannot compromise with any evil thing and remain in the Land of Promise. We cannot abide in His love without keeping His commandments.

"Wherefore come ye out from among them, and be ye separate, saith the Lord, and touch not the unclean thing; and I will receive you, and ye shall be my sons and daughters, saith the Lord Almighty."

3. Perhaps the most serious cause of their failure was their inability to understand their own weakness. It was the spirit of self-sufficiency, and self-confidence that brought about their ruin. There was a deep meaning in the words of Joshua which they could not understand, "Ye cannot serve the Lord," said their faithful leader. He knew better than they the weakness of their own hearts.

They were ready enough to promise and to purpose, but they knew not how certain they were to go back again to the forbidden sin. Their fathers at Sinai had been as ready to answer, under the terrors of the mount, "All that the Lord hath spoken we will do," but before the month was ended they were dancing around the golden calf. Peter was ready enough to promise, "Though all men should deny Thee, yet will not I," and yet, before the next noonday, Peter was among the enemies of his Lord, a blaspheming, broken-hearted man.

The deepest need of our spiritual life is to know our utter helplessness, weakness and liability to err. Then we shall lean on His stronger arm, and in self-distrust abide in Him, knowing that apart from Him we can do nothing.

This was the great lesson of the Old Testament discipline. "The law made nothing perfect, but," praise the Lord; "the bringing in of a better hope did." " What the law could not do, because it was weak through the flesh, God, sending His own Son in the likeness of sinful flesh, and for sin, condemned sin in the flesh, That the righteousness of the law might be fulfilled in us, who walk not after the flesh, but after the Spirit." "For the law of the Spirit of life in Christ Jesus hath made us free from the law of sin and death." "If we walk in the Spirit, we shall not fulfill the lusts of the flesh."

The secret of victory is the profound consciousness of our utter inability and helpless nothingness. Our insufficiency is measured by His all-sufficiency, and as we decrease, He must increase. Most of our failures are meant to teach us our inability and worthlessness, that we may learn that apart from Him we can do nothing.

4. The review of God's faithfulness and grace is fitted to establish us and encourage us in fidelity and steadfastness. Joshua led them back over the history of the past, and recalled to their mind the marvelous dealings of Jehovah with them and their fathers and then reminded them of the good land unto which He had brought them, and all the blessings with which He had

surrounded them, and by all these considerations He called them and bound them to remember their covenant obligations, and be true to their faithful God.

And so, God holds us to Himself by the memory of His grace and love. What marvelous promises He has given us, and how vast are the prospects and the recompenses that He has in store for us! By all these things, let us be true to our covenant and faithful to our heavenly Friend.

God would awaken us to a sense of our true dignity and our glorious future, that we might "walk worthy of our high vocation." Behind us there lies a high and heavenly calling and a past full of His faithful love. Before us is a kingdom of incomparable and everlasting glory, and both are calling us to be "steadfast, unmovable, always abounding in the work of the Lord, for as much as we know that our labor is not in vain in the Lord."

CHAPTER XV.

FOUR MIGHTY ALLS.

Joshua 21.

"And the Lord gave unto Israel all the land which He sware to give unto their fathers; and they possessed it, and dwelt therein. And the Lord gave them rest round about, according to all that He sware unto their fathers: and there stood not a man of all their enemies before them; the Lord delivered all their enemies into their hand. There failed not aught of any good thing which the Lord had spoken unto the house of Israel; all came to pass." – Josh. 21:43-45

WHAT a glorious collection of majestic and magnificent *alls*! Four *alls*, four glorious *alls*! *all* the land, *all* the rest, *all* the victory, and *all* the promises.

I.

All the land of their inheritance. The Lord gave them *all* their inheritance. Has He given it *all* to you? Have you got *all* of your inheritance? Have you accepted it? And when the close comes shall you be able to look back and say, "I have had all that the Lord meant to give me, all that He created me for, all that He redeemed me for, all that He sanctified me for, all that was purchased for me in Christ, all that was revealed by the Spirit, all that He ever made me think of, long for, expect and claim, all that was meant for me to be. I have had all.

"That thing which even my brothers could not be, that thing which was specifically my part in the Redemption of Christ. God gave it *all* to me, not mutilated, not abridged, not in the slightest diminished; but like the full orbed sun, largest at its setting, my sun is going down a perfect sphere. I have had *all* my inheritance." That is what God wants for you. That is what God meant for you. Are you going to have it? Have you got it *all* now? Your sun may go down today, there is no time to waste in dreaming. Haste to make sure of that higher calling to which you are chosen. The calling which He has set His heart upon for you, more than you have yourself. Have you got all your land?

Your land is not mine, remember. There is something for each – your own inheritance. There is something for you nobody else can fill. No garment will fit you but your own. You have a service which no one can perform but you. There is a joy no one can have but you. There is a white stone with your name written on it. Are you going to have it? That is what God wants for you. He wants to give you the land. He has taken you up to the mount of vision and shown it to you. Will you take it?

II.

Then He speaks of all *the rest*, according to which He sware unto their fathers. Have you got the rest? Have you got that perfect peace which the Lord says He will keep him in whose mind is set on Him. The peace of God which passeth all understanding – rest round about, as well as rest inside. The whole horizon clear, the whole sweep of life free from an anxious thought. The "great peace which nothing can offend." That is what God means by the Land of Promise, the type of perfect rest.

There are some things good, without being perfect. You don't need to have a whole regiment cannonading outside your room to keep you awake. It is quite enough that your little alarm clock rings its little bell. It is not necessary to fret about everything, it is quite enough if the devil gets your mind rasped with one little worry, one little thought which destroys your perfect peace. It is like the polish on a mirror, or an exquisite toilet table, one scratch will destroy it; and the finer it is the smaller the scratch that will deface it. And so your rest can be destroyed by a very little thing. Perhaps you have trusted in God about your future salvation; but have you about your present business or earthly cares, your money and your family, your reputation, your own spiritual keeping, or your future in this life. God wants you to take the perfect peace He gives.

What is meant by the peace that passeth all understanding? It does not mean a peace no one can comprehend. It means a peace that no amount of reasoning will bring. You cannot get it by thinking. There may be perfect bewilderment and perplexity all round the horizon, but yet your heart can rest in perfect security because He knows, He loves, He leads, He fills my heart with His own perfect love, with His infinite peace. He gives perfect rest round about.

According to *all* which He sware to give them. Have you ever noticed that? God not only promised but swore. God's mighty oath is pledged to give it. His honor is involved in its fulfillment, and though heaven and earth pass away He will fulfill it. How condescending! He binds Himself to show that He will not evade the responsibility of keeping His great word to us and giving His mighty blessing to those that will hold Him to it.

He gave them the land which He sware, the rest which He sware to give unto their fathers. Do you realize, beloved, what this means? Many of you are accustomed to think this is a sort of extra for a privileged few, and that once in a while someone else may get rest. But it is not so. God has bound Himself to sanctify and fully save every soul that will claim salvation, and rest through Jesus Christ. He has bound Himself to do more than merely forgive you your sins. The oath which He sware unto Abraham, as is expressed so beautifully in that chapter in Luke, that He would grant us, that we, being delivered from all our enemies and the hand of all that hate us, "might serve Him without fear in righteousness and holiness before Him all the days of our life." God has sworn that He will give this inheritance of rest to all who claim it.

III.

Then we come to that other "all" – victory. One by one their enemies were permitted to confront them that Israel might gain a great victory. There was no other way of bringing them into the fullness of their conquest. Thirty-one kings had to be successively subdued, the most difficult citadels, fortresses and fastnesses of the land had to fall into their hands. But not a place could resist them, victory floated on their banners until they waved triumphantly over all the land and the whole of Canaan lay at their feet. Not one of their enemies remained, the mighty Hittites, the giant Anaks, the Amorites and the people of the Heshbon. He never once failed them when they were right with Him. Once they were beaten, but the failure at Ai was due to His absence, and the scar of the single failure was more than wiped out.

And so, beloved, God calls us to victory. Have any of you given up the conflict, have you surrendered? Have you said, "this thing is too much?" Have you said, "I can give up anything else but this?" If you have, you are not in the land of promise. God means you should accept every difficult thing that comes in your life. He has started with you, knowing every difficulty. And if you dare to let Him, He will carry you through not only to be conquerors but "more than conquerors." Are you looking for all the victory?

God gives His children strength for the battle and watches over them with a fond enthusiasm. He longs to fold you to His arms and say to you, "I have seen thy conflict, I have watched thy trials, I have rejoiced in thy victory; thou hast honored Me." Not in one place was there a failure; there stood not a man of all their enemies. You remember what He told Joshua at the beginning, "There shall not any man be able to stand before thee all the days of thy life; as I was with Moses, so shall I be with thee, I will not fail thee, nor forsake thee." And again He says to us, "Fear thou not for I am with thee; be not dismayed, for I am thy God; I will strengthen thee; yea, I will uphold thee with the right hand of My righteousness, and they that were incensed against thee, shall be ashamed and confounded."

He wants to give you victory, victory over yourself, over your own heart; we must all begin there. You must conquer yourself first. God wants victory over your heart; not a victory that will crush you, I don't mean that; but a victory, a triumph through Jesus Christ.

There are three great victories that God wants to give to every one of us. The first is, victory over ourselves; the second, victory over our circumstances; and the third, victory over our enemies and all those who rise up against us.

Look at Joseph, the type of all these. It was not easy for him to turn away from his father and his home, to go into the kitchen as a slave, and then to be thrown into a prison as a criminal, unjustly charged with the sin of another and forced to languish there for long months, with no one to plead for him until the iron entered into his soul, and it seemed as if God had forsaken him.

But Joseph endured all this, quietly learning the secret of victory over himself.

Then came the victory over his trying circumstances, and all the difficulties that had surrounded him soon passed away, and he forgot even his sorrow, and rose as high as his descent had been deep and low.

Then came the victory over others. God brought his brothers who had wronged him to his feet, and gave him the power – if he had wanted it – to have sweet revenge. Oh, how natural it would have been to have reminded them of their cruel crime and make them feel the bitterness they had caused him long days before?

But no, Joseph had a greater victory. He would not even allow them to feel too keenly the sense of their wrong, but longed to forgive them and make them feel his love, and throw his arms about them with all a brother's forgiving tenderness.

Ah! that is the victory that satisfies a Christ-like heart. It is heaping coals of fire on the heads of those who have wronged us. And yet there is a way of putting coals of fire on others' heads that has more meanness in it than an open revenge. There is a way of doing another a kindness in such a manner as to make him feel that we are doing it just to make him feel badly.

Sweeter by far is the revenge which God has promised to the overcomer: "I will make them to come and worship at thy feet and to know that I have loved thee" and to acknowledge you as the instrument of the highest spiritual blessing.

Beloved, God is bringing all these things into your life, In order to give you an opportunity of making eternal history. There is a day coming, when your biography will be written in the Bible of the eternal ages the same as Joseph's; that is to say, if it is worth writing.

Ages to come will read the story of your trials and your triumphs, and glorify your Saviour for what He has done in you.

IV.

The last "all" includes all God's promises. "There failed not aught of any good thing which the Lord hath spoken to the house of Israel; all came to pass." Blessed be His name for that glorious promise! How it sweeps out to the far horizon, and reaches the length and breadth of meaning beyond all that we can ask or think!

How it speaks of a finished life, of an accomplished career, of a home-coming for us, too, that will have no regret in it, and no abatement from all His highest, greatest will!

It is the spirit with which God wants each of us to finish our earthly career. When life's battle is over, and life's mystery about to end, oh, that each of us may look back from the closing portals of the past and say: "There failed not aught of any good thing that God had spoken; all came to pass."

It is so blessed to feel and to know that God wants to gives us this. We are not holding a reluctant heart to an enforced obligation, but we are simply cooperating with our truest Friend to bring about that on which He has set His own heart for us.

Beloved, there is not a promise in your catalogue of promises, there is not a thought of blessing in your inmost heart, there is not a purpose of victory in your soul, which did not originate with Him. You can depend upon His love and His loyalty. His great heart is set upon blessing you, if you will only let Him; nay, we may almost say, in blessing you in spite of yourself.

I do not know that there is a more inspiring study than to trust the exact fulfillment of the very words of God. There is nothing more wonderful than to take the ancient prophecies of this book and read them along with the parallel columns of human history and see how they correspond in their minutest details.

Take, for example, the first chapter of Genesis and the story of the creation. Four thousand years ago, Moses wrote the record that light was created on the first day, and the sun on the fourth day.

The scientists used to love to laugh at that incongruous statement and say that it is impossible to believe the story of creation, and the existence of light before the sun.

They had their day and their laugh, and then – it was God's turn. A few years ago, science discovered the solar spectrum, and the fact was declared, – on scientific authority, – that light could exist apart from the sun, and Moses' record was shown to be scientifically true, as well as Divinely in advance of the times in which it was written.

The Word of God was right, after all, and even more right than all the modern ideas of the age, perhaps even before the days of Moses.

Job in one of his sublime flights, spoke about "the sweet influences of the Pleiades, and the bands of Orion." Until very recently, no one could imagine what was meant by "the sweet influences of the Pleiades," but modern astronomy has discovered the fact that these Pleiades are probably the physical center of the whole universe, and that all the stars and constellations are perpetually moving around that distant spot in far immensity, where mighty Alcyone, the chief of the Pleiades, twelve thousand times larger than our own sun, reaches out his tremendous force of gravitation, and holds all these constellations in their orbits.

Again, we read in ancient prophecy, two strangely contradictory announcements regarding Zedekiah, – the last of Judah's kings, – one to the effect that he would go to Babylon, and the other to the effect that he would never see Babylon. They looked like contradictions until the fact was brought out, in the fulfillment, that after the fall of Jerusalem, Zedekiah's eyes were blinded by the cruelty of Nebuchadnezzar, and he was carried in chains to Babylon, but he never saw it, although he ended his days in one of its dreary dungeons.

Thus every jot and tittle of this faithful word shall stand, and the day will come when wondering angels and saints will exclaim again, "There failed not aught of anything which He had spoken; all came to pass."

Even his very judgments are an evidence of the faithfulness of His everlasting word. Two Hebrew Rabbis were standing on Mount Zion, looking at the desolations of Jerusalem, and the very foxes that ran on the ruined walls. One of the old men wept, and his brother smiled. Then they looked at each other, and one asked, "How can you weep?" and the other asked, "How can you smile?" One answered, "I weep because I see how God has fulfilled His word, spoken by the mouth of the ancient prophet, that 'the foxes shall run upon the wall of Zion.'" "Ah," said the other, "that is just why I smile, because the same prophet has said: 'Zion shall be restored,' and I know therefore, that as one word has been fulfilled, the other shall also come to pass."

How true this promise has been, and will yet be to Israel as a nation! True, they have hindered God in the fulfillment of His promises, and forced Him to interpose many a long delay in the accomplishment of His purpose, but every word shall yet be entirely fulfilled.

"The gifts and calling of God to Israel are without repentance", and the seed of Abraham shall yet gather on the heights of Zion, and join in the chorus of the Millennial world "There failed not aught of any good thing which the Lord hath spoken to the house of Israel; all came to pass."

Rabinowitch has told us that the ancient Hebrew Bible has the letters Alpha and Omega, just after the prophecy in Zechariah, "They shall look on Him whom they have pierced, and they shall mourn." For long ages, Israel's Rabbis could not understand that Alpha and Omega; but even those two little words were not in vain, and if you turn to the Book of Revelation, you will find John recalling the prophecy and applying it to Christ: "Behold He cometh with clouds and every eye see Him, they also who pierced Him", and then Christ, applying it to Himself, and saying: "I am Alpha and Omega, the beginning and the end."

No! not a single *yod*, the smallest letter in the Hebrew alphabet, shall pass away until all be fulfilled.

And so, beloved, it has been fulfilled and yet will be fulfilled in your own heart and life. You may trust His faithful promises. He will bring it all to pass. You can send up the prayer of David, and say: "Remember Thy word unto Thy servant upon which Thou hast caused me to hope."

Yes, if He has even caused you to hope in it, He will not disappoint you. His heart is so true that He will not let you trust a misleading word.

With infinite delicacy and confidence He says: "If it were not so, I would have told you." You may not understand all the promises or their fulfillment; you may not understand all the trials of the way; you may not quite understand all the meaning of His words. They may mean to you what they mean to no one else; they may speak to your thoughts and hopes, what your own circumstances suggest; but all that He has meant for you and all that He has let you claim in the spirit of humble trust, He will weave into the pattern of your life; He will work out in the chain of His providence, and He will cause you to say, with rejoicing heart as you look back from the heights of eternal recompense, "there failed not aught of any good thing that He hath spoken unto my heart; all came to pass."

What He said to Jacob of old, on the stony pillow, He will fulfill to your trusting heart: "I will not leave thee until I have done all that I have spoken to thee."

Yes, He will be faithful even to the erring. "If his children forsake My law, then will I visit their transgressions with the rod, and their iniquities with stripes; nevertheless, I will not utterly take My mercy from them, nor suffer My faithfulness to fail."

Even your faith may sometimes falter and seem to fail, but, above all your sighs and tears, the promise will often come ringing back: "If we believe not, yet He abideth faithful; He cannot deny Himself."

Blessed be His name for all the faithful words He has kept to us hitherto, but He will lift up the vision of our faith to the greater things which He has yet in store for us.

His eye is upon the glorious ending. He wants to have you enter in, saying: "I have fought a good fight, I have finished my course, I have kept the faith, henceforth there is laid up for me a crown of righteousness."

Some day, even you, trembling, faltering one, shall stand upon those heights and look back upon all you have passed through, all you have narrowly escaped, all the perils through which He guided you, the stumblings through which He guarded you, and the sins from which He saved you; and you shall shout, with a meaning you cannot understand now, "Salvation unto Him who sitteth upon the throne, and unto the Lamb."

Some day He will sit down with us in that glorious home, and we shall have all the ages in which to understand the story of our lives. And He will read over again this old marked Bible with us, He will show us how He kept all these promises, He will explain to us the mysteries that we could not understand, He will recall to our memory the things we have long forgotten, He will go over again with us the book of life, He will recall all the finished story, and I am sure we will often cry: "Blessed Christ! you have been so true, you have been so good! Was there ever love like this?" And then the great chorus will be repeated once more – "There failed not aught of any good thing that He hath spoken; all came to pass."

Beloved, will you take these old promises afresh? Will you make an edition of your Bible not printed by the Bible Society nor the Oxford Press, but a Bible written by the Holy Ghost upon your heart, and translated into the version of your life? And some day He will let us write upon its last page, this glorious inscription – "There failed not aught of any good thing which He spoke unto the house of Israel; *all* came *to pass*."

CHAPTER XVI.

THE CHURCH'S INHERITANCE.

"And Jesus came and spake unto them, saying, All power is given unto Me, in heaven and on earth. Go ye, therefore, and teach all nations, baptizing them in the name of the Father, and of the Son, and of the Holy Ghost; teaching them to observe all things whatsoever I have commanded you; and lo, I am with you always, even unto the end of the world. Amen." – Matt. 28:18-20.

THE whole story of the Book of Joshua may be applied, in a broader sense, to the people of God collectively, and especially to the New Testament church. In an important sense the whole body of Christians may be called the spiritual Israel. And the history of God's ancient people is full of interesting parallels and lessons for us, even if they may not be exact types in this respect.

1. The failure of Israel to enter into the land of promise through unbelief, had its parallel in the rejection of Christ by His own countrymen, and the consequent rejection of the Jewish people from the privileges of the Gospel. But as, for ancient Israel, there was still a period of probation and long-suffering, which lasted for forty years, affording individuals the opportunity of entering into the spiritual blessings of God's covenant, so there intervened a similar period after Christ's rejection by His own people, before the final destruction of Jerusalem, and the dispersion of the Jews.

And as there were some of even the first generation of Israel who believed, so there were exceptions in the ministry of Christ and His disciples, from among even that unbelieving nation, who gladly accepted their Messiah, and entered into their spiritual inheritance.

2. The glorious career of Joshua, the crossing of the Jordan, the conquest of Canaan, and the dividing of the inheritance among the tribes of Israel, find their striking parallel likewise, in the death and resurrection of Jesus, the descent of the Holy Ghost at Pentecost, and the triumphs of Christianity, when the Church, to a very great extent, claimed her inheritance of power, purity, and blessing, and entered upon the conquest of the world for Christ, until there was scarcely a region of the globe where the Gospel was not at least planted, and the strongholds of Satan challenged and shaken.

The crossing of the Jordan may well illustrate the Cross of Calvary, and the experience of death and resurrection which was so emphasized in primitive Christianity. The new covenant has its counterpart in the coming of the Holy Ghost, and the Gospel of full and free salvation.

The death of Moses and the advent of Joshua, whose very name is suggestive of Jesus, suggest the transition which then actually came, from the law to the Gospel. The victories of Canaan had their counterpart in the triumphs of Christianity. Dividing the inheritance foreshadowed the various gifts of the Holy Ghost distributed to the Church.

The supernatural element which runs through the entire story of the conquest of Palestine, was more than realized in the first centuries of Christianity in the manifestations of the Divine presence and power, in signs and wonders and mighty deeds. And the choice possessions won by Caleb, Othniel, Achsah, and others, remind us of the transcendent examples of piety, faith, love, knowledge, and holy power and usefulness, which adorned the annals of the early church.

3. The failure of Israel to enter promptly and fully into their whole inheritance, also finds its counterpart in the church of the New Testament. With all its fresh beauty

and Divine glory, still there was much of human imperfection and melancholy failure.

The old cry, "There remaineth much land yet to be possessed," "How long are ye slack to go up and possess all the land which the Lord your God has given you!" is echoed back in more than one of Paul's sorrowful admonitions to the churches he loved; and still more strongly in the appeals and warnings of the Son of God to the seven churches of Asia, through the last messages of the Holy Ghost, sixty years after His ascension. There we find Him saying to the strongest of these churches, "I have somewhat against thee, because thou hast left thy first love. Therefore, be watchful and strengthen the things that remain that are ready to die, for I have not found thy works perfect before God." And to another, "Thou hast a name that thou livest, and art dead." And yet again, "Thou sayest, I am rich and increased with goods, and have need of nothing; and knowest not that thou art wretched, and poor, and miserable, and blind, and naked."

Already, even in the lifetime of Paul and John, the primitive church had allied itself sufficiently with the world to open the door for many of the errors which afterwards entered and overwhelmed the purity of the early church.

4. The fearful declension of ancient Israel, leading ere long to the dark chapter of the Book of Judges, and their shameful compromise with the heathen world and subjugation to its power, is more than paralleled in the story of the dark ages of mediæval Christianity, through the same cause, namely, the failure of God's people to separate themselves from sin and worldliness, and to enter into their full inheritance. The purity and strength of apostolic Christianity were speedily lost in the unspeakable corruptions of an apostate church, with all the errors and abominations of that anti-Christian system which took the place of the church of God for twelve

hundred years, and has been well called a "baptized heathenism."

Many of the pictures of the Book of Judges might find a vivid counterpart in the story of the Middle Ages. The graphic picture of Micah and his mother, with its strange intermingling of dishonesty, religion, and ritualism, almost seem like a parable of much of the religious life of such a period, and, indeed, is not without its parallels in our own days. Like Micah's sanctuary, many a formalist has folded his arms in the midst of violence and sin, and said, "Now the Lord will do me good, seeing I have a Levite to be my priest."

Notwithstanding this there were many exceptions in ancient Israel – a wise and patriotic Deborah, a brave and faithful Barak, a Divinely-called Gideon, a single-hearted Jephthah, and a mighty Samson. And, so, even in the darkest ages of Christianity, there have not been wanting those who have not defiled their garments, and who, at times, dared to rise up for God against those that did wickedly, and shed a Divine luster on their times and names. Such were the noble army of the martyrs, and confessors – a Waldo, a Wickliffe, a Huss, a Savonarola, a Bernard and a Bede.

At length the time of reformation came to ancient Israel, when Samuel, the prophet, arose to recall his people to their ancient faith and prepare them for the coming kingdom. Such a ministry of our own time was that of Luther and the Reformation, calling back the Church of God to her ancient faith, and arousing her to claim her lost inheritance. But, as even Samuel's mighty work was in a measure ineffectual, and was followed for a time by the counterfeit kingdom of Saul, and the false and worldly aims of his countrymen, which led them into a separation from God that left its effects for half a century, so even the revived Christianity of the Reformation has not been perfect; and, like ancient Israel, the church, delivered from her immediate foe, has given herself up, to a great degree, to a spirit of worldliness, and to look for her kingdom in a forbidden world.

There is much today of the spirit of Saul in nominal Christianity; the pride that finds its satisfaction in earthly gifts, talents and successes, and fails to recognize the true King, who, like the rejected David, waits for His throne as the "despised and rejected of men."

The kingdom of David seems to prefigure the true triumphs of our coming King, and the ushering in of His dominion in the final victory of Christianity.

5. The peaceful and splendid throne of Solomon completes the picture of the millennial glory which is to be the consummation of the Christian age.

Then will come the full inheritance of grace and glory, both for God's ancient people and the church and the bride of the Lamb.

What, then, for us, in the Church of God today, is the teaching of this ancient Book?

1. It summons her to her glorious crusade of conquest against the enemies of Christ. Never was there an age more full of encouragement for the good fight of faith and the conquest of the world for Christ. The whole land is before us; every avenue of influence at home, every missionary field abroad, is open for the church's zeal and holy enterprise. The triumphs of the Gospel in the past fifty years have not been unworthy of comparison with Pentecost, or even with Joshua's campaign. True, it has been but a small section of the church that has dared to claim these victories, but the recompense has been sufficient to call forth far higher achievements and aspirations.

Especially should the near prospect of the coming kingdom arouse us to go forth and win for our glorious Captain the crown of all the world, until every citadel of heathendom, and every stronghold of sin shall have become a monument of His grace and power.

More emphatically still, let the tender lesson of Rahab in the beginning, and the Cities of Refuge at the close, remind us that our supreme conflict is for the souls of sinful men. And beyond all the questions of dogmas, and the discussion of principles, and the undermining of systems of error and iniquity, let our objective point be individual men and women, and our highest and brightest trophies, the transformed lives of the most helpless and degraded of our race.

2. Let us, like Joshua and Israel, go in and possess all our inheritance. The church has been slack to do this, and is still slack. She has not claimed her full inheritance of knowledge and truth, nor entered into all the fullness of God's precious promises.

She has not entered into her full inheritance of holiness, but has been content to look upon a life of sanctity and devotedness as an exceptional exhibition of individual temperament rather than as the duty and privilege of every child of God.

She has not entered into her full inheritance of faith, nor recognized the power that lies latent in taking God at His word and daring to claim all that He has spoken. A life of becoming faith and remarkable answers to prayer is regarded as something special and wonderful, a sort of peculiar calling on the part of some individual of exalted piety.

She has not entered into her full inheritance of love and unity, but has been rent with strifes, divisions, jealousies and controversies, which have left Hebron in the hands of the Anakims and her Lord "wounded in the house of His friends."

And she has failed to enter into her full inheritance of supernatural power. The gifts of Pentecost have never been recalled, but have only been imperfectly claimed, and natural talent, human learning and worldly influence have been their weak and insufficient substitutes. Let us go in and possess all the land. All power is given unto our Joshua in heaven and in earth, and lo! He is with us alway.

"God hath not given us the spirit of fear, but of power, and of love, and of sound mind." Let us, therefore, "stir up the gift of God that is in us;" Let Zion hear her Master crying, "Awake, awake, put on thy strength, thy beautiful garments;" "Arise and shine, for thy light is come, and the glory of the Lord is risen upon thee."

The Almighty Presence of our risen Lord is sufficient for any obedient service which we will dare to attempt in His strength and name. Let us put on the whole armour of the Lord, "Be strong in the Lord, and in the power of His might," and clothed in all the fullness of the unchanging Paraclete, let the church of God go forth to the last campaign of the great conflict.

3. Let the church remember the necessity of separation from sin and the world if she would overcome her enemies and possess her full inheritance. She must cross the Jordan and let its unbridged torrents roll between her and the world. She must know the true meaning of circumcision and let Gilgal roll away the reproach of Egypt from her spirit and person. She must watch against the sin of Achan, and not let the accursed thing touch her spotless hands. She must take no tribute from the Canaanites, nor lean upon the world in the slightest measure for her support.

She must separate from unbidden alliance with the ungodly, and stand "fresh as the morning, fair as the moon, clear as the sun, and terrible as an army with banners." Alas, this is the secret of her weakness and failure; she has gone, like Israel, into a forbidden league with the tribes of the land. She has put her head, like Samson, in Delilah's lap, and her locks are shorn, and all her shaking of herself will not renew her strength until she has taken the place of the Nazarite and separated herself from a defiling and hostile world. "Come out of her my people," is the Master's call; and as the church obeys it, will she stand forth in her primitive purity and power and draw all men unto her Lord.

CHAPTER XVII.

THE MILLENNIAL INHERITANCE.

"Whose voice then shook the earth; but now He hath promised, saying, Yet once more I shake not the earth only, but also heaven. And this word, Yet once more, signifieth the removing of those things that are shaken, as of things that are made, that those things which cannot be shaken may remain. Wherefore we receiving a kingdom which cannot be moved, let us have grace, whereby we may serve God acceptably with reverence and godly fear." – Heb. 12:26-28.

CHRISTIAN hope has always loved to link the land of promise with our heavenly inheritance. The sacred poetry of the past is full of this sweet imagery. Jordan is the swelling flood of death, and the sweet fields beyond are the images of that heavenly land.

"Where everlasting spring abides,
And never withering flowers,
And death, the narrow stream, divides
That heavenly land from ours."

The vital objection to this theory is that heaven essentially differs from the earthly Canaan in most of the features which chiefly distinguished the latter. That was a land of conflict and hard-won victory, while heaven shall have no foes to overcome, and all its crowns shall be those of accomplished triumph and peaceful recompense. Heaven will have no Jericho, no valley of Achor, nor failure such as that of Achan, and no sad declension such as that which followed Israel's entry into Canaan.

And yet, there are some points in which the misinterpretation is not without its lessons. Canaan was Israel's home, their place of rest after the conflicts in the wilderness, and the realization of long-deferred hopes and promises.

And so, there remaineth a rest for the people of God on the heaven side of the grave where they shall be at home, and "shall rest from their labors while their works do follow them;" and where the long-deferred hopes and expectations of life shall be realized at length, and all their wanderings and trials shall forever cease. God forbid that we should abate aught of the blessed meaning of heaven, where all the ransomed wait in unspeakable felicity for the greater inheritance that lies still farther beyond!

It is of this better inheritance that the ancient Canaan was really the type; for there is a better inheritance even than heaven. Christian hope is always connected in the New Testament Scriptures, not with death and the state of the departed, but with the second coming of the Lord Jesus, and the millennial glory which is then to be ushered in. Even the earthly Canaan itself was but the transient home of the seed of Abraham; it looked forward both in type and promise to a future age when Israel shall inherit their full patrimony, and when all the children of faith shall possess, through the age of glory, their true Land of Promise.

1. Like the ancient Canaan, it is to be introduced by the true Joshua, the Lord Jesus Christ. There is no millennium promised in the Scriptures apart from His personal coming. The heavens have received Him, according to the language of the apostles, "until the times of restitution of all things;" but He is coming again, and His appearing and His kingdom will be simultaneous.

There came a day, in Scotland, when the great heart of the Reformers went out to John Knox. They felt it was he whom they needed, and his coming would settle every question.

When at last the tidings went abroad, over hill and valley, and hamlet and city, "John Knox has come!" all hearts were thrilled with confidence that the crisis was passed, and strong men gathered at the rallying-places, and tyrants trembled on their thrones; for they knew that his single presence was worth the combined strength of all their armies.

And so, the need of our world is not institutions, and organizations, and people, but the coming of the King Himself.

2. Like the ancient Canaan, only the children of faith and obedience will possess this inheritance. Perhaps many of the ancient Israel were saved who never entered the Land of Promise; and so it is possible to belong to the people of God and yet lose much of the glory and recompense connected with the hope of His appearing. "Unto them that look for Him will He appear the second time without sin unto salvation." "They that are with Him are called, and chosen, and faithful."

There is a faith that brings salvation, but there is a faith that will bring the recompense promised at His coming, and there will yet be a generation whose faith will keep them from the power of death, and bring them the translation glory.

Often have we seen the children of God struggling through some tremendous trial of soul or body, and it seemed as if their faith did not quite win the victory here. But it was sweet to believe that what they had missed in this world would be given as the recompense of their faith, at His coming.

Not one single grain of true faith is ever lost, and although it may seem to have missed its mark on this side, it is all reserved for His coming, and many a soul that has wept and wondered will wonder yet more, when it beholds the crown laid up for it there when the tears shall have long ago been forgotten.

But obedience is as necessary as faith. They who are to be among the first fruits of His appearing have followed the Lamb whithersoever He goeth. "Ye are My friends," He says, "if ye do whatsoever I command you."

3. The Millennium, like Canaan, must be conquered, too. Not without resistance shall He enter upon His kingdom. The world's greatest conflict will just precede its millennial Sabbath. The mighty Captain of the millennial armies sits upon a white horse with garments dyed in blood, and a name upon His vesture and upon His thigh, King of kings, and Lord of lords; and comes forth as a mighty Conqueror, treading under His feet the hosts of Antichrist and the powers of hell, and scattering His enemies at the feet of Nebuchadnezzar's image, like the chaff of the summer threshing floors; for "He must reign until He put all enemies under His feet." The battles of Joshua and the conquests of David are the living types of the advent struggles, and the Armageddon war.

The promises of His coming are all given to the overcomer. God is not going to throw away His crowns and thrones on those who have lived for earthly rewards. He has a "little flock" to whom He will "give the Kingdom," and He is picking them out every day, through the tests that come to them and the victories which they win.

Gideon started with thirty thousand men, but God only took three hundred of all that army. They were not only picked, but they were picked again and again.

The first thirty thousand were taken out of Israel, then ten thousand were taken out of the thirty thousand, and then three hundred were taken out of the ten thousand, and with these three hundred the victory was won.

Day by day, each of us is meeting the enemies who come to prove whether he can be trusted with a crown.

4. The Lord's coming will bring not only conflict, but victory. Joshua's campaign was an uninterrupted and complete triumph until it was finished. There was no king in all the Hittite confederacy that had not been overthrown; and so our Lord is to put down all authority

and opposition and reign without a rival over the millennial earth. The day is surely coming when every evil thing that lifts its head in proud defiance shall be laid prostrate at His feet. Not forever shall right be on the scaffold and wrong upon the throne. "He will avenge His own elect."

Error shall at length cease to delude, selfishness to prey on holiness, and injustice, vice and crime to defile and destroy the creation of God. The hour is coming when the adversaries of the church and of the soul shall be remembered only as a vanished dream. We shall seek for them and they shall not be found. The proud empires of the world, the blasphemous and defiant power of Antichrist, and even Satan himself shall be given to the saints of God and the Prince of Peace. The conquests of Canaan were not a truce with the adversary, nor an attempt to transform their adversaries to peaceful friends; but their utter extinction.

And so the coming of the Lord is to involve the destruction of His enemies. The Gospel age is the time for evangelization and the day for the world's peaceful submission and conversion, but when the Master comes it will be to "consume with the Spirit of His mouth, and to destroy with the brightness of His coming, everything that exalted itself against the obedience of Christ."

5. His coming will bring to us our inheritance. Then will Abraham and David possess the literal fullness of their ancient covenants, and the land on which their feet rested for a time shall be their own and the home of their offspring. Then shall the disciples who followed Jesus in His days of rejection, "sit on twelve thrones judging the twelve tribes of Israel." Then shall we possess our complete redemption, spirit, soul and body, perfectly restored to the image of God, and our lost dominion over the earth given back through our exalted Head. Then shall the saints of God receive the recompense of their lives of service and suffering, and those who have overcome shall wear the crowns of victory and glory

which He hath promised to the faithful and triumphant. Then shall each soul find its perfect sphere and enter upon the service for which its earthly training has qualified it; and doubtless there will be a Hebron of exalted fellowship and love for every brave Caleb; a Kirjath-sepher of boundless knowledge for every conquering Othniel; a fountain of life, with its upper and nether springs, for every true Achsah who has dared to claim her full inheritance; a double inheritance for every true Ephraimite that has dared to conquer it in the days of earthly battle; a city of honor and service for every Levite who has been true to his consecration and a Timnath-serah of everlasting light and glory for every faithful Joshua.

Our full inheritance is yet to come. All we know of Jesus in His indwelling fullness and victorious life is but the type of the glory that awaits us at His advent. All we know of truth here is but through glass darkly, then "shall we know even as we are known!" All we know of holiness here is but a shadow of that hour when "we shall be like Him," as we see Him as He is. All we know of physical redemption is but a prophetic foretaste of the glorious life that will thrill every frame with the resurrection joy. All we know of service for the Master is but the blundering attempt of the schoolboy as he learns the mere alphabet of knowledge, compared with the mighty faith and Divine power with which we shall be workers together with Him, in the transformation of the millennial earth, at the inauguration of His glorious kingdom.

He is educating us to bear a far "more exceeding, even an eternal weight of glory." Let us be apt learners and by-and-by we shall look back with amazement to our earthly childhood and scarcely recognize the trembling and blundering beginner who once struggled through the years of time, and claimed the inheritance that was to be so much more vast and transcendent than his brightest earthly dream.

6. And best of all, He will be Himself our Eternal Inheritance. "Behold the Tabernacle of God is with men and God Himself shall be with them and be their God."

How much is meant by the presence of Jesus! How much it used to mean in the old apostolic times! What a difference it made to that little company when suddenly He stood in their midst, and thrilled their hearts with the sweet words: "Peace be unto you." "Then were the disciples glad, when they saw the Lord."

Only four or five times did that wondrous Presence appear to Paul, but oh, the power of one such moment upon his life!

What cared he, that day, as he rode into Damascus, for any earthly or heavenly power? What to Him was the name of Jesus? But suddenly, like a flash of lightning from a clear sky, the face of Jesus blazed out from the glory, the voice of Jesus spake to him, and Paul was prostrated upon the ground broken and subdued, and crying, "Lord! what wilt Thou have me to do?" One moment with Jesus had transformed the mightiest will of the age.

Look at him again, crushed and discouraged, in that dungeon in Jerusalem, wondering if he had made a fatal mistake, and sinking, doubtless, in deep depression. But suddenly the Master appears, and with one word assures him. "Thou hast testified for Me at Jerusalem, thou must bear witness for Me at Rome." Instantly Paul's heart was on the heights of glory, and for two years of persecution and apparent failure, that one moment bears him on in unbroken glory, even as the one flash the sailor gets from the sky and the one observation he takes of the sun, will carry him through long weeks of clouds and storms.

Look again at that little company on the stormy Adriatic.

For days the ship has tossed on the wild Euroclydon, but, suddenly, Jesus appears to Paul. One single message is all – "Fear not, thou must be brought before Cæsar; I have given thee all these that sail with thee."

Paul is a victor again, and standing on that tossing vessel, he inspires with his own courage the sinking hearts of the men with him. They reach the shore, and by-and-by, the capital of the world.

Oh, what will it be to have that wondrous Presence with us forever, and every moment be able to look into His face, to hear His voice, to have Him with us, and to be "even as He?" Thank God that blessed Coming is near at hand! God is saying to many hearts today, as He has said so often in His Word: "Yet once more, (it is a little while) I shake not the earth only, but also heaven." Yea, I will shake all nations, and the Desire of all nations shall come.

Surely, He is shaking the nations today. Surely this terrible financial trouble that is distressing all the world, making hundreds of thousands of paupers, bringing distress of nations and perplexity, surely this is one of the harbingers of the coming of the Son of Man, and the quaking earth is keeping time to the tread of the heavenly march.

Only a few days ago, tidings reached us from across the ocean and the continent, that the very heart of Asia had been shaken by the most significant earthquake of modern times. Surely, if there is one place on earth that is the seat of heathenism and the very citadel of its strength, it is Thibet, and that great monastery, where thousands of priests surround the Grand Lama of Buddhism, the Pope of five millions of Asiatic people; and yet, a few weeks ago, that very spot was shaken by the hand of God, that great monastery crumbled into a heap of ruins, and the Grand Lama himself has disappeared, with hundreds of others and filled the minds of his followers with consternation.

God help us to understand the meaning of our times, and to hear Him saying to us, "How knowest thou but thou hast come to the Kingdom for such a time as this?"

THE

LAND OF PROMISE,

OR,

OUR FULL INHERITANCE IN CHRIST.

BY

REV. A. B. SIMPSON.

The Land of Promise;

OR,

OUR FULL INHERITANCE IN CHRIST.

CHAPTER I.

LOOKING OVER.

"And Moses went up from the plains of Moab, unto the mountain of Nebo, to the top of Pisgah, that is over against Jericho: and the Lord showed him all the land of Gilead, unto Dan, and all Naphtali, and the land of Ephraim, and Manasseh, and all the land of Judah, unto the utmost sea, and the south, and the plain of the valley of Jericho, the city of palm-trees unto Zoar. And the Lord said unto him, This is the land which I sware unto Abraham, unto Isaac, and unto Jacob, saying, I will give it unto thy seed; I have caused thee to see it with thine eyes, but thou shalt not go over thither." – Deut. 34:1-4.

WHEN God took Moses up into the top of Pisgah He showed him all the Land or Palestine. There are few scenes on earth that could afford such a prospect as was spread out before him there. There are few such views of natural beauty and grandeur as can be seen from the heights of Moab, from the sides of Olivet, or from the mountains of Lebanon. The picture is exquisitely beautiful in itself, and there is an added charm to it from its historical associations. There is a sacred meaning connected with every scene which one would think must appeal even to the heart that cares little for heavenly things.

It is not our intention now, however, to look, at the land topographically, historically, or geographically; but to find in it a symbol of our great inheritance in Christ – a special type of what God would have us see in Him, and enter upon as our own spiritual possession.

Moses had now led the hosts of Israel for forty years. He had shared in all their trials, and had led them to the borders of the inheritance promised to their fathers; but now at the last, by an act of unbelief, he had forfeited the right to enter it with them. This scene upon which he was looking now was the last view God gave him of the land which he could not enter. From the top of Pisgah God gave him a view of the glorious inheritance that others were to enter upon. There is given still to the soul, a revelation, by the Spirit of God, of every experience before it becomes real. We see Christ as a Saviour, before we take Him to be ours. So also is it with the deeper experiences of His grace.

Moses was only allowed to look over into this possession from the heights of Nebo. God is calling us not only to look upon it, but to enter into it and enjoy it.

I. It was a supernatural vision. No one could have shown it to him but God. "It hath not entered into the heart of man to understand the things which God hath prepared for them that love Him, but God hath revealed them unto us by His Spirit." "The natural man receiveth not the things of the Spirit of God; for they are foolishness unto him; neither can he know them, because they are spiritually discerned." The most intellectual and cultured minds often fail most utterly to comprehend the simple gospel of redemption. They cannot understand the atonement of Jesus Christ. The mystery of an indwelling Saviour, a life of victory over sin, and of rest and peace in God, are beyond their comprehension. If you talk to them of a constantly victorious Christian life, it seems to them like foolish sentimentalism.

From their high, intellectual standpoint they look down with a kind of pity upon the morbid fancies of an emotional religion, and can have no sympathy with the idiosyncrasies of the people who profess such things. They consider them an uncultured class who are living on the lower plane of their emotional nature. Yet how often you have seen such people changed by the power of the Holy Ghost. Through the pressure of some heavy trial, or by means of a personal revelation, God has shown to them a new world of blissful reality in Himself. He sets their feet all at once on Pisgah's heights, and what before had seemed to them meaningless and insignificant, suddenly becomes tangible and sublime.

What they had considered as the toys of a child, now take their true place above the higher conceptions of genius. God has brought them to the land of promise, and He only could have done it. The Holy Ghost has begun to reveal to them the things of Christ. "The Spirit searcheth all things, yea, the deep things of God." So the Spirit has shown them the land. They perhaps could not tell how, but somehow He has done it.

Thus God brought Moses to the top of Nebo and somehow gave him a view of all the land. He had taken all the clouds out of the sky, and left it clear and transparent. He gave to the eagle eye of His servant, not yet dimmed by age, supernatural strength to take in the glorious vista spread out before him. His eye took in all the details of the picture, from the snowy summits of Lebanon away down to the southern limits of the land, and from the sparkling waters of the Mediterranean to the palm trees nestling around the city of Jericho at his feet. It was all one exquisite picture of loveliness. I believe Moses not only took it in topographically, but that he saw, too, the spiritual meaning of it all, as it was afterwards unfolded in the teachings of the Scriptures. I believe his mind was illuminated by the Holy Ghost to see in this land a type of the experience of the church in the ages to follow.

Have you so seen it, beloved? Perhaps you have not become simple and humble enough for it, and teachable as a little child. "If any man among you seemeth to be wise in this world, let him became a fool that he may be wise;" for it is written, "He taketh the wise in their own craftiness." You cannot see the land with your heads; the view must come from the heart. The apostle prayed for the Ephesian church that their hearts might be enlightened to know the riches of the glory of their inheritance.

There are many intellectual Christians who do not see all that God has for them in this life. The church needs to get her eyes open to see the land. She may admit there is much yet unattained, but she has not seen it. Ask the Lord to show you your full redemption rights in Christ." Ask Him to show you the unappropriated promises of your Bible. Only He can give you the vision of your inheritance; and He is ready to anoint your eyes with eye-salve that you may see.

II. Like Moses, many do not see the land until they are about to die. Like him they wander about all their days, and at last, near the close of life, they catch a glimpse of what they might have had all the time, but which they cannot enter upon now. They must leave the picture for others. All they can see before them is the banks of Jordan. They cannot cross them and enter the fields beyond. They will be with Christ yonder and will see Him at His coming, but they have missed forever what might have been theirs in their earthly life.

However much we may admire the character of Moses and reverence his memory, we must not forget that he lost something. He gained many crowns, but he did not gain the land of promise. I believe many Christians realize on their death-bed what they have lost. If they had known earlier what they find out then, theirs would have been a life of more constant joy, victory and usefulness – but it is too late; they are saved, but they lost much out of their life that God would have given to them.

It is possible, beloved, for you to see too late what God had for you in this life. It is a blessed thing to know about it, and tell Joshua to enter in. It is more blessed to enter yourself. God help you not to disappoint yourself or Him! May you not have too late a vision of a life that has ended in disappointment instead of triumph! May your soul perceive the vision of the end, and enter at once upon the possession of all the fullness or Jesus!

III. In order to see the land of promise you must get above the level of the natural world. You cannot see it while you are wandering on the plains below. You must get to the top of the Pisgah to behold it. You must get on higher ground, the ground of consecration. You must be above the world, with your back to its allurements. Everything else must be counted vain and worthless beside the privilege of that glorious view. Lift up your eyes to the place or separation, then go up there alone like Moses. He did not see it in a prayer meeting, or amid the noise of thousands. He was alone with God. With Him he climbed the steps up that dizzy height. It was a difficult and solitary way, but it was necessary for God to get him apart from human counsels, and, in the silence of that lonely mountain, to speak to him face to face. Moses did not fear that all-penetrating light upon his heart of hearts. Have you thought what it must be to be absolutely alone in His presence? It was a blessed place to Moses. All heaven was open to Him there with all its possibilities of blessing.

IV. To get a view of the land of promise you must get to the place of death. You must go up that mountain-side to die. Moses knew he would never come down from Pisgah. He saw his own sepulcher first, then he saw the land. He did not go up there to become glorified or exalted in himself. It was death to his own pride, and goodness and wisdom. He saw his lonely grave in Moab's land. Then God could show him all the land.

When we get there, beloved, God can show us the land too, and bring us in as He did not Moses. The veil of the flesh is in the way of the Holy of Holies. It must be rent by crucifixion to self. The glory must be opened up to us as it was to Jesus on Calvary, in His crucifixion. We must die, like Moses, to our own self-will, our glory, our pride, our sensitiveness, the affections that are not utterly of God and for God, our gratifications, our personal aims, our very fear of dying. Perhaps you are afraid of missing something when you are thus dead; well, go to Him and die to that fear. No harm can come to you if you are in the hand of your Father and Saviour.

I don't know that we can actually die, but we can be willing to die. Moses did not fear when God took his hand and laid him in the grave. I am glad we have not to crush out this evil thing, and tear out that sin. I am glad we have only to go to Nebo's top and look up into the face of love, and then pass away upon His bosom. We shall awake and find somehow the old life is gone, and "henceforth it is no more I, but Christ that liveth in me."

God has buried the old will and strength, and we do not know what has become of it. We have gone out of self, and we have no consciousness but of God. He has separated us unto Himself. The apostle says it is possible for us to be in this place. "If ye, through the Spirit, do mortify the deeds of the body, ye shall live." Are you willing to go there and have the sentence of death pronounced upon you? It is a solemn hour in the lives of many. It seems as if you must actually die. There are things which you hold almost dearer than life, that must go out forever. It will be an unutterable surprise to you when the surrender is really made, to find out that nothing is lost after all. When Isaac lay upon the altar, it must have seemed to Abraham that all was lost. The bitterness of death was past when God spoke, "Stay thy hand, Abraham." The inner life of self, the strong will of both Abraham and Isaac died in that hour. When all is yielded to God, absolutely and unconditionally, come what may, there is no place so safe or so sweet as the altar of Moriah, the grave of Nebo, or the sepulcher of Jesus.

V. Not only did Moses behold the Land of Promise with his outward eyes, but he saw its deeper, spiritual meaning as no other perhaps of the ancient prophets. In his ministry and in his writings, Moses revealed the deeper and higher experiences and truths of which Canaan was a type. They are all one great object lesson revealing the Land of Promise. Who is the grandest type of faith in all the world? Who was told to turn his back on his kindred and his land, and to step out in the darkness upon the bare promises of God? Abraham. And who gave us the character of Abraham? Moses. Who gave us that other picture of the death of self which we must pass through before entering Canaan – Jacob, the crookedest and most perverse of God's children, until slain by the hand of God at Peniel, after which he could go forth as a prince having power to prevail with God and men? It was Moses. Moses, too, gave us that redemption-picture of the blood of the Paschal Lamb, the sacrifices on the brazen altar and all the continuous portraiture of Jesus displayed in the tabernacle services.

What is it all but Moses viewing the land and showing it to us? Jesus Himself said, "Moses wrote of me." From the top of Pisgah he saw the luxuriant fields and forests of Bashan; then his eye swept past orchards and meadows to the snow-crowned peaks of Lebanon, or followed the silver line of Jordan down to where the sea of Galilee lay among the hills like a diamond set in emeralds. From Hermon, his eye glanced over to the bosom of the Mediterranean, then down the broad lands of Ephraim and Manasseh, and to the hills of Judah and Jerusalem. Perhaps it rested last upon a little hill outside of Jerusalem, where in vision he may have seen a cross erected and One upon it in the agony of death. Perhaps the spirit whispered to him that was the meaning of the Paschal lamb, and the brazen altar, and the tabernacle of Israel.

Then as his eye rested for a moment upon the white peaks of Hermon, he may have beheld another scene in which he himself should take part, as the heavens opened, and the transfiguration-glory descended upon the Son of Man, even Him who was to come as the fulfillment of the law and the prophets, Jesus Himself, the Son of God, who afterwards came to fulfill the vision He had given to Moses. He it was who revealed Himself to Moses no doubt as the significance of all he saw. He would not show the land to him apart from His own coming and His redeeming work. Moses must have seen Jesus through all his own types as the end of the law and the substance of all truth and life.

The teachings of Moses unfold the deeper truths of the spiritual life. The cleansing of the leper speaks to us of cleansing from the deep poison of sin, which has gone through all our nature. The ordinance of the red heifer teaches the need of keeping the soul from the touch of death, and a defiling world.

So too, the Feasts of Moses point also to Jesus and His finished work. The Passover speaks of redemption; of the feast of Pentecost; of the outpouring of the Holy Ghost; of the Feast of Tabernacles; of the glorious fruition of His whole redemption, when He shall come in the glory of His Father and all the holy angels with Him to sit upon His millennial throne. All this was pictured in the annual feasts.

Nowhere do we find Rest more beautifully typified than in the sabbatic feasts. The weekly sabbath, the sabbatic year coming every seventh year, the year of Jubilee every fiftieth year, all speak of rest in God. The whole Mosaic system teaches the closest communion with God. The tabernacle itself is the very picture of a sanctified life more full and deep even than the highest Christian experience has ever fathomed. Probably Moses knew much of this, and in the vision of the land he saw in vision all he had taught in symbol. We too shall understand the meaning of the Land of Promise as we stand with him and look over its broad fields in the light of the later Scriptures and in that of the Holy Spirit.

Not only does Moses unveil it, but all the Scriptures are full of the vision. David wrote of this land in the Psalms, "Blessed is the people who know the joyful sound; they shall walk, O Lord, in the light of thy countenance. In thy name shall they rejoice all the day: and in thy righteousness shall they be exalted." "Blessed is the man whom thou chooseth, and causest to approach unto thee, that he may dwell in thy courts: we shall be satisfied with the goodness of thy house, even of thy holy temple." "They shall be abundantly satisfied with the fatness of thy house: and thou shalt make them drink of the rivers of thy pleasures."

Isaiah saw a vision of the ransomed coming to Zion with songs and everlasting joy upon their heads. "And an highway shall be there, and a way, and it shall be called, The way of holiness; the unclean shall not pass over it; but it shall be for those: the way-faring men, though fools, shall not err therein. No lion shall be there, nor any ravenous beast shall go up thereon, it shall not be found there: but the redeemed shall walk there."

As he looked over the land, he saw it bathed in the very sunlight of heaven, and radiant as with the very joy of the Marriage Feast. "Thy sun shall no more go down; neither shall thy moon withdraw itself: for the Lord shall be thine everlasting light, and the days of thy mourning shall be ended." "Thou shalt no more be termed Forsaken: neither shall thy land any more be termed Desolate: but thou shalt be called Hephzi-bah, and thy land Beulah: for the Lord delighteth in thee, and thy land shall be married."

Joel, Micah, Habakkuk, Zechariah, indeed all the ancient prophets wrote of this glorious land.

How has Jesus painted it? "Come unto me, all ye that labor and are heavy-laden, and I will give you rest. Take my yoke upon you and learn of me; for I am meek and lowly in heart: and ye shall find rest unto your souls."

"These things have I spoken unto you, my peace I give unto you." "In the world ye shall have tribulation, but be of good cheer, I have overcome the world."

Paul speaks of the Land of Promise in this way. "That Christ may dwell in your hearts by faith; that ye, being rooted and grounded in love, may be able to comprehend with all saints what is the breadth, and length, and depth, and height; and to know the love of Christ, which passeth knowledge, that ye might be filled with all the fullness of God."

John lived in the land. "There is no fear in love: but perfect love casteth out fear: because fear hath torment." "We love him because he first loved us." "Whosoever abideth in him sinneth not." "Whosoever is born of God sinneth not; but he that was begotten of God keepeth him, and that wicked one toucheth him not."

So we might go up to the top of many a Pisgah and see what the departing saints saw as they passed away. The martyrs of the primitive ages, the Christian heroes of the past, the sainted ones of all time, found this land real. You know something of it too. You may not be able to write of it, but you know it. You can say,

"I cannot tell the art
By which such bliss is given;
I know thou hast the heart,
And I have Heaven."

Let us get up into the mountain and look over, and then enter upon it. I am glad that it is not a far-away land. Its borders are close beside you. One step into yonder stream, and you are there.

VI. Let us sum up the landscape in conclusion.

1. In that land there is reality. It is not all promise, and hope, and make-believe, and trying to get at things. It is getting at them. There is reality in faith. Jesus becomes a real Sanctifier and a lasting sanctification.

2. It is a land of rest, not only from care, and fret, and trouble, but rest in the living God. It is the peace of God which passeth all understanding. There is something imparted to the soul that is full of rest. There is a calm upon the heart, as though a heavenly hand had been laid upon it and had stilled all its flutterings. The peace of Jesus has taken the place of your fears and distractions. You have His rest. It is a supernatural calm, and you almost wonder how in the midst of things that are enough to drive one crazy, the soul can be kept in peace, like the very breath of heaven. This is what the land has for you, beloved. You can always find it in the bosom of Christ. He wants to put it into your breast. Have you entered into His rest?

3. It is a land of victory. You are not to be beaten and baffled always in your life, but to overcome sin and Satan. You are to be triumphant in the hard places, to be master of the difficulties and trials, pushing through the obstacles and accomplishing your work for God in spite of them. That is the Land of Promise. Have you hard places in your life? Have you got over them? Is God overcoming them for you? Can you look behind you and see many foes vanquished, and can you say, As He overcame those for me, so shall He ever triumph in me? We have not enlisted for a battle, but for a campaign. He who has led you through a hundred battles, will lead you through a hundred more. It is a hard fight, but it is glorious. Have you this line of victory, beloved? Are you being beaten, or are you overcoming? The battle is not too hard, the Anakims are not too great. Say as Caleb did, "If the Lord God be with us we will be able to overcome them." Take care lest you think the difficulties cannot be overcome. Take care how you fail to go forward to meet them in Christ. There is a life of victory for you even if you are not in it; but do not stop until you have it in all its fullness.

4. There is not only deliverance from guilt, but there is real holiness in the land. God wants and means to have

all the beauty and grace of Jesus Christ put into your life and wrought out in your character. What would the land be without the grapes of Eshcol? What are the fruits of this land? Paul speaks of them in the epistle to the Galatians, "The fruit of the Spirit is love, joy, peace, long-suffering, gentleness, goodness, faith, meekness, temperance." These are the grapes of Eshcol. They do not grow out of you, beloved, but out of the land. You cannot make them. Get the heavenly vine and they will be on it. If you are a part of the vine they cannot help growing upon you.

5. The inheritances in that land are not confused and jumbled together, so that everyone shares alike. Each has his own inheritance. They had theirs in the literal Canaan, and it is true also of the spiritual land. Each of us can have the best thing possible for us in the will of God. He will give to us just what will yield us the greatest real blessing, and which will in every way, make the most of us. Not that we will all become Edward Paysons, or Madame Guyons. She had her inheritance, and you will have yours.

God has a place for you as a bookkeeper, a carpenter, a missionary, or a humble shepherd of the flock. Have you got all there is in life for you? Have you missed nothing? Have you taken into this short life all God would press into it? Can you say as Joshua did: "There failed not aught of any good thing which the Lord had spoken unto the house of Israel: all came to pass." It would be a terrible thing to miss what He made and redeemed you for. The soul may not be lost, but there will have gone out of your life beautiful, precious things like clusters of radiant gems. God help you to take them and make them your own.

6. There is power and blessing for others in the land through your ministry. Your life will tell for good to them. It will never thus tell, until you have risen to a higher level in your own experience.

7. And the land was not far away from the mountain where Moses stood, it was lying at his feet; a few days after, the children of Israel entered upon it. Don't say, it is at such a distance and will take a long time to reach it. The land is very near. What did Caleb say? "Let us go up at once and possess it." They were willing to go some time afterward, but God was not. They tried to go on the morrow, but God would not go with them. Before this evening sets you can be in the land. Nay, before this chapter closes your feet may have taken the first step of full committal. Before tomorrow morning, you may have fought a hundred battles, and overcome in all. May the Lord say to you this morning, "Go up at once and possess it."

How sad that Moses saw the land but could not enter it. He was a good man, yet he yielded for a moment to doubt and haste, and lost a great blessing. There are people of God today who are missing much of the precious things they might receive. I am glad Moses was under the law, and we are under the gospel. Moses could not enter in because he represented that law. Joshua alone could go into the land because he represented the gospel. Jesus has come to lead you in, beloved.

Don't waste time in trying to get there yourself. Christ only can lead you in. Can you say, as you look over from Pisgah, "Now we have received, not the spirit of the world, but the Spirit which is of God: that we might know the things that are freely given to us of God." We know them now. But they are also "freely given to us." We can have them as a free gift of His infinite grace. Shall we take them and rejoice forever that we said this hour,

"Lord, I believe a rest remains
To all thy people known;
A rest where pure enjoyment reigns,
And thou art loved alone.

"A rest, where all the soul's desire
Is fixed on things above;
Where fear, and sin, and grief expire,
Cast out by perfect love.

"Oh! that I now that rest might know,
Believe and enter in;
Now, Saviour, now the gift bestow,
And let me cease from sin.

"I rest upon His promise sure,
I come, I wait to prove
The cleansing of my heart from sin,
The fullness of His love."

CHAPTER II.

SETTING OUT.

"Now the Lord had said unto Abram, Get thee out of thy country, and from thy kindred, and from thy father's house, unto a land that I will show thee." – Gen. 12:1.

"And the Lord said unto Abram, after that Lot was separated from him, Lift up now thine eyes, and look from the place where thou art, northward, and southward, and eastward and westward: for all the land which thou seest, to thee will I give it, and to thy seed forever. And I will make thy seed as the dust of the earth: so that if a man can number the dust of the earth, then shall thy seed also be numbered. Arise, walk through the land in the length of it and in the breath of it; for I will give it unto thee." – Gen. 13:14-17.

THE act of setting out for the Land of Promise is beautifully exemplified in the life of Abraham. At the command of God he left his home in Ur of the Chaldees, and emigrated to Palestine, to him, a new and strange land. There are three steps in this pilgrimage which exactly typify the stages of Christian experience at the beginning of a life of entire consecration. First, we see him setting out from the old life, and separating from it. Next, we see him coming into the land; believing in it, appropriating it by faith, and taking actual possession of it. Lastly, we find him walking through the length and breadth of it; and actually entering upon the possession, of it day by day in all its fullness.

I. SEPARATION.

This word was the keynote of Abraham's life, and it is a most important thought in connection with full salvation. We must separate from sin unto holiness; from the old nature unto the new; from the earthly life unto the heavenly. The idea of separation runs all through the history of Abraham.

1. He was separated from his country. God's call came to him, "Get out from thy country." So, beloved, before we can enter the Land of Promise we must be out of the other land. What is the land God calls us to leave? It is the world. We cannot enter upon the fullness of Christ's salvation and have the pleasures of the world at the same time. The two things cannot go together. The command is as imperative as it was to Abraham, "Get out from thy country." "Come out from among them, and be ye separated, saith the Lord, and touch not the unclean thing; and I will receive you, and ye shall be my sons and daughters, saith the Lord Almighty."

It was not to old Terah that God said this, but to young Abraham. It is not old people, who have taken their fill of pleasure and are tired of it, that God calls to leave their country; but it is to young, fresh hearts, to whom everything is fascinating and delightful, that the word is given. There is great blessing for those who can turn aside from the cup of pleasure, even when it is at their lips, and while the ardor of youthful passion is glowing in their hearts. There is no consecration in turning from these things when the taste for them is lost, and passion has burned itself out by indulgence.

If we would enter into the land and secure our inheritance there, we must have no aim on earth but to know God and do His will. We must get so stripped of all longings for other things that there will be nothing left of them. Ah! it is blessed to have the heart and will consent unto God in this entire surrender, and He does surely fill the soul that is so given up to Him.

2. Abraham was called also to leave his kindred. So we, too, are called to lay on God's altar all the ties of natural affection, all the selfish passions and the loves of earth. His is not the cold and cruel mandate of an

unfeeling master. He calls for them that our hearts may be consecrated on Him alone. Then, if they are pure and held only for His glory, He will give them back to us. If they are not so possessed, there will be, there must be, loss.

We must have everything cut off from the earthly side, that we may be compensated by a richer growth on the heavenly side. It is a furnace of fire through which the heart must pass. The friendships that are dearer than life cannot be laid down on God's altar without deep anguish, but He is calling for it, He will have us get out from our kindred. If the wife you count your dearest earthly treasure, or the friend on whose wisdom and affection you depend so implicitly, are hindering God's work in your heart, though it be like taking out your very life, they must be laid down. Then, though you can only give Him a broken heart, He will bind it up and fill it with His own holy presence, which will bring a joy and peace utterly unknown before.

3. The next call to Abraham was to leave his father's house. I think there is figurative reference in this to our natural descent from our first parents, and our relations to the fallen human race. God would have us get out from that life into which we were begotten by our father. The very nature itself must be left behind. There is where the hardest death comes. The severest strain of all is not to leave your race or your country, or even your human affections, but it is to part with that which is far dearer than them all, your will. You must be separated from the sinful, despotic, old self-life enthroned in the bosom.

The instincts of our nature are not to be our guide. We must cease to be directed by them. They can never bring a blessing to those who obey them, whether they are the promptings of self-will, of earthly desire and lust, or what may be termed the highest tastes of refinement and culture. We are not to follow the guidance of human intellect and reason alone, because these things came to us by the creative hand of God, and they have been injured by the fall. Everything that pertains to us naturally is corrupt and fit only for death. God makes no account of them. We must lay all that came to us from the old Adam life upon the block. It must be given up to die that we may be wholly dedicated to the will of God.

Abraham three times suffered this separation from his father's house, and each time the stroke must have been a severe one. The first was in Haran where his aged father died. Then his nephew, almost the only relative that came with him, was one who would not work in harmony with him; his will was corrupt, and so there had to come another separation. We can imagine with what sorrow the old patriarch parted from Lot, but how grand the unselfishness that gave to his meaner nephew the choice of the best land, as he left him! Lot took it, leaving to Abraham the barren hills upon which to feed his flock, while he went to the rich vale of the Jordan, well watered and fertile as the garden of the Lord. Keenly the old man must have felt the selfish ingratitude, yet for the love he bore his nephew, he made the sacrifice. Lot deliberately chose the world, wounding and disappointing a noble nature in doing so, and many a deep trouble it caused Abraham afterward to deliver him from the result of folly.

The trial that must have gone most deeply to his heart, however, came afterward, when he was called upon to separate himself from the child of promise. Isaac had come as a wonderful fulfillment of the faith that had waited twenty-five years for him, and he had grown to be the center of all his hopes. God came again and tested his heart more deeply and could say to him when it was over, "Now I know thou lovest me more than these, because thou hast not withheld from me the child of thy affection." Isaac was the very link of Abraham's faith and hope, nevertheless, when God called, he became separated again. That which God had given, he must learn to hold only for Him. He would not cling to it for himself.

There is a precious lesson in this for us, beloved. The things which God gives to us, and which we hold so dear, are not to be prized for the joy they add to us, but we are to receive them in Him, and as a means of increasing our usefulness in His service. The friends that are so dear to our heart, we must not cling to for ourselves, they are to be held only for God. This is, perhaps, the most necessary lesson to be learned in Christian life. God would teach it to the very depths of our souls, and make it a part of our spiritual life. We must surrender all to Him. We must hold everything subject to His will, and yet not be afraid that He will do something harsh if they are so yielded. Isaac must be laid on the altar, but he is not lost. He could not be. We, too, shall hear God say, as Abraham did, "Now I know that thou lovest me, because thou hast not withheld thy dearest one from me."

This is to be "pure in heart." The word pure simply means unmixed. "Blessed are the pure in heart." That is, blessed are the single in heart. "If thine eye be single, thy whole body shall be full of light. But if thine eye be evil, thy whole body shall be full of darkness."

Have you learned all these lessons of separation, beloved? Have you heard God calling you to this; and have you yielded without fear? You need not dread the knife that cuts so deeply into all the quivering flesh of the proud self-life, it wounds only to heal, and all you gave up of your selfishness will be restored to you a thousand-fold in Him.

II. FAITH.

The next step in Abraham's life was that of faith. He had to take as well as leave.

1. He had, to exercise faith without clear light. There was no consciousness before his mind except the consciousness of God. He had no way by which his pilgrimage could be guided. He did not go by an express train that was engaged to let him off at the right station.

He had not an itinerary of the desert he was to cross, that would show him even when he reached the end of it. He had only the naked word of the Lord, "Get thee out unto a land that I will show thee." There was nothing definite in the promise. The call was clear but nothing else was. God would be with him and show him the way as he needed to know it. That was all.

When God calls us out of our own land to go to the land of promise, the first thing we have to leave is our preconceived notions of what is to be done. We must set our own ideas aside. God is to be the chief object of our faith and hope. Like the disciples on the Mount of Transfiguration we are able to see no man but Jesus only. Many of you have got the way all mapped out. You have heard someone's experience, and want that itinerary for your journey. He will not lead you, beloved, as He has led me. The Lord will show the way Himself. The road will develop as you go on; you cannot even see twenty-four hours ahead.

Sometimes God may keep you waiting as He did Abraham, for twenty-five years. You will be tempted today and tried tomorrow. What you have to do is to lean constantly on Jesus. There is no life apart from Him. Nothing else is definite or clear. God will show you the way day by day. Learn to lean on Him more than on His promises. That is the lesson that Abraham learned. He saw Him first and the land afterward. He leaned on Him and went out not knowing whither he was going. You, too, do not know how He will lead you; but choose Him anyhow. Happy indeed the heart that can sing—

"I have called thee, 'Abba, Father;'
I have stayed my heart on thee:
Storms may howl, and clouds may gather,
All must work for good to me."

Can you say this in the midst of deep sorrow? Have you truly got nothing but Him? If you have, He will show you many things. He will draw you constantly nearer to Him, and lead you constantly farther on your way, explaining much that is dark to you now. This cannot be, however, until you have Him alone in the world. The heart must be centered on Jesus. You must see nothing but Him in the heights above or in the depths below. He must be to you the substance of all blessing. Then you can take everything else as He gives it. Abraham believed, not the word, he "believed GOD, and it was counted to Him for righteousness." Oh, beloved, learn to lean on God, to trust the person of God. Later, you can learn to trust His promises. You can then, as surely as you expect salvation, expect to have your prayers answered. You can cling to God, not merely to His word, for the thing you want. He loves to have you cling to Him. You too, may then be called the friend of God.

2. A distinct promise comes after a little. It is easy to believe that now, for he has already believed the Promiser. When Abraham reached Palestine the Lord said unto him, "This land will I give unto thee, and unto thy seed after thee." As if to make the meaning of the promise clear to Abraham's mind, it was coupled with another promise – that he should have a son.

Abraham believed both promises, all the more because he had believed God before. It was hard to believe that the land into which he had come, which was then inhabited by the Canaanites, was one day to be his own. He had to leave it almost as soon as he entered it and go down to Egypt for food. It was hard to believe he should have a son in his old age, to become the head of the redeemed race. He waited for the fulfillment of this for a quarter of a century. God wanted the promise to mean something to him. The more difficult it was, the more it would show His own almighty hand. Abraham had got God, and so he had the guarantee of the promise. God could not fail and so the promise was secure. Oh, the blessedness of thus leaning on God! You can never know the happiness of a deeper and higher life in Christ till you have learned it.

Again, Abraham believed God for the land and for the seed long before he had any evidence of possessing either. He believed not only when he had no sight, but when everything seemed to be pointing directly the other way. He waited for it not one year, not two and a half years, but many, many more. Twenty-five years passed before the promise was redeemed, yet Abraham was no more sure of it when his child was born than he had been during the years of waiting. He had been satisfied that God would keep His word, and it had all along been real to his faith. It is an important lesson for all who would enter into the fullness of Christ. Faith must be the basis of a life of consecration to God. We expect Him to remove the difficulties. That is not God's plan. He would have us step out in the midst of the opposing elements and trust Him. We cannot stand steadily in the hard place of testing, unless we are sure beyond a question that He will stand true to His promise. That is what Abraham did.

If you would come to Christ for sanctification, beloved, the first step is to dare to believe that He accepts you as fully as you give yourself to Him, and becomes to you all your need. If you saw it all first, you would not have the blessing of faithful Abraham, who believed the promise while yet its fulfillment was unseen. It is the same for other blessings even in temporal things. All that you will dare to stand upon and claim as yours with unswerving faith, you will receive.

Do not say this is not for you, and that it is a higher style of Christian life than you can reach; be willing to believe and wait. Perhaps He will not keep you waiting an hour.

Abraham believed God and received the rewards of his faith in the possession of that for which he trusted. The apostle said of him in the epistle to the Romans, "He staggered not at the promises of God through unbelief; but was strong in faith, giving glory to God, and being fully persuaded that, what He had promised, He was also able to perform; and therefore it was imputed to him for righteousness."

3. Abraham so believed God that he "counted the things which are not as if they were." He allowed Lot to have his choice of the land, and when he, full of his strong self-life, claimed the best, Abraham let him have it. When we believe God, we can let people have many things which really belong to us. If God has them for us, no one can possibly take them from us. So Lot took the rich plain of the Jordan. God had given it all to Abraham, and he knew he could not lose it.

Can you believe God for your reputation enough to let people say what they like about you? Can you be meek and suffer, knowing that God is your vindicator? Can you let failure and difficulties of all kinds come if He sends them? Can you lose means and friends and yet say, "God has promised all to me, and it is right?" Can you let things seem to be taken from you rather than fight to retain them? Do you understand the meaning of this verse, "He that believeth shall not make haste." Do you believe God enough to put Isaac upon the altar and be quiet in the time of testing? Did Abraham believe Isaac would die! Not for one minute. He was the seed of the promise, and Abraham knew he would be preserved. He doubtless did not understand God's leading, but this call could not hinder Isaac's being the child of promise.

Beloved, if we are sure our Isaacs are the children of promise, if God has told us they are ours, we, too, can lay them fearlessly on His altar. They cannot die, but they must be surrendered. Then we shall know that they cannot be lost. Indeed we do not truly believe God until we are sure of this.

4. And yet, on the other hand, while Abraham would not contend with Lot for the land, he did contend for it

with his enemies. When a band of invaders from Chaldea came into the land, claimed Abraham's inheritance, and took Lot prisoner, the old man rose up for the defense of his inheritance. He used the sword for the first time in his life. He went against the invaders with a small band of trained servants, brought back the fugitives and the spoil they had carried away and reclaimed the land from the touch of the Alien.

So we shall resist Satan's attack upon our promises. It is not our province to contend with men, especially our brethren, but the attacks of the devil call for a courageous resistance. We should fear no enemy here, for we shall be more than conquerors through Him that loved us.

5. After Lot was separated from Abraham, God gave him a glorious vision of faith, and a renewal of the promise. He said to him – "Lift up now thine eyes, and look from the place where thou art northward, and southward, and eastward, and westward. For all the land which thou seest, to thee will I give it, and to thy seed forever. Arise and walk through the land in the length of it and in the breadth of it."

Abraham's outlook upon the land was not like the one given to Moses from the wilderness on the other side of Jordan, from which he saw a land he could, not enter upon. Abraham looked upon it from the midst of what was already, by faith his inheritance. Moses looked at it from Pisgah; Abraham, probably, from Hebron, or some mountain in the interior of Palestine. It was a vision after he was in the land. Moses looked only in one direction; Abraham looked north, and south, and east, and west. Lot was down in the valley of the Jordan; Abraham was on the barren hilltop, and his view was unobstructed. Lot, from his position on the low, alluvial plains, could not see very far; he was sunk so low in his selfishness that he could only see the fertile plain. But the grand old patriarch, away upon the Judean hills, had a magnificent outlook over all the land.

Have you ever stood thus upon the barren heights of some great self-denial and looked down upon your land of promise, away up to the distant north, down to the sunny south, yonder to the sunrise in the east, yes, all the way to the setting sun, and heavenly horizon in the west! All is yours; all you can apprehend in the vision of faith is your own. Look as far as you can, for it is all yours. The vision of faith is the prophecy of blessing. If there is nothing revealed to you, there can be no meaning in the land for you. No instincts can be put in you by the Holy Ghost but He purposes to fulfill. Let your faith then rise and soar away, and claim all the land that you can discover.

All that you long to be as a Christian, all that you long to do for God, are within the possibilities of faith. Then come still closer, and, with your Bible before you, and your soul open to all the influences or the Spirit, let your whole being receive the baptism of His presence; and, as He opens your understanding to see all His fullness, believe that He has it all for you. Accept for yourself all the promises of His word, all the desires He awakens within you, all the possibilities of what you may be as a follower of Jesus. All the land you see is given to you. Let faith follow hard upon vision, and Joshua enter into all that Moses sees.

III. POSSESSIONS.

One thing more. It was not enough for Abraham to stand upon the mountaintop and look over the land; he must go down, from the height, and walk through the length and breadth of it. So, every moment of life, to the very end, we must make the land ours step-by-step. Every little circumstance of life, every minute detail, is to be but another hold upon the land of promise. It is as long as twenty-four hours in a day, and as sixty seconds in a minute. It is as broad as our spirit's need, as our temptations and our trials, as our body's pains and infirmities, as the cares of the family, the toils of the kitchen, the labor of your workshop, the transactions upon the street tomorrow, the business of your office, the religious world you live in, the social circle in which you mingle, the whole world in which you move. It is as long as life and as broad as human need.

Don't say this life cannot be lived in real, practical experience. The best time I know for true consecration is from Monday morning to Saturday night. The hard pull of every day is the best test of the grace of God. Take Jesus this afternoon, this evening, this night. Tomorrow morning begin the day in His presence. Take Him for the fifty things that must be thought of perhaps in an hour, so that nothing shall be neglected. It is a practical life. Arise and walk through the land, a step at a time. These little steppings alone will make it all your own.

Travelers, who would most thoroughly understand and enjoy the scenery of Switzerland, walk through the valleys and passes of the mountains. Thus only can we know all the fullness of Christ.

"Jesus, my all in all thou art,
  My rest in toil, mine ease in pain;
The medicine of my broken heart;
  In war, my peace; in loss, my gain,
My smile beneath the tyrant's frown;
  In shame, my glory and my crown.
In want, my plentiful supply;
  In weakness, mine almighty power;
In bond, my perfect liberty;
  My light in Satan's darkest hour;
In grief, my joy unspeakable;
  My life in death; my heaven; my all."

CHAPTER III.

Coming Short.

"And Moses sent them to spy out the land of Canaan, and said unto them, Get you up, into the mountain: and see the land, what it is; and the people that dwelleth therein – whether they be strong or weak, few or many; and what the land is that they dwell in, whether it be good or bad; and what cities they be that they dwell in, whether in tents, or strongholds; and what the land is, whether it be fat or lean, whether there be wood therein, or not. And be of good courage, and bring of the fruit of the land. Now the time was the time of the first ripe grapes. So they went up, and searched the land from the wilderness of Zin unto Rehob, as men come to Hamath. And they ascended by the south, and came unto Hebron; where Ahiman, Sheshai, and Talmai, the children of Anak, were. (Now Hebron was built seven years before Zoan in Egypt.) And they came unto the brook of Eschol, and cut down from thence a branch with one cluster of grapes, and they bare it between two upon a staff; and they brought of the pomegranates, and of the figs. The place was called the brook Eschol, because of the cluster of grapes which the children of Israel cut down from thence. And they returned from searching of the land after forty days. And they went and came to Moses, and to Aaron, and to all the congregation of the children of Israel, unto the wilderness of Paran, to Kadesh; and brought back word unto them, and unto all the congregation, anti shewed them the fruit of the land.

"But the men that went up with him said, We be not able to go up against the people; for they are stronger than we. And they brought up an evil report of the land which they have searched unto the children of Israel, saying, The land through which we have gone to search it, is a land that eateth up the inhabitants thereof; and all the people that we saw in it are men of a great stature." – Num. 13:17-26, 31-32.

"Let us therefore fear, lest, a promise being left of entering into his rest, any of you should seem to come short of it." – Heb. 4:1.

THIS is the most vivid and mournful picture of the children of Israel halting on the borders of the promised land.

What spiritual lessons can we learn from this story of their failure? May we not discover it in some of the causes that are keeping many back from entering into the land? There were four general causes for Israel's failure, and they will be found to correspond very closely to the causes of spiritual failure in the church of today.

I. The first of these is dependence on human wisdom. The very appointment of the spies implies a leaning upon the counsels of man rather than taking the word of God. It is singular that the names of these men are strongly suggestive of human wisdom and confidence.

The first was Shammua the son of Zaccur. The word Shammua means fame, and Zaccur stands for distinction. They both suggest human wisdom, and are typical of those things which would lead us to put confidence in the opinions and traditions of men. They were leaders who seemed likely to give wise and good counsel, but they kept Israel from their inheritance. The preponderance of the brain over the heart and the simplicity of faith are the great hindrances to spiritual life. Brilliant qualities may give intellectual power, but they can never bring us to the teachings of the Holy Spirit, or to the feet of Jesus, and therefore they stand in the way of spiritual progress.

There are such leaders as Shammua, the son of Zaccur, in the world still. They lead their followers into the realms of culture and earthly distinction, but never into the life of faith, or the Land of Promise. A highly cultured intellect, though it is God's gift, is not meant to be the guide of His people until it has been consecrated at His feet and filled with the Holy Ghost.

There is no lack of intellectual power in the leaders of Christianity at the present time, but they only keep back the children of God from their true place. Christ was constantly meeting Shammua, the son of Zaccur, in his ministry. He warned the people against the teachings of the Rabbis and Pharisees, who could not lead them into the land of rest. Paul had to contend against the wisdom of the Jews and the philosophy of the Greeks. It is the light of God we need, not the conceit of man. "If any man will be wise, let him become a fool that he may be wise."

The next leader was Shaphat whose name means judge. He was a man of strong common sense and sound judgment. He was able to judge wisely and discreetly. It is just as bad to rely upon our own judgment as to lean upon the wisdom of other people.

Joshua was the next leader. His name meant Jehovah, my Saviour. He represents the spirit of faith and the leadership of Jesus.

We have not time to examine all these names. One other only will we look at, Ammiel — "My people are strong." This man did not trust in wisdom, but in numbers and strength. Does not Christianity sometimes look at its vast machinery, its splendid forces, the strength of its missionary bands, and other associations, and say, "My people are strong and great?" Indeed, they are strong collectively. They have force enough to go up and take the world for Christ. They have talented men and gifted women in abundance. The people are strong. Ah! beloved, that is not the way to take the kingdom. "Fear not, little flock, for it is your Father's good pleasure to give you the kingdom."

The confidence in our strength is always an obstacle to real advancement. It will stand in the way of dependence, and whatever keeps us from getting at the feet of Jesus, must be a hindrance.

The very thought of sending the spies was the suggestion of human wisdom. God had said the land was good. Where was the sense in sending to see if it was good? God had told them there were mighty tribes there, but that they should cast them out. What was the use of going to see how strong the Hittites were? God had told them He would be their leader. Why should they try to make a way for themselves?

So man is always doing. He asks God for direction, gets an answer, and then goes and talks to man about it. He receives a message from the Holy Ghost, and immediately begins to question and reason about it, and gets into darkness at once. Be careful, beloved, of the wisdom of others and of your own reasoning, unless both are under the full control of the Spirit of God.

There are two or three particulars in which this thought needs to be applied.

1. We should be guarded against the traditions and opinions of men. Jesus charged the Pharisees that they made void the Word of God through their traditions. The apostle Peter tells us that we have been redeemed through the blood of Christ from our vain conversation received by tradition from our fathers.

2. We need to be guarded also about our own wisdom. We would not discourage careful, deliberate thought before making any important decision in life, nor the seeking of judicious counsel, if there is not a certainty in the mind as to the will of God about it. But when His word has been given, when the voice from heaven has spoken clearly, then there should be implicit, unquestioning obedience. There must be a walking alone with God henceforth, and a going forward in His work without fear.

3. Another thing we need to be guarded against is prejudice. This often gets in the way of God, and induces many Christians to turn away from some of the most precious truths in the Bible, because they have not been taught in that way. Their belief has crystalized into a rigid creed, perhaps much of it human, and there is no moving them. Many are held back from the fullness of perfect liberty in Christ by a set of opinions they have always held, or the doctrine taught in their church, and

this deep prejudice it seems impossible to uproot. They are prejudiced in favor of certain things and against certain other things. They do not care for this class of meetings, it is too sensational or emotional. They will lose their blessing because some heart, on fire for God, breaks out in praise in the meeting, and disturbs their dignity.

The trouble is, although they do not see it, their own prejudices are in the way. It is the head again instead of the heart. Shammua or Shaphat is taking the lead once more. The spies are bringing a false report and are being believed instead of the Holy Ghost. The one most used of God to bring to me God's message about the deep things of religion, was the last person I should have chosen with my head for that purpose. A dear old saint, who knew the Lord better than I, was used to teach me of the indwelling life of Jesus Christ, and if I had not been willing to receive the teaching God sent me in that way, I should have lost it. Someone has said, we have to be beheaded first, and then headed up anew before God can bless us. Well, be sure the old head is really cut off. Prejudice, dislike for some person or some set of people, unwillingness to receive the blessing in some way, have kept many of God's children out of the land of blessing for years. We have to come down. Personal prejudice must be given up, if we would have the fullness of the blessing.

II. The next cause of Israel's failure was their fear. Some Christians have always a ready ear when the devil speaks of difficulty. The spies said the land was good, and the grapes were rich and abundant, but the people were mighty. They said the cities were walled up to heaven, and their fears undoubtedly exaggerated also the strength of the enemy. In the eyes of these ten they were giants, and they themselves were like grasshoppers before them. It was all the language of fear. Job says, "I feared a fear and it came upon me." The solemn charge given to Jeremiah was, "Be not dismayed at their faces, lest I confound thee before them." God looks upon such fear as sin. It is the certain prelude to failure, confusion and disaster. It would be possible to get a complete gospel by stringing together all the "Fear not's" of God's Word. Oh, beloved, be afraid of your fears!

Discouragement and fear on the part of Israel at this crisis sprang from several causes:

1. The chief one was the dwelling upon the greatness of the difficulty itself. It is well to know at the outset that all sorts of difficulties are to be met with in this life. They are there in the path, and they must be overcome, for they are tremendously real. Your home, your associates, your very minister may seem to hinder you in your life of consecration. You must be true, and yet you must keep constantly the sweet spirit of Christ, and there are a hundred difficulties that will seem to forbid it. But God is a sufficient power against all these things, whether they come from your disposition and temperament, or from the outward difficulties that meet you in life.

Your body may be weak, and physical infirmity may depress you. But God makes no account of difficulties; take it for granted that they will appear, and do not yield to fear and worry. Stand in His strength. Lay the difficulty over upon Him; He is able to give you the victory. Expect things to be at their worst. If they prove to be easy and delightful, let them come to you as a pleasant surprise. Take hold of His strength expecting you are going to have conflict.

2. The next cause of Israel's failure was looking at their own weakness. Not only did the cities seem too strong to be taken, and the men of the land like giants, but they themselves in their own eyes were like grasshoppers. When the soul is ever turned inward upon itself, a great deal can be found that is discouraging. If you look at self, you have no end of trouble. The language of faith will cease. Your difficulties will seem like great cities walled up to heaven, your foes like

giants, and you like grasshoppers before them. Even if you are like grasshoppers, what difference does it make anyhow? God is not measuring your strength if He has undertaken to fight your battles for you. He does not expect you to be strong. There are no resources in you at all for the work. Trust in Him and let Him be the victor.

Do not say you have so little talent you have nothing for God, or you cannot speak for Him because you have no tact to influence others. The great majority of people expect God to excuse them from service because they are so small. What God expects of you is victory under all circumstances. It is just as egotistical to think of your weakness as of your strength. All you can possibly bring to God is an empty hand, and the spirit of nothingness. He starts in you as the Alpha and He will become the Omega. He is all the real strength you will ever have. He will become faith to you, if you will cease from yourself and learn to trust Him.

Take the Holy Ghost as the true gift of wisdom, and He will become in you power for all your Christian service. God wants you to be weak. He hath "chosen the weak things of this world to confound the things that are mighty; and the foolish things of the world to confound the wise and base things of the world, and the things which are despised hath God chosen; yea, and things which are not to bring to nought the things that are; that no flesh should glory in His presence."

3. We can but notice, too, that many are afraid of their reputation and what they may suffer in stepping out too decidedly in Christian life. They are afraid of what people will say, or that the step will cost them some suffering, perhaps the sacrifice of something which is very dear to them if they consecrate themselves fully to God. This one fear stands in the citadel of their will, and refuses to surrender. How it makes everything seem black and forbidding that obstructs in any degree the way of this new life; but then, this once given us, the self-life

within wholly yielded, the world entirely renounced, how different everything is!

When the Israelites got into the Jordan, they found they were walking through it on dry land. Not a bit of the slime from its bed, or even a drop of its water touched them. It was only a seeming death. There was no real sacrifice after all. So we too find it when we are willing to give up everything to Him. We receive all back from Him, and there is nothing that really amounts to a sacrifice.

All that God wants is a full surrender of the will. Be afraid of your fears, beloved. They will pierce your heart and hinder your advancement. God is calling you forward, the devil is trying to discourage you, and so puts a fear within you. Dismiss it as an evil thing. The cloud that seems to surround you will turn into the cloud of God's presence, with Jesus in the midst.

III. Israel failed also because of unbelief.

1. They did not believe God's promises. They did not doubt His power exactly, but they did not set a firm belief in that power over against the difficulty that met them. That is unbelief. You may believe God can do all things, but, unless you make that belief of practical use in your hour of trial, you are not really trusting Him. They should have put the power of God over against the Anakims and the walled cities of the plane. Caleb did that. He said, "We be well able to go up and possess the land." They said, "We be not able." When a pressure of trouble comes, it is so easy to look at it and fail to see the help God has for it. They needed to take His power for the difficulty.

David says, "I have set the Lord always before me; because He is at my right hand I shall not be moved." That is faith. Everything else is unbelief. If you really believe God you will take hold of His omnipotence for every difficulty, whether it be great or trifling. Have you got a bad temper? You will see that God is able to fill it with His sweetness. Have you a strong, dominant will?

God is able to make it pliable by His touch. Are the people around you holding you back from the place you long to occupy in Christ? God is able to manage them and make them instruments of blessing in your life. The harder the place, the more He loves to show His power. If you wish to find it real, come to Him in some great trouble. He has no chance to work until you get into a hard place. He led Israel out of the usual way till he got them to the Red Sea. Then there was room for His power to be manifested. God loves the hard places and the narrow places.

Rejoice, if you are in such a place. Even if it is in the very heart of the foe, God is able to deliver you. Let not your faith in Him waver for a moment, and you will find His omnipotence is all upon your side for difficulty in which you can be placed.

2. The Israelites doubted His love. "Wherefore hath the Lord brought us into this land, to fall by the sword, that our wives and our children should be a prey?" They thought God had brought them there to destroy them; that he was against them and no longer loved them. Everything seemed to work adversely in their life, and they could give no other reason for it than that God had ceased to be their friend. Can you see in this state any mirror of your mind, beloved? Does doubt of His love ever come to you when difficulties increase?

Temptations may attack us like a fierce tempest, but we should be able to believe that God is in the very midst of the whirlwind. You are not going to perish if you will but trust Him. The enemy is always ready to come back with his old serpent's hiss, and whisper in your ear that these troubles have all come because you have done something wrong, and that you are not one of God's chosen ones; and by listening to him you are sure to grieve away the Spirit. He presses the barb deeper and deeper into your soul, until he plunges you into the darkness of despair.

How often in the moment of temptation doubt comes into the weakened soul as to whether it is saved, and distrust of God's love is sure to follow! I think it would be better to doubt the power of God even, than His love. Never do that, beloved. Though unworthy, believe His love to you without a question. It hinders many from receiving the fullness of His salvation, and it comes because they do not know the heart of God.

He loved us when there was no beauty in us; but He looked ahead and saw what He could make of us in Christ; and so He took us, all unlovely as we were, and is transforming us into the loveliness of Christ. It all comes from the wealth of His grace to us, and when the change is completed we shall see that through it all God has had nothing in His heart for us but love. It was a revelation of heaven when I dared to believe the promise, "I have sworn that I will never be wroth with thee, nor rebuke thee." Only as you believe this word can you go forth and take the word of victory.

3. The Israelites doubted the word and promise of God. They refused to believe in His truth. He said He would bring them into the land and they doubted it. At the very entrance of it they were thrown into bewilderment and confusion by the report of the spies and they did not believe that God would be with them in every step if they entered it. They failed, as too many people do today, to count God's word a perfect word and already fulfilled in His sight when it is given to us. It is not a future thing, but a past one to God. "I have given thee the land," He said.

This is another reason why so many fail to enter into the fullness of Jesus. They want to feel the help He has for their body, or for their life. God wants them to believe it anyhow, without doubting, no matter what they see. That is what He calls faith. "Take heed lest there be in any of you an evil heart of unbelief, in departing from the living God." This spirit of departing from Him is manifested by doubting His word because something else is wanted to confirm it.

We need to have appropriating faith in regard to His promises. We must make God's word our own personal possession. A child was asked once what appropriating faith was, and the answer was, "It is taking a pencil and underscoring, the me's, and mine's and my's in the Bible." I know not a better answer. It is saying, "My Lord and my God." "He loved me and gave Himself for me." "I am my beloved's." It is standing isolated from everything, and feeling as if there were no one anywhere but God and you. It is claiming the largest share of His love for yourself. This does not give offence to Him, but greatly pleases Him.

Put the power of God over against all the difficulties of life. Believe that He loves you today, and is making the best out of everything for you forever. Take any word you please that He has spoken and say, "That is my word." Put your finger on this promise and say, "It is mine."

IV. The last and greatest sin of the Israelites at this time was disobedience. This was shown in two ways. They refused to obey God and enter at once into the land, and they did afterward what God had not commanded them to do.

God told them to go up and possess the land. They held back and disobeyed. The next morning they said, "We will go up now," but God said, "That would be disobedience a second time." He did not send them this time, and the result was that they were hurled back by the enemy. Whether we go or not, it must be as He commands. The minding of the Spirit is life, but the minding of the flesh is death.

When we obey the strong will in us, dear friends, the self-directing force that is not subdued to God, we are always in the greatest peril. God calls it rebellion. How terribly He speaks of it later in the Bible, calling it "The day of provocation and temptation in the wilderness, when your fathers tempted me forty years, to whom I sware in my wrath, They shall not enter into my rest." So the whole three millions of men, women and children, were turned back into the desert to wander day after day, and year after year, panting from thirst; mothers seeing their children crying for water and having none to give them; and all eyes straining to catch a view of some green spot on the distant horizon. The blazing sun from a cloudless sky shone down constantly upon them, but still they went on, many falling sick by the way and leaving their ghastly skeletons to whiten on the sand.

No wonder Moses looked on and sang the mournful wail of the ninetieth Psalm, "Thou carriest them away as with a flood; who knoweth the power of thine anger? Even according to thy fear so is thy wrath." And yet this spectacle is not half so sad as the strangely useless lives going on in the church today. Many young men who started out with glorious prospects of usefulness have had their lives blighted for many years because they have made some other things than God the idol of their heart, and they wake up at last to see that their lives have been wasted. They are saved, but oh, what they have missed because they were not brave enough to step out immediately at God's command, and enter into all the blessings that would have followed their obedience. Great peace and joy were before them, but they turned from them.

Believe the picture given here to be true of what you, too, will become, beloved, if you do not enter into rest. Perhaps you are even now at the crisis hour of your life. God has led you up to this point and waits for your decision. Put aside everything that would lead you in the other direction, and dare follow Jesus fully. Step out at once and be all the Lord's. Take care lest your refusal to do so may make this your day of provocation to God, and your life, too, become blighted. Blessings are waiting for you, and no hand but your own can push them aside, and no will but your own prevent their coming. God save you from refusing to enter into your purchased possession.

May the Holy Ghost Himself keep you from a rebellious heart! He will lead you and teach you if you are yielded to Him, and your self-will laid down. God will perfect that which concerneth you. The Lord bless you and lead you into the Land of Promise, and may none of you ever seem to come short of it.

CHAPTER IV.

ENTERING IN.

"Moses, my servant is dead. Now therefore arise, go over this Jordan, thou and all this people, unto the land which I do give to them, even to the children of Israel. Every place that the sole of your foot shall tread upon, that have I given unto you as I said unto Moses." – Josh. 1:1-2.

OUR subject leads us up to the gate of the land, not any longer to look over into it, but to enter upon it and possess it. It is as real an experience as the setting out from Egypt.

The steps for our entering into the promised land are very definite.

I. Moses must die.

The first sentence of the book of Joshua is – "Moses, my servant, is dead." The children of Israel could not go in as long as Moses was alive. He represented the law, and the law could never save any human being. There is in it no salvation either here or hereafter. The Ten Commandments are not Christianity. They made nothing perfect, but the bringing in of a better hope did. They show us what they have to do but they cannot make us do it. Punishment never makes an offender do better. The example of a good man never has this effect. It is all law. We may try our best to do better, but we cannot. We may resolve and re-resolve, but at the end we are the same. All the efforts we can bring to bear upon our life and character will not make us good. That is the law.

Moses himself could not enter into the land; he was killed by his own law. He disobeyed, and so the Lord took him up into the heights of Pisgah and showed him the land upon which he could not enter. It is blessed to have the law and make strong clear stand upon the side of right, but we want more. Many people today are trying their best to keep, perhaps, a new year's resolution to live a different life, but before the year is past, they fail. They do this over two or three times and finally give all up in despair. This is what the devil wants. He knew you would fail all the time. Many Christians are doing the same thing and perhaps think God has put them in hard places and their efforts are vain to live in them.

Beloved, it is not what we can do but what God can do. Jesus Christ came not to impose taxes but to pay them. He does not command you to be right, that was the work of Moses. There is a great difference between law and grace; as great as between demand and supply. The law says, "Thou must," grace says, "I will enable you to do." The law says, "Be strong and be holy," grace says, "I have come to bring you the blessings of holiness." The first words spoken to Joshua were – "Go over into the land which I do give to thee." Jesus comes to give, not to demand. He says, "My yoke is easy and my burden is light."

Beloved, have you passed from under the law into the blessed freedom of the gospel? Have you ceased from your own efforts and your best endeavors to do what is right? And have you received the full grace of the Blessed One so that He lives in you, keeping there the righteousness of the law so that while, in a sense, you are still living in the flesh you are walking after the Spirit? Do not think we would depreciate the law in speaking of it thus, but we can not keep it if we try our best, and yet it is as grand as it ever was. It is righteous but can never make you righteous. Jesus has come to give us the power to keep it. A mirror will show us a dirty face, but we cannot wash the stain off with the mirror. The law shows us the sin, Jesus gives us the cleansing from sin.

You will never get into the Land of Promise till you are through striving against sin, resisting the evil one, and laboring to be pure and holy, apart from Christ. You must come to the Lord Jesus for Him to be in you holiness and victory.

God said, "Moses my servant," not, my son. While you are under the law you are only a servant. "As many as received Him, to them gave He power to become the sons of God, even to them that believe on His name." When you become as children, when you are really living in His bosom, then you have in you the very heart to do His will, because He hath sent His Spirit into your heart, crying, Abba, Father. Henceforth you are no more servants but sons, because you have within you the nature and life of God.

Beloved, God will give you this blessed experience. Come to Him, telling Him how you have striven to obtain it but cannot. Then believe that he gives it to you as a free gift and you shall receive it. You will pass at once from the deep poverty of your baffled life into the possession of that blessed peace which passes all understanding. It is a blessed life, for there is not only consciousness of His presence always in blessing, but there is both the will and power to do His will.

II. Not only must Moses die, but Israel must die also. "Now therefore, arise and go over this Jordan." What is Jordan? From time immemorial it has been taken to represent death. The meaning of the type certainly is death and judgment. It is the act of putting off the past life, of stepping down into the floods of Jordan and coming out on the other side as the Israelites did, not the same people anymore. We are to go over Jordan, not stay in it. The past life is to be buried with its imperfections and its sins, and we are to go forth in resurrection life on the other side.

It is the figure of new life for the Christian heart. It is a definite committal of self in all its forms, to the waves of death, and a parting with everything in this life that we ought not to have. It is saying goodbye to the world, to our past life and everything in our present life that is less than the will of God. It is a separation from the world, and a coming forth from this death as if we had dropped down from heaven, made over anew; thenceforth we are citizens only of the heavenly world. "Ye are dead, and your life is hid with Christ in God." "They that are Christ's have crucified the flesh with the affections and lusts." There is now no dragging around of the old life or any efforts to make it better. We have got something better, even Christ Himself, our life.

In the river Jordan the Israelites built a pile of stones to mark the place of their death. They built it there in the slime as a perpetual memorial of this fact. Then on the other side they built another heap of stones to mark the place where the dead were made alive. The one marked the death of sin, the other marked the new life in Christ.

This second experience of the resurrection life we must come into if we are to have abiding purity and victory. We must gather up what God condemns, what the Holy Ghost condemns, what our own sense of right condemns, and hand them over to death without sparing one of them. They must die; we cannot kill them, but we can hand them over to God and give Him the right to slay. He will do it when they are completely given up to Him. Then we are to seek His help to keep them from coming back.

The sacrifice must be bound to the horns of the altar, but we cannot do that either. We must give even that over to God. He will keep us. Our business is not with our old nature any longer. It may knock at the door and try to get in, but it must not be admitted. Paul speaks of it in this very language; he calls it "The old man," and he refers to the mean, despicable nature we once had. When it is given over to God we are henceforth always to reckon it dead and under the flood of Jordan. And if we are dead with Him we shall also live with Him.

Reckon from some special time when you died in Him; build a pile of stones there to mark the spot, and then build another on the life-side, the resurrection-side. As certainly as you have handed over self and sin and all carnal desires to God, so certainly has He handed over His life, and power, and glory, to you. Take it today, beloved, build a heap of stones to mark the time, and never fight the old battle again. Christian life is not definite enough; we should not be dying and rising, and dying and rising again and again; we should build our memorial stones once for all, and then ever date from that time.

After the Israelites had passed over Jordan they were circumcised at Gilgal. This type was more vivid even than the passing of the Jordan was, of death to the flesh. It typified the handing over to God of the old, natural life, and nature which you received at birth from your father and your mother. The apostle calls it flesh, and says it is to be slain. It does not mean the body, there is nothing wrong in that in itself.

The flesh means the natural character, not merely the physical life. It is the carnal mind that will not submit to the will of God. It includes the natural tastes, the aesthetic pleasures, and all the desires that center upon self instead of upon God. It is centered in the will, in the mind, and in the tastes. It is not necessary to be a drunkard, or to be a glutton, or to be given up to earthly passion, to have a fleshly nature. There is a beautiful self which is full of culture. Many Christians are hindered by it from rising up into a true, spiritual life. Paul calls it the psychical man. It is fond of fine arts and refinement. Beautiful things have a keen fascination for it. A coarse and uncultivated nature will offend its finer tastes. All this is merely natural. It has nothing to do with the Spirit of God.

I asked a young man some time ago if he had received this heavenly Guest. His answer was, "I am not sure; sometimes I think I have, for when I hear fine music now, it affects me more than it used to." He is not the only one who mistakes this taste for the Holy Ghost. The aesthetic nature is not the spiritual oratory; eloquence may move the soul when the heart is very far from God.

While the streets of Paris were flowing with blood, during the Revolution, men and women were shedding tears every night in the theatre over the fine acting that was given there. Often I have known cultivated taste to be a hindrance in the divine life, keeping people back from the position they ought to have taken, perhaps because some Christian did odd things which they could not stand. We are not dead, beloved; the fleshly life has not left us if we are disturbed by these things. We must be dead to all kinds of flesh. It is not enough to slay what is apparently evil in us; the devil exults when we stop with that. The physical nature must be dead also. The whole thing must be laid over at the feet of Jesus.

We cannot even rejoice in the affections of the heart, or the natural ties of human life, until they are handed over to God and He has given them back to us as strong as they were before, but no longer selfish and earthly. This was the way with Abraham when he was able to offer up Isaac to God.

Dear friends, have you crossed the Jordan? Have you received the circumcision of the heart? Have you laid your whole throbbing self at the feet of your Lord, there to find yourself raised and filled with His life? I heard of a warrior in ancient times who, with his helmet and coat of mail on, pointed his sword at the breast of his child, and sent it screaming in fright to its mother. The mother smiled and said, "My dear, that is only papa." The father then took off his helmet and coat of mail, and with a smile, pointed his sword again at the breast of his little one, who rushed into his arms, and said, "I am not afraid of you now, I know you are my papa." So, beloved, may you rest in the arms of your father without fear; and if He pointed His sword at any evil thing in you, let it go, He cannot hurt you. He will only slay the evil and let you lie there upon His breast and die in the arms of His love.

III. They must claim the fulfillment of His word. "Unto the land which I do give unto them," was the command. He did not say the land which I will give them; that was the promise to Abraham. To Joshua it was, the land which I do give them this very day. The whole land was theirs, but they had to take it by one great claim. It is well to understand the grammar of the Bible, especially its moods and tenses. There God can always be found. His great name is "I am," not, I am going to be. That is the way all the promises come to us. He says to the sinner, "You are saved now if you accept the Lord Jesus as your Redeemer." He says to the weak Christian, "You are made whole by taking Him to be your sanctification." He says, respecting our prayers, "Believe that ye receive the things you ask for and ye shall have them."

In the very moment we trust Him, God gives us the fullness of salvation, and afterwards it comes to us in detail. He gives it at once, but we enter upon the possession of it step by step. It is ours as fast as we go forward and step into it. Jesus Christ comes to you this morning with all the blessings you can ever need in life, and offers all to you. If you accept it as all yours from the start, then you have to go on and take it little by little, whether it is forgiveness; sanctification, healing, or power for service.

IV. Not only must they claim their inheritance by faith, they must also step out into it. "Every place that the sole of your foot shall tread upon, that I have given unto you." They had had the promise of it before, now they must go forward into it and place their feet upon it. The promise now is in the perfect tense, and denotes an act just now completed: "That have I given unto you." If we dare to place our foot upon anything God has promised, He makes it real to us. So, take Him as the supply for all your needs, believe He is yours, and never doubt it from this moment. It may be your need is for spiritual cleansing; His promise covers this. "Now ye are clean through the word I have spoken unto you."

If you can believe that, you shall be sanctified and kept. Take the promise that suits your need, and step out on it; not touching it timidly on tiptoe, but placing your foot flat down upon it. Do not be afraid it will not hold your weight. Put your whole need on the Word of the eternal God for your soul, for your body, for your work, for the dear ones for whom you are praying, for any crisis in your life; then stand upon it forever.

V. The next step is courage. Make up your mind at the beginning that the devil will frighten you if he can, but make up your mind also not to be terrified by him. "Be strong and very courageous." He will be strength for you in the time of conflict. Fear keeps many persons out of the Land of Promise. They are afraid of the sufferings they may have to endure, afraid of what some one may think or say, afraid of themselves, afraid of everything. God commands us "Fear not."

Fear is the beginning of failure. God's word to Joshua about it was almost stern. "Have not I commanded thee? Be strong and of good courage: be not afraid, neither be thou dismayed." He warns us about it all through the Bible. He took Jeremiah, weak as a woman and timid as a baby, and made him stand before kings and princes as a witness against them for fifty years; and when Jeremiah tried to evade the difficult work, saying, "I am but a child, I cannot speak," the Lord rebuked him with this message: "Say not I am a child; for thou shalt go to all that I shall send thee. Arise and speak unto them all that I command thee: be not dismayed at their faces, lest I confound thee before them."

If you get into the midst of a hard battle, the only thing to be done is to stand like flint against the enemy, and nothing shall hurt you. It is always harder to run away. When Paul speaks of the different parts of the Christian armor, he mentions no defense which was provided for the back. Therefore, in Peter's catalogue of the advanced steps of Christian progress, we find him speaking first of this grace – "Add to your faith courage."

VI. The next quality required was obedience. "Thou shalt observe to do according to all the law which Moses my servant commanded thee." We are to go according to the Scriptures in everything, carefully adhering to all its commands. We are to observe to do them. This includes watchfulness and the careful study of their requirements. If we expect to make any progress in the higher life taught in the Scriptures, we must live according to the teaching of God's word. They are not difficult to follow if we love them. It is easier to live a holy life than a wicked one. God has cast up a highway for His redeemed ones to walk in, and it easier to stay there than to go back into sin.

It is not impossible to walk as He would have us, if we are watchful and obedient. His spirit is ready to put these qualities within us if we will receive them. He expects to have them. "The minding of the flesh is death, but the minding of the Spirit is life and peace." The Holy Ghost seems to say to us, "Now mind me." It is not hard. The way of obedience is full of comfort and blessing. "If ye be willing and obedient, ye shall eat the good of the land."

VII. The Lord Himself. "The Lord thy God is with thee whithersoever thou goest." He walks before you into the thickest of the conflict, and He is not going to let you fail. The watchword of the higher Christian life is, we are to give ourselves wholly to God and let Him be all in all to us. We can count upon His presence. The secret of this life is "Christ in you the hope of glory." He is not there as an influence but as a person. It is as though a presence from another world had dropped down upon us and encompassed us with a world of light to go to Heaven in.

This is sometimes very different from the vain struggles of nature, and the weary reaching out of this human heart after holiness. It is the holiness of Another revealed within us, and so shining out that we glorify not ourselves, but our Father which is in Heaven. The Lord wants to make Himself thus real to us. He wants to become sufficient for all our needs. Has he become this to you – everything to you? This is the land of promise. "This is eternal life, to know thee the only true God, and Jesus Christ whom thou hast sent."

O, may He make you lonesome for His presence, and show you your self and your need, until you shall cry "Lord, if thy presence go not with us, carry us not up hence"; and the answer shall come back:

"My presence shall go with thee and I will give thee rest."

Jesus, my Saviour, is all things to me,
Oh, what a wonderful Saviour is He!
Guiding, proteoting, o'er life's troubled sea,
Mighty Deliverer – Jesus for me,

He is my Prophet, my Priest and my King,
He is my Bread of Life, Fountain and Spring,
Bright Sun of Righteousness, Day-Star is He,
Horn of Salvation – Jesus for me.

He is my Refuge, My Rock, and my Tower,
He is my Fortress, my Strength and my Power,
Life Everlasting, my Daysman is He,
Blessed Redeemer – Jesus for me,
All the time, everywhere,
Jesus for me.

CHAPTER V.

OVERCOMING.

"Joshua made war a long time with all those kings. There was not a city that made peace with the children of Israel, save the Hivites, the inhabitants of Gibeon; all others they took in battle. For it was of the Lord to harden their hearts, that they should come against Israel in battle, that he might destroy them utterly, and that they might have no favor, but that he might destroy them as the Lord commanded Moses." – Josh. 11:18-20.

"Be strong in the Lord, and in the power of His might. Put on the whole armour of God, that ye may be able to stand against the wiles of the devil. For we wrestle not against flesh and blood, but against principalities, against powers, against the rulers of the darkness of this world, against spiritual wickedness in high places. Wherefore take unto you the whole armour of God, that ye may be able to withstand in the evil day, and having done all, to stand." – Eph. 6:10-13.

THE first thought that arrests our attention, as we look at the children of Israel after they have really entered upon the land of promise, is the fact of conflict. The same thought must at once attract our notice as we look at Christians who have entered upon a higher experience in the land of rest. One might suppose that all battles would be over after reaching such an experience, and that the Canaan of the soul must be a land entirely without conflict. Yet the apostle speaks of "wicked spirits in the heavenly places," and "wrestling with the principalities and powers." We read of "the evil day" in which we are to "stand." Indeed, the nearer we get to the heavenlies the fiercer will be the foes. They are only to be overcome in the power of His might. No strength but that of the Lord can be sufficient to withstand them. There were no conflicts so terrible as those which met the Israelites on the Canaan side of the Jordan, at Jericho, at Ai, at Beth-horon, at the waters of Merom, and in all the battles by which the thirty-one kings of the land were at length subdued.

We know little of the power of temptation till we attempt to overcome it. We are not able to estimate the force of evil, till we have attempted to match our strength against it and found we are not equal to the task of resisting it. It is said that two Scotchmen were once talking on a beautiful Sabbath day, and one said to the other, "Do you never feel a temptation on these lovely Sabbaths to go out fishing? It is very hard for me to keep back from going." "No," said the other, "I never feel tempted, I just go." I believe there are too many in the world who yield just as easily and have an easy time because there is no struggle against sin. But let a man set His face like a flint for the truth and for the right, and be determined, come what may, that he will not yield, and all the batteries of hell will be opened against him. He will find out soon enough that there is a personal devil.

A life of victory is not a life of freedom from the attacks of the enemy. He is always ready to spring upon us, and there can be no victory without conflict. The greater advances we make, the more will sin and Satan resist us. The nearer heaven we can get, the more of these wicked Spirits we shall meet. They throng the regions above us, and they are "principalities and powers." If we go on expecting peace, we shall be unarmed to meet them. If we go armed for war, we shall not be taken unawares, but shall be mailed and panoplied for victory.

II. We must next look at the captain of this conflict. Before Joshua did any fighting he had a vision of His captain. One night before the battle of Jericho he went out reconnoitering, looking over the defenses of the city, and, perhaps, arranging the plan of his attack, when there flashed upon his vision the light of a flaming sword, and looking up, he saw an armed warrior standing before His path. Joshua was no coward, and he advanced with true soldier courage, and asked, "Art thou for us or for our adversaries?" Then there fell upon his ear a voice that thrilled his very soul, and that brought him prostrate to the earth in humility and adoration. "Nay, but as the captain of the Lord's host have I come." "You thought you were going to be captain in this battle! nay, that is my place. You thought you were going to take Jericho. I am to lead the forces, and you are but to follow me. Put off thy shoes from thy feet, for the place whereon thou standest is holy." And as Joshua yielded up the command to this glorious leader he was led forward into victory.

The next place the army went up against was Ai, and although God had marvelously given them victory, through faith and simple obedience, at Jericho, Joshua sent spies up against this place to see how strong were its defenses. There is no mention made of any counsel being asked of the Lord. They used human wisdom alone in reference to it and they were ignominiously defeated. They were not following the captain closely. The promise had been given that if He were leader, no man should be able to stand before Joshua all the days of his life.

We are only strong, beloved, when strong in Him. We are more than conquerors through Him that loved us. We are commanded to be "strong in the Lord and in the power of His might." We are not to take a little strength from Him, and rely a good deal upon our own. We must be impotent in ourselves if we are to have the Lord's help. When we are willing to lie at the feet of Jesus and let Him lead all the battle we shall be led to victory. Joshua thought three thousand men sufficient for Ai, and he did not even consult the captain in this case. He would have been led in victory against this as against every foe if he had. It is the worst thing that can happen in our Christian life for us to trust ourselves. We need to come with Peter to the cross with downward head, and when we get there the Lord can always lead us in triumph."

III. The victory in the land of promise is one of faith alone. This was God's first charge to Joshua, "Be thou strong and very courageous." The whole book illustrates this principle, but especially the battle of Jericho. The author of the book of Hebrews speaks expressly of this. "By faith the walls of Jericho fell down, after they were compassed about seven days."

1. It must be faith that follows the leader. The priests and the people followed the ark, they did not go ahead of it. You cannot walk with God and yet do all the time as you please. We must see God's way and then follow. We must have a "Thus saith the Lord" about things before we act. Some people seem to think all that is necessary is to have faith and they claim anything they please. Nay, the will must be surrendered to God, and His word must be accepted about all things before we shall be able to believe them. We cannot risk our faith on the whims or caprices of ourselves or others. Let it be fixed on the eternal foundation of God's will and word. Then you shall not trust in vain.

2. Faith steps out after its leader. Faith can walk seven days around Jericho and not mind the rough places; and it can go seven times around on the seventh day. It is not dreamy, it is intensely actual. It goes forward putting its foot down firmly on every part of the promised land, following closely the footprints of the leader, not falling back, or faltering till its march of victory is gloriously complete.

3. We must learn, too, the patience of faith that can wait for its possession and not be uneasy if it does not come right away. Seven days the Israelites waited for their victory, but did not falter. Perhaps the inhabitants of the city were watching them from the walls and

making sport as they passed, but they marched on without being at all discouraged.

The first day there was no sign of victory, nor the second, nor the third, but on they marched in the confidence of faith. "Ye have need of patience, then after ye have done the will of God, ye might receive the promise." "Though the vision tarry, wait for it; because it will surely come, it will not tarry." The margin reads, it will not tarry too long. The fulfillment may be protracted but it will not come too late.

4. There comes a time when faith not only expects but accepts the promise. The word comes at last: "The Lord hath given you the city." Then faith sends up a shout that makes the earth and heaven ring, and marches in to its possession. "This is the victory that overcometh the world, even our faith." In another place we are told, "Cast not away, therefore, your confidence, which hath great recompense of reward." There is an allusion in this text to an ancient practice that a soldier who threw away his shield could not come back into the army. Cast not away therefore, your shield, the apostle says, for it hath great recompense of reward. Only believe. Satan is a conquered foe and we need to remember this always. The sixth of Ephesians is a parallel with the book of Joshua.

After Paul had mentioned the different pieces of armor, he says above all, that is over all, have the shield of faith. This was a larger shield, large enough to cover the whole person and armor too. God wants you, beloved, to have a great big faith that will cover all. He has promised all, whether for soul or for body. Our shield must be long enough to cover the sixty seconds in every minute, the sixty minutes in every hour, all the hours in every day, and all the days in every year.

I am glad, however, that David had not only a shield but a buckler. Not only the large shield to cover all the person, but a little one to fasten on the arm and which could not be lost. Our faith in God must not only be large, but it must be so fixed that we cannot lose it. Then the enemy can have no more power over us than he had over Christ.

IV. Faith has to learn also the secret of failure. It was not always victory with Joshua, and it is not always so in the highest Christian life. It ought to be, but it is not. But the failure often brings wholesome lessons with it. The Lord often lets trouble come upon us as He did upon Peter, to let us get firmly established upon the rock. Don't be discouraged, dear friends, if you sometimes fail, even after you have reached high ground. Don't expect the failure, but if it comes, why, learn how to take the devil prisoner, and make him fight your battles for you. Learn such good lessons from the failure that the enemy shall be afraid to touch you.

What have you been learning, beloved, from your failures? Have they filled you with discouragement, or with vigilance and wisdom? Has it been true of you as Paul rejoiced that it was of the Corinthians, that "godly sorrow worketh repentance." "What carefulness it wrought in you, yea what fear, yea, what vehement desire, yea, what zeal, yea, what revenge." It has not been altogether an evil, if it has made you more watchful, humble and holy. Don't be distressed about it, and moan and cry over it.

The Lord was not pleased with Joshua's morbid prayers and tears about the defeat at Ai, and He gave him a bracing word of kind reproof, "Get up from your knees. There is a cause for this failure which must be put away. Israel had sinned and the camp must be purged from the accursed thing." When this command was obeyed, Israel was stronger than before. If you have failed in life, there is at the root some secret cause; something in your spirit that God is not pleased with.

Separation from God must follow till the sin is put away. He will not be with you anymore until the accursed thing is removed. There is no use in attempting to fight the foe outside until the foe within the citadel is conquered. The heart needs to be laid open for the inspection of God. Be still before him. Stop crying to the Lord to help you, and say as David did, "Search me, O God, and know my heart; try me, and know my thoughts; and see if there be any wicked way in me, and lead me in the way everlasting." When the sin is confessed and put away, He is always ready to restore the soul to His favor and deliver it from the power of evil, and there must be faithful work about it. If the sin remains, it will surely defeat you.

There are two fires in the spiritual world. One is the fire of the Holy Ghost that burns out the evil from the soul, the other is "the unquenchable fire" that burns and yet never consumes. Bless God that He lets you know about them before it is too late. The time is coming when we shall be glad we have already found Him "a consuming fire." We are getting ready for that last great battle, and "there is no discharge in that war." We are in the drill-room now, not ready yet for the conflict, but if we are true now, our Captain will not let us fail then. Failure here is not hopeless. Deal faithfully with the thing in you that wants to sin, and you shall rise into new strength and victory.

In the next chapter, after Achan's sin God told Joshua, "Fear not, neither be thou dismayed: take all the people of war with thee, and arise, go up to Ai. See, I have given into thy hand the King of Ai, and his people, and his city, and his land." The army won a glorious victory just where it had failed before. God led them over the same ground again, but this time it was in blessing. Have you failed in a certain place in your life? Be sure you will be tested in that same place again. You cannot go on till you have had victory there. The same thing will meet you until there has been such a triumph over it that it can never trouble you anymore. You cannot go on and leave Ai behind. Only be true. God's word shall not fail you, and you shall yet be able to look back over your whole life and say, "There hath not a word failed of all the Lord hath promised."

V. Then there are deeper and higher lessons for the conflict to be learned afterwards. Joshua had not only to meet the open attacks of the enemy, but he had to encounter their wiles. The devil comes in disguise sometimes and deceives the children of God and lures them into sin.

After Joshua had won the victory at Ai, there came to him a deputation of the queerest people he had yet seen. They were dressed in old clothes, their shoes were worn out, and they were covered with dust. They looked like a company of modern tramps. They represented that they had come from a long distance, and were tired pilgrims whose bread was moldy and their water gone, and they asked Joshua to give them shelter, and they would become hewers of wood and drawers of water for his people. Joshua listened to his good-natured impulse, and, without inquiring of the Lord about it, made a league of peace with them.

Very soon he found, to his horror, that they were his near neighbors and inhabitants of the land, whom the Lord had told him to exterminate. He had listened to the voice of worldly and human sympathy, and had not got divine counsel. But his word could not be broken, and the league must now stand. However, these people became an endless source of evil to Israel afterward, teaching them lessons about idolatry, and opening the way for those forbidden alliances and intermarriages which afterward were so ruinous to their spiritual life.

If the devil cannot cause you to fall in open conflict, he will send his emissaries, disguised as angels, to deceive you. Perhaps it will be to make you act quickly from your own impulses, and sometimes make a decision in this way which will be a snare for life, and which will bring you many a heartache in the future. Many a one has acted thus quickly and brought trials which have caused him to go mourning all his days. Sometimes it is a partnership in business, or social friendship, or a more intimate alliance. God only is able to detect the evil in these things.

There are foolish things that cause us to trip in ten thousand places, and we fall into them by having wrong views of life, and taking that for good which is really evil, because we did not go to the Lord and ask light from Him about it. We sit in judgment on others, we decide matters by our hasty ideas of what is right, we sympathize with people and think we are doing them good. The only secure place is to be in constant communication with Him who, has said, "In all thy ways acknowledge Him, and He shall direct thy steps." "The meek will He guide in judgment." "The soul that is wholly yielded to Him, and that is afraid of taking a step alone shall walk safely. The devil may come to such a soul with ten thousand flattering devices, but he cannot win it from the path of safety and victory.

VI. There come in Christian life, occasions that Paul calls "the evil day" – pitched battles when the heavens are black and the earth is resounding with the tramp of the oncoming foe. Your little force is shut in on all sides, and there seems no chance of deliverance. Such were the battles of Beth-heron and Merom, when all the kings of Palestine met, determined to crush out the invaders. Joshua met these fierce bands with steady courage. Not waiting for them to attack him, he steps out in faith and attacks them, and finding the day not long enough for the battle, he calls upon the sun and moon to halt in the heavens, and the day is lengthened out till he has finished his victory.

We, too, have critical conflicts to meet, in life, when all the forces of the evil one seem to combine for our destruction. Such a Gethsemane comes in every life, and perhaps leaves some of God's dear children with a feeling that they have lost very much by not standing steadily in it. God will give you grace to hold your ground. Even there you can stand out in His strength and power and be able to bring glory to Him by a successful resistance. He sees the battle and will give the power to be victorious. We little know how much frequently hangs on the result of these conflicts. Often the conflict comes in the closet hour.

There are many battles where I think I know what Paul meant when he said, "We are made a spectacle unto the world, and to angels, and to men." From the air around us there are millions of glorious beings looking down upon these issues. If it is lost, even upon the brow of the dear Redeemer, there must come a blush of shame and a shout of delight from hosts of devils who also are spectators.

Beloved, do not look upon these conflicts as unimportant. Years of service for the Master have been the outcome of more than one such moment, though no one knew the battle had been fought but God alone. If you have not passed through them, they will surely come, but God has promised to be your strength, your rock, and the arm of your power. As you trust that mighty power in the fiercest attacks, you will find it all-sufficient, and the day will come when you shall be able to raise the victor's song: "Thanks be unto God which always causeth us to triumph."

VII. We learn the still more important lesson that life has not only its evil days, but also its long campaigns. "Joshua made war a long time with all those kings. There was not a city that made peace with the children of Israel, save the Hivites, the inhabitants of Gibeon." When the thirty-one kings were all subdued, then the land had rest from war. We have enlisted not for one Gettysburg, but for the whole period of conflict. Do not think you have one or two sharp battles merely; they will come again and again, and we shall not have rest from war until the whole thirty-one kings are subdued. With not one of our enemies should we be willing to make peace.

The city that Joshua made a compact with was a curse to Israel after. "It was of the Lord to harden their hearts that they should come against Israel in battle, that he might destroy them utterly." It was the only way of safety for the Israelites. How could they be destroyed unless they were led into conflict? The only way the Lord can destroy the evil in us, is by letting it come out and show itself to us. These hard places we come to so often in life are of the Lord, who would have the thing in us destroyed that counts them hard. He is deeply interested in the slaying of the evil.

The land is not subdued in a day. We read in Ephesians that we are not only to withstand in the evil day, but having done all, to stand. Then we shall be able to say with Paul at last, "I have fought a good fight, I have finished my course, I have kept the faith; henceforth there is laid up for me a crown of righteousness which the Lord, the righteous Judge, shall give me at that day."

Let us take this lesson of perseverance, and go out trustfully to meet the things that surely will oppose us. Let the poetry of the subject go; let the glow of the inspired feeling give place to the downright reality. Go forth with a watchful heart, but with fear. The difficulties will not be too hard. He is able for your battles. It is always true, "God is faithful, who will not suffer you to be tempted above that ye are able, but will with the temptation also make a way of escape, that ye may be able to bear it." "In nothing terrified by your adversaries: which is to them an evident token of perdition but to you of salvation, and that of God."

I'm more than conqueror through His blood,
  Jesus saves me now;
I rest beneath the shield of God,
  Jesus saves me now.
I go a kingdom to obtain,
I shall through Him the victory gain,
  Jesus saves me now.

Before the battle lines are spread,
  Jesus saves me now;
Before the boasting foe is dead,
  Jesus saves me now.
I win the fight, though not begun,
I'll trust and shout, still marching on,
  Jesus saves me now.

I'll ask no more that I may see,
  Jesus saves me now;
His promise is enough for me,
  Jesus saves me now.
Though foes be strong and walls be high,
I'll shout, He gives the victory,
  Jesus saves me now.

Why should I ask a sign from God?
  Jesus saves me now;
Can I not trust the precious blood?
  Jesus saves me now.
Strong in His word, I meet the foe,
And, shouting, win without a blow,
  Jesus saves me now.

Should Satan come like 'whelming waves,
  Jesus saves me now;
Ere trials crush, my Father saves,
  Jesus saves me now.
He hides me till the storm is past,
For me He tempers every blast,
  Jesus saves me now.

CHAPTER VI.

INHERITING.

"Now Joshua was old and striken in years: and the Lord said unto him, Thou art old and stricken in years, and there remaineth yet very much land to be possessed." – Josh. 13:1.

"And Joshua said unto the children of Israel, How long are ye slack to go and possess the land which the Lord God of your fathers hath given you?" – Josh. 18:3.

THE Land of Promise is not a place of ceaseless conflict. There comes a time when we enter on that which we have conquered, and really possess that which we have claimed.

I. What is meant by possessing the land?

There are two thoughts suggested by the term. First, we are to appropriate the land, that is, make it our own, then we are to sit down and occupy it.

The personal pronoun my, expresses the first of these acts. You know what is your own. You need no interpreter on that subject. What is yours you take a strange interest in. The little cottage yonder; that poor deformed child, are far more to you than all the world, because they are your own. It is in this way you are to make the promises your own. The Bible is to be read as if written expressly for you. Jesus is loved because He is your blessed Saviour. The Holy Ghost is your own personal Sanctifier, belonging to no one as He does to you. God is your own God, to be used for all things you need Him for. The promises are made yours by appropriating faith, you rejoice in them in hope, and soon you find they are really yours in blessed experience.

After that you go on into actually living them out. It is not merely going to an agency and entering your name for a farm in the public domain, but it is really going out West upon the land, building a house there, cultivating the land, eating of the fruit of it and making the place really your home. There are many things we believe for in Christian life, but have never entered into by realizing that they fully belong to us.

The root of the word means to sit down upon. We are not to step over into our inheritance once in a while, but we are to settle down upon it; we must live and know all there is in the possibilities of Christian life. This is as blessed in the workshop as in the sanctuary, as true down at the foot of the mountain with the foaming demoniac as upon the height where Jesus was transfigured, and heaven poured down its celestial glory upon the bewildered disciples. It is blessed thus to enter upon this possession and find it practical and real. Have you gone on to possess the land, beloved? Have you not only claimed and conquered it, but are you living in it?

II. What is meant by the inheritance?

1. Israel's inheritance was given them by promise. So our inheritance is all the fullness of God's exceedingly great and precious promises; all the unclaimed wealth of these forty thousand checks in the Bank Book of the Bible; promises for the soul, promises for the body, promises for ourselves, promises for others, promises for our work, promises for our trials, promises for our business, promises for time, and promises for eternity.

2. Israel's inheritance was given on account of Abraham. So our inheritance has been purchased by the Lord Jesus Christ. It includes all for which He died. There are redemption rights, for which He has paid the full, the tremendous price, and we should be willing that no part of that mighty purchase should go by default, or be lost to us. Did He die for our own sins and rise again for our justification? Then justification is our redemption right. Did He bear our sicknesses and carry

our infirmities? Then it is all right to lay them upon Him. Did He "by one offering perfect forever them that are sanctified?" Beloved, then by that one perfect offering we have the right to claim our sanctification. Has He received from the Father all the fullness of grace, power and holiness for them that abide in Him? Then these are our rights of inheritance. Has He sent down from heaven the gifts and presence of the Holy Ghost? Then we may claim all His fullness of grace and power for ourselves. It is the children's bread, and let us not fear to take our place at the Father's table. There is bread enough and to spare, why should we perish with hunger?

3. Israel's inheritance was given on account of Abraham. So our inheritance has been bestowed on account of the Lord Jesus Christ. The patrimony of each was distinct, and the land was equitably divided among them by a prescribed divine plan, and according to the allotment of the will of God. So our inheritance in Christ is an individual one. To each of us Christ gives our own salvation, sanctification, Christian experience and special service. No one should wish to copy another's life. God has for every true soul a white stone with a name written thereon, that no man knoweth but he that receiveth it. Just as the same sun will shine upon your garden and produce yonder a little blue-eyed violet; and there a gorgeous rose, and there a pure white lily of the valley, so Christ develops in every soul according to its kind, and would have all to be as varied as the flowers of the field and the stars of the sky.

Our inheritance like theirs is a matter of divine apportionment. The gifts of the Holy Ghost are not all bestowed upon one, but "all these worketh that one and selfsame Spirit, dividing to each severally as He will." He exercises a loving oversight in His blessings; and, while He freely gives to all who ask and trust Him, and there is no limitation in the measure of our blessings but our faith and obedience, yet even when He gives most largely it is in the line which His wisdom and love see most consistent with our highest good and His supreme glory.

III. What does God mean by the complaint, "There remaineth very much land to be possessed; how long are ye slack to possess it?" It implies much neglect and failure on our part. The apostle says, "Let us therefore fear, lest a promise being left us of entering into His rest, any of you should seem to come short of it." He is speaking of the land of promised rest as a land of realization and of blessed victory over enemies, foreshadowed by Canaan, and He bids us fear, not that we shall miss it altogether, but come short of it, that is, not quite receive all its promises. We may miss it by just a little, and fail, perhaps by a hairline of fully reaching all that it means.

1. Do you possess all the land about which you know? There has been a great deal promised, but is it all yours by actual possession? "If ye know these things, happy are ye if ye do them." Are you living out all about which you have been taught? A brother told us the other night that God would not let him say a certain grace was his own without putting him in a place where he would have to show it before the week was over. Whatever you know about Christian truth, God will make you put in practice. Many of you have been studying this subject of Christian holiness. Have you lived it out? Are you coming up in daily practice to what you know about it?

2. Have you received all that you have believed for, or are you talking about having it by faith, but have not really had it given to you yet? Faith is the substance of the possession; it is not a sham. It is the evidence of things not seen. We often hear Christians say, "I have victory by faith, but I have not the evidence yet." Then you have not got the faith, for faith is the evidence. It is a deep, inwrought conviction coming to you right from the heart of God, that the thing you have believed for is yours. Have you thus entered on that which you have believed for?

3. Have you come up to all the meaning of God's words and promises to you? We are easily satisfied with a little, without all that there is in the promises. We limit them so limit Him, and we lose much of the blessing that would be ours if we did not so dwarf them down to the miserable level of our indolence or fears.

4. Are you coming short in any particular of God's blessed will and purpose for you? Are you reaching "all the good pleasure of His goodness, and the work of faith with power"? God has a will for us. There is a lofty ideal in his heart for each one. Are we coming short of it? We cannot fail of his conception for our life without disappointing Him. If we do come short of the Holy Spirit's peace for us, it will be vain to make spiritual progress without it. There can be no forward movement until His will is first met. If He has been saying to us, "Come up higher," we must obey before there can be any blessing in any other direction.

The high consciousness of this call of God in the heart is often a sad contrast to the miserable experience of failure the life represents. Men are afraid or reluctant to obey it, especially if it be in the direction of leaving off something that is dear to them. The apostle says, "I will follow after, if that I may apprehend that for which also I am apprehended of Christ Jesus." Paul felt a hand upon him pressing him on; he knew it was God's hand, and he was fully meeting it.

Are you abreast with God, beloved? He will not lead you forward faster than you are able to go. He knows all the depths of human weakness, but His high ideal reaches down to every part of it. God lets down to you as much light as you can live by today. There will come brighter, clearer revelations tomorrow. If today's light is missed, tomorrows' cannot be received. There is never light enough to see very far ahead. It is given only as you use it. Are you fully doing so?

5. What about the great fields of Christian service that are left unoccupied? Have you missed opportunities for

work, which will one day be silent witnesses against you? Will any souls be lost through your failure? Have there been any openings in the providence of God which you have not entered into? There is no use in seeking more supplies of grace for Him, while there remains so much land to be possessed.

It is a very sad fact, and I believe it is typical of the state of Christianity today, that seven whole tribes of Israel failed for a time to enter into their possessions. They held back from the self-denial, and remained encamped around the tabernacle of Shiloh. There was no progress there. It seems to foretell the mournful truth that the church would one day lie down in supreme indifference to much that Jesus died and rose again to secure for her. She is not pressing forward into her possession. It seems to hint that even yet the great mass of Christians are coming short of their inheritance.

This is not true of all, but there is many a disciple who goes for years and years without even the assurance of salvation. Indeed, it is a rare thing to find in many quarters. They think it is presumption to say they have such assurance. If you should ask in an ordinary Christian gathering how many were living holy lives, overcoming temptations day by day, and enabled by Christ's power to follow in His will according to all the light that has been given, you would find multitudes who would hesitate to make such a confession. I have been able in some places to count on my fingers the Christians who would dare to say so.

This is sad. The least inheritance in the land of promise means full salvation. The church needs to be roused up from its sleep of centuries, from the low standard of Christian life, which it has accepted, and which make a life of holiness such a wonder. It is deemed exceptional to find such lives as Fletcher, or Wesley, and other saintly lives. It ought to be the rule. Faith like Franke's or George Muller's is considered a prodigy in the spiritual world, but God expects all His people to believe Him perfectly.

The epistles speak of all Christians as saints. The letter to the Corinthians was addressed to such. They were all "called to be saints." "All the saints salute you," Paul says in another place. God expects nothing less of us. "Follow me as I follow Christ," was the apostle's direction. God does expect us to be pure and holy up to our knowledge of His requirements, and to know and do the full measure of His will.

This is the land upon which it is our privilege to enter. These are the possibilities that are placed before us. All may secure them, for the land was the common inheritance of all the tribes. There were special prizes beyond this claimed in it by Joshua, Caleb, and a few others; and there are still some brave spirits in the Church always, who gain special crowns of victory as rewards of unusual faith and service; but the ordinary inheritance of every Christian should be at least a full salvation.

Don't excuse yourself from receiving this by any false humility. Don't talk about "not expecting ever to be a saint." If you are willing simply to get into heaven, as Job says, by the skin of your teeth, the Lord help you. There will be crowds there at the gate just like you, and whether they will ever get in is doubtful. I am sure at least they will so block the way, that it will be a long time before you will see the gate. I don't believe the soul is saved at all that is satisfied to miss any of God's blessings, or that does not care whether or not it brings glory to God during its earthly life.

God hates sin and wants it overcome, and any Christian who can sit down at ease, not caring whether his spiritual life is gaining in power, had better look into the matter of his conversion. Perhaps he will find he is a backslider. The apostle says, "Let us fear lest we seem to come short." It is a fearful thing for a Christian to be willing to be half saved. He is in tremendous peril. His life should be a constant growth, a continual pressing out after new attainments.

IV. What was the cause of the Israelites coming short of their full inheritance?

1. One cause is hinted at in the expression, "Ye are slack to possess the land which the Lord God of your fathers hath given you." The word implies that they were indolent, and quite satisfied with their present condition. There was a lack of holy energy and aspiration after the inheritance promised. They were taking things easy. They were little concerned about failure and sin. They would have gone on forever in their present state of apathy and distaste for conflict. They were breathing the atmosphere of the enchanted ground.

Have you never, perhaps even while on your knees, had such an influence thrown over you – the very anodyne of Satan, who would thus lull your spiritual senses to sleep. How it has made you shrink from the pain of holy inspiration, and made you willing to fall back into a passive contentment! God is calling you to press forward, "to lay aside every weight"; and "be not slothful, but followers of them who through faith and patience inherit the promises."

Is this your spiritual state, beloved? If not, ask the Lord to awaken you out of your sleep. There may come a very terrible awakening some day if you do not. He may have to strike the chords of deep anguish to awaken you out of this sleep of death.

2. Timidity was another cause of failure. They dreaded meeting the foes that were still in the land, and so left them unconquered.

3. They failed also because the majority hung back. Nearly all Israel was encamped around Shiloh. It was a lonely thing to step out into the regions beyond, the homes of the Anakims, and they shrank from it. So long as the larger number of the people stood back, the rest were contented to be as they. We have got to step out, beloved, from the majority. The path of life is "a narrow

road with here and there a traveler." God help us to be singular, if that is necessary. Better to have God on our side, whether we be in the majority or the minority.

4. They were hindered by a spirit of self-complacency. Their past history they counted a good-enough record, and this increased their spiritual apathy. Martin Luther said, "If thou say enough, thou shalt perish." We have not got enough until we have received all His will. Yesterday's victories were only for yesterday. Count not that you have already attained, but press on for all the fullness of His blessed will.

V. What meaning is there for us in God's tender appeal to Joshua, "How long are ye slack to possess the land"? Is He saying to any of you this morning "How long are you going to remain unsanctified"? Until some terrible trial wakes you up, or some fearful fall makes you realize your condition? Or, are you waiting for death to do that work within you? That is a poor time to be saved, and a poorer one to be sanctified, when the mind is clouded by the power of disease. "How long are ye slack to possess the land?"

Now, while your brain is clear and your choice is not compelled, make the wise choice, and give yourself wholly to God. Use all the light He has given you. Make your own all that Jesus died to bring you into. Let not your inheritance go by default. Let not the grace of God be received in vain. There is not a promise He has made but He is anxious to make good to you. The alluring visions of grace and glory He has held before you, He will transcribe upon your heart, and engrave deeply into your whole life if you will let Him. There is not a crown hung up in yonder mansions but somebody is to wear it. Do not let these dreams become a mockery to you. They may be real, and God wants them to be real for you. He has a separate inheritance for each one. You cannot get into mine, and I cannot get into yours. Do not fail to enter upon yours. If you do, you shall suffer eternal loss, even if you do not lose your soul.

2. The day will soon come when you, too, will be old and stricken in years. Time is rushing by; God has not given you a day too many. They are going fast. Suppose they should stop tomorrow, and you never have another opportunity to gain a victory for Him. You would give all the world for a chance to resist temptation, or for another hard place in which to glorify God as you had before dishonored Him. The days once gone can never come back. You will not pass this way again.

There will be no chance in heaven to learn holiness, to have patience with unholy people, or to love your enemies. There will be no enemies to love. If you have not grace enough here to learn these lessons, there will be no other chance for it. This is the only place in which you can be a soldier, or endure suffering, or show forth the graces of sanctification in trial. You have abundant opportunity for that now. You will find them waiting for you in your homes when you go back to them today. If there were no giants on the hill there would be no inheritance for you to gain. Caleb would never have won his crown if it had not been for the Anakims. He met them in the name of God and conquered them, and Hebron became significant of the place of fellowship and the friendship of God.

If you find difficulties in your homes, or enemies in your own heart, or trouble anywhere in your life, God has given them to you as opportunities for victory. There you will find the crown of glory and the land of promise. It is always the place where God plants His paradises. Eden is always in the midst of a wilderness. The place of springs is always upon the barren mountains. It is the desert of life that is to be made to blossom like a rose.

When God wanted to build a temple, He first sent Abraham to purify the place by the consecrated offering of Isaac; then it was again used as a place of sacrifice at the threshing-floor of Araunah. After that God could use it as the place of His sanctuary. When He wanted a capital, He sent David to take a hill so difficult to capture, that its inhabitants laughed at him, and defended it with the blind and lame. Yet David conquered it, and it became the Zion of the Lord, the holiest, dearest place in all the world forever.

Go out into the field in which He has cast your lot, beloved, meet the temptations and difficulties in the strength of the Lord and turn them into Edens; and thus show forth to others, through them, the grace of Jesus Christ, and the power of a consecrated life. You do not need to go into the land which is very far off to do this, for the opportunity is very near you.

May He send you forth to gain all this large inheritance and give you the joy of saying at last, "It is finished; there hath not one word failed of all that the Lord hath spoken."

> Transform us! Let us bear
> Thine image everywhere,
> The living witness of the living Word:
> We would in thee abide,
> In thee be glorified,
> And shine as candles lighted by the Lord.
>
> Jesus, in us fulfill
> Thine ever blessed will!
> We breathe a glad 'amen' to thy decree.
> We would henceforth entwine
> Our darkened lives with thine,
> Nor ever find the selves we lose in thee.

CHAPTER VII.

CHOICE POSSESSIONS.

"Though I speak with the tongues of men and of angels, and have not love, I am become as sounding brass, or a tinkling cymbal. And though I have the gift of prophecy, and understand all mysteries, and and knowledge; and though I have all faith, so that I could remove mountains, and have not love, I am nothing. And though I bestow all my goods to feed the poor, and though I give my body to be burned, and have not love, it profiteth me nothing. Love suffereth long and is kind; love envieth not; love vaunteth not itself, is not puffed up, doth not behave itself unseemly, seeketh not her own, is not easily provoked, thinketh no evil; rejoiceth not in iniquity, but rejoiceth in the truth; beareth all things, believeth all things, hopeth all things, endureth all things. Love never faileth; but whether there be prophecies they shall fail; whether there be tongues, they shall cease; whether there be knowledge it shall vanish away. And now abideth faith, hope, love, these three; but the greatest of these is love." – 1Cor. 13:1-8, 13.

THERE are some special possessions spoken of in the book of Joshua, besides the common inheritance of the land. These were meant to illustrate the special possessions which we may still obtain through courage, faith and obedience.

We have, first, an account of the taking of Hebron by Caleb. A few years after they entered the land when the conquest of the great kings had been completed, and the Israelites were in possession, Caleb came to Joshua and asked the fulfillment of a promise made to him by Moses more than forty years before, that he should have the city of Hebron for his inheritance. It was a place already sacred to the people by many associations. It had been the home of Abraham and near it was the cave of Machpelah in which were the graves of their forefathers.

It was a place of natural beauty, surrounded by a valley of great fertility, and was one of the chief cities of Canaan, older indeed than even the oldest city in Egypt. Caleb had set his heart upon it when he had gone through the land with the spies, and Moses promised that it should be his as soon as they entered upon their inheritance. Then came the rebellion of the tribes and their turning back into the desert. Yet, though Caleb had to wait half a century for it, he did not despair. He knew that he should have his inheritance. The long years of waiting were now over, and as soon as it was fitting that he should prefer a personal request, Caleb asked that the promise given so long ago should be redeemed.

It was not an easy possession to take, and he was now an old man of eighty-five, yet he was as strong as on the day he left Egypt both to go out and to come in. To gain his possessions he must drive out the giant Anak who was then its ruler. Later, the city became David's capital, and still later it became the home of Elizabeth, and John the Baptist was probably born in the neighborhood.

But dear as Hebron is to the Bible student historically, the lessons connected with it on account of the significance of its name are still more precious. The word means "friend" and it is significant of our spiritual inheritance of fellowship and love. It is a choice spiritual inheritance, the highest of all the victories of grace – that of love. Paul says love is the greatest of all the graces, and superior to all other spiritual gifts.

After Caleb had gained possession of Hebron, another special inheritance was gained by Othniel, one of the brave leaders of the same tribe. His name means the "lion of God." He claimed an old literary city in the neighborhood of Hebron – Kirjath-sepher. The civilization of some of those ancient kingdoms was as remarkable as our own. They had splendid libraries, with thousands of volumes, many of them works on philosophy and natural science.

Kirjath-sepher was the City of Books. Literature probably flourished there, and schools and colleges. It was doubtless the seat of instruction about the Canaanitish worship. Celeb promised his daughter to anyone who would take Kirjath-sepher. Othniel said at once, "I will take it!" He went forth with the same faith in God that Caleb showed, conquered the enemy, took the city, and won Achsah for his bride. It, too, is the type of spiritual blessing, as Hebron was of love. Kirjath-sepher is significant of truth. It represents our deliverance from spiritual blindness and the old carnal mind with all its foolish ideas. It means taking Christ's thought in everything, and possessing the illumination of the Spirit. Hebron is the place of love, Kirjath-sepher of light and truth.

Connected with all this story is a romance of singular beauty, that is very suggestive of other spiritual truths. Othniel had won his bride, and with her came a splendid inheritance, but it had one very serious defect. The land lay facing the south, exposed to the scorching heat of a tropical sun, and there was no water on it. Then Achsah, as she came to her husband, petitioned her father that, as he had given her a rich inheritance which yet had no springs upon it, he would give her also a spring of water; and he gave her the "the upper and the nether springs."

From the upper spring the hillside could be irrigated. By pipes the water could be carried along the ridge of the hill and liberated there at will, and the burning and arid sands could thus be changed into a very garden of fertility. The nether spring would irrigate the valley in the same way. Springs in the valleys are very unusual. They are frequently found in mountains, but not often in the valleys. The word Achsah means grace. The prize Othniel won by giving up his natural wisdom was grace, suggesting the complete fullness of God's grace.

Beloved friends, what is the meaning of all these types to us?

I. The first is that our very choicest inheritance, the highest place we can possibly take in the land, is the place of love. When we enter the land of Canaan the first thing we must do is to stand in the place of faith with Joshua, but, when the battles are over and we are ready to sit down in our possession, there comes another experience, typified by the taking of Hebron.

The battle of Jericho was a victory of faith, the capture of Hebron was a victory of love. We overcome by faith, we remain overcomers through love. Faith may indeed remove mountains, but faith without love is like sounding brass, or a tinkling cymbal. I have seen Christians who have had a wonderful experience in the line of faith, but who seemed to have no love, and their lives have been blighted by the lack. You may be able to take Jericho and conquer the kings at Beth-horon, but you will fail if you do not win Hebron and slay the sons of Anak. Sometimes it seems as if God were leading only to the development of the experience of faith, and there are few calls for the higher grace of love.

Then it seems as if the school of love were suddenly opened and all the testings are in that line, and the scholar is learning such lessons as these: "Love is not provoked. Love maketh no account of evil. Love doth not behave discourteously." If this experience has not come to you yet, dear friends, be sure it will meet you before God is through with you. If it has not come, your experience is like the barren rocks where there are no springs of water – the very essence of God and heaven. Love is to cover the sides with verdure. Love is the fulfilling of the law. If you are willing to be overcomers in this field you may walk ever with a glowing heart and a sweet and loving spirit, and without these all else is worse than vain.

2. This love must be divine. It is not our natural spirit or affection springing up in the bosom. It is not

something which we can compel by our own will. You must feel the lack of it, beloved, and lie down prostrate at the foot of the cross, and God will baptize you into it by pouring into you the very nature and spirit of Christ Himself.

It is not man's love, it is God's Love shed abroad in the heart by the Holy Ghost. If you try to get it in any other way, you will find how helpless you are in this direction. You will come sharp up against people whom you will find it impossible to love, and God has meant you to fail in it to show you the weakness of your own fancied strength in this very matter. You are deeply ashamed of the failure, and see, too, that if you are not victorious here you perhaps have no certain hope of salvation. You become painfully aware of the necessity of having love for them, and see also the perfect helplessness of your heart to give it. Then comes the humbling of proud self, and a readiness at last to be the spirit of love within you.

How sweetly then He comes, changing Boanerges into John the loving disciple who rests on Jesus' bosom! Ah, beloved, Hebron is the stronghold of Canaan. It is the citadel of the Lord. The things that were most opposed to God in your spiritual nature may be most fully consecrated to Him, and you become strongest for Him where you were the strongest for the devil, so that men will say, how wonderful is the grace of God!

Do you believe this? You are saying, perhaps this spirit of gentleness and love is not your nature. Of course it is not. It was not my nature. We have all come to a place where all our nature revolted against love, especially to the unloving, but God has made it easy. He will not let you off without it. He will not, because He has it for you. Are you going to take Hebron, dear friends? The Anakims may be mighty, but by God's help you can drive them out.

3. Hebron is called Kirjath-arba, or the city of Arba. Arba was the father of Anak, and Anak had three sons – all giants like himself. It will help us out a little to look

at the meaning of their names. If you think it is too fanciful you can let it go. The truth is not fanciful if the frame is. The name Arba suggests the spirit of self-will. Literally it means "the strength of Baal," or masterhood. Whatever this is, it is the strength of self, the spirit of self-will, that thing in you that wants to be master.

Arba was the type of the spirit of self, and the victory of Caleb over him was the victory of love over selfishness. It is the anti-Christ of the spiritual life, the same self. It. does not appear so strongly at the beginning of the Christian life. You find it a long way in, after sin has been slain for years. The Israelites had left Egypt more than forty years ago. Even when sin has been slain, self remaining in the heart must be brought into subjection to God. All that we call natural strength, even what is usually termed "the better self," must be laid upon the altar. Old Arba, the giant of self-will, must be slain and the will of God brought into the soul in his place.

The love of God is not an emotion of ecstatic feeling. This is often manifested by people whose love breaks down upon little provocation. God does not care so much for effervescent joy as for a will that chooses His will and holds to it in the very teeth of temptation, a stern determination that we will die before we either please self or distrust God. This is called in the Word "a perfect heart." It stands firmly with the hand on the helm, the will fixed, and the eye on God. The life will not be all an easy holiday, but there will be in it what is far better, a faithful living up to the requirements of God and a constant sense of living always in the city of Hebron, the place of His unclouded presence.

Arba had three sons, and their names are also typical of evil. The first of these was Anak. His name means "long-necked." Do you know what that means? A long-necked animal holds its head very high and looks down on things below it. There are some professing Christians who have such necks. It is the spirit of pride that God hates. He loves the meek and humble spirit, but He knoweth the proud afar off. "I dwell in the high and holy place, with him also that is of a contrite and humble spirit."

Beloved, if you are to dwell in Hebron, Anak must die. The long neck must be hewed off by the sword of Christ. What is the principal thing that hinders our love from going out to other people? It is our abominable pride. You measure yourself with them and seem in your own eyes better than they. Measure yourself with God instead, and learn how you appear in His sight. Then see how abominable a thing your pride is, and never venture to criticize a human being again. Job got right with God when he got a view of himself. "Wherefore," he says, "I abhor myself and repent in dust and ashes."

How sweetly Christ linked together love and humility by getting down and washing the disciples' feet – a lowly service, but He was not ashamed of it. The spirit of lowliness is the spirit of love. If you have it you will not be able to see the spots in other people's lives. The critical eye sees them very quickly, but overlooks the great faults in its own life, which Christ says is like a beam in your own eye. It seems the other way to you. In the eye of God there is a great forest tree in your own vision, and but a little speck of dust in your brother's. When once you see yourself in the true light, fit only to be nailed to the cross, to be spit upon and scourged, you will never be able to lift up your head again or sit in judgment upon your brother. May God give to all of us the true spirit of humility!

We do not know the names of Arba's other sons, but we will call the second of the Anakims the giant of Prejudice. He stands for the spirit of dislike, especially dislikes that are capricious and unreasonable. Many Christian people harbor such feelings, and think they are simply exercising good judgment and discernment of the characters of some of their neighbors. Their whole feeling is probably built on a misunderstanding. If you knew them as God knows them, you would be ashamed of your misjudgment. You have a distorted view of them.

I have seen people lifted up out of disease and sin, and helped marvelously over the darkest, hardest place in their life, who almost lost their blessing afterwards through prejudice. Many people have been seriously hindered in their spiritual lives by impressions which after all were false. When they laid down these impressions, and came like Nathaniel to see what they really are, and what there is of Christ in other people, they have found their mistake and entered into a fullness of blessing they never before possessed.

If you have a feeling of dislike or prejudice against any of God's dear children, it probably hides the greatest blessing of your life. The dislike is the devil's cloud. Hidden away behind the alienation, lies Hebron, the very mountaintop from which you may see the King in His beauty, and behold the land which is very far off. The people turned from Jesus because He came from Nazareth, asking scornfully "Can any good thing come out of Nazareth?" They did not want any blessing which came from that source. You may make up your mind, beloved, that your great blessings are to come to you from the most forbidding places.

Dislike of eccentric people, perhaps, will hinder your spiritual life, till you lay it down at the feet of Christ. Then the thing you disliked will become a means of great blessing. Put away your malice, and prejudice, and hatred. You cannot have Jesus in the heart and keep them there too. Become open and frank as a babe toward every child of God. You will find that love is always twice blessed to him that gives and to him that receives.

We shall call Arba's third son, Pleasure, including the love of ease, the love of the world and all other selfish loves. This may have power over us through any thing to which we give our heart. It may be an idol in the household, or love of some dear friend, or earthly possessions. No matter about the size of it, if it gets the heart away from God it is wrong. We are to do the things that please not us but God. We are not to follow our fancy or our choice about things, but say always "Lord what wilt thou have me to do?" If we would have His blessing constantly, we must love what He loves, and, indeed, receive our very preferences from Him. Living to please God is the true aim of the holy heart and the true secret of happiness. We are to "walk worthy of the Lord unto all pleasing;" but "she that liveth in pleasure is dead while she liveth."

The capture of Hebron suggests these four forms of evil in the heart, antagonistic to the life of God in the soul. They are self-will, pride, prejudice and pleasure. When these are cast out, the soul can live the life of love and consecration. Then we shall walk constantly in the light of His love. Jesus said, "The Father hath not left me alone, for I do always those things that please Him." This is Hebron.

II. The second choice inheritance was Kirjath-sepher, which was taken by Othniel. We have already seen that this was the City of Books, and it teaches us that the wisdom of the flesh is of no value in God's sight. Hebron, however, was captured first. There can be no great spiritual light till love has come. We do not want much freight for the head until the heart has been ballasted. A ship will founder if it were top-heavy, and so will a Christian. Get the heart filled first, then will come all the illumination from the Holy Spirit that is needed.

There are two sides to this subject. 1. The old library must be burned. Then God's light can come in. Are you willing to part with your old books? Here are some of them.

The traditions of men perhaps come first – your old ideas, maxims and traditions, the things that have been handed down for centuries. As the fathers thought and lived, so do the children.

Here are books full of superstitious nonsense, signs, ill-omens, and all such satanic shadows. God would have you go straight against the whole of these silly lies.

The best things that ever come to me, generally come on Fridays. Burn up all these natural books, and take God's thoughts instead.

Here are books full of your own natural reason. They teach you to walk by your common sense, and exercise your own clearheaded judgment about things. They do not tell you to look to the Holy Ghost for guidance. You may think it uncalled for to turn away from these things. But God says, "Trust in the Lord with all thine heart, and lean not unto thine own understanding."

The library contains books on theology, written by good men. They are full of man's reasonings about the Bible, and they teach you to believe only on the certificate of one of their doctors. Take no man's leadership apart from God's word. The wisest and best theologians disagree on almost every department of truth. There must be something wrong somewhere. Take God's word only. Truth is not five-fold nor two-fold. It is one-fold. Do not lean too strongly on the wisdom of any man, and least of all take my opinions unless they are sustained by the Word of God.

2. But it is not enough to burn the old library of Kirjath-sepher. We want a new one. And God has it for us. There is first, His precious Word of Truth, with its inexhaustible fullness. Deeper and deeper shall we now fathom its glorious teachings and receive the unfolding of its light as we dwell in the Land of Promise. There is no interpreter of Scripture like a spiritual experience. How it glows with light and glory when we can trace in it the echo of all our most sacred, inward experiences! And above all other teachers the heavenly Comforter leads us into all truth.

How precious is the Bible to a holy, consecrated heart! How its pages glow with light and love and transcribe themselves upon the memory and the soul! What a choice possession has it become to many a land of Light and Truth, flowing with milk and honey indeed! "More to be desired are they than gold, sweeter also than honey and the honeycomb."

But there are other Books in this blessed City. There is the light of personal revelation through the Holy Ghost. He would indeed be poorly honoring the Written Word who denied the reality of the Living Word, the law written in the heart, the Voice of the Shepherd, the Light of His Face, and the inward communications of the Comforter Himself directly to the heart, guiding, comforting, commanding, and suggesting impulse, thought and feeling, devotion, praise, prayer, or holy gladness as He is pleased to impart. From Hebron, beloved, the place of love, God waits to lead us over to Kirjath-sepher the place of heavenly light and unerring guidance.

III. There is a beautiful story connected with Achsah in this account. When Othniel won Kirjath-sepher Caleb gave him his daughter Achsah for his wife, and she claimed and received from her father springs of water, and he gave her the upper and the nether springs.

1. What are the upper springs? They surely are typical of those things in the divine life which touch the higher parts of our being, the spiritual elements in the soul. The divine life within us should be a spring flowing spontaneously, like water from an Artesian well.

There should be springing life and light. The springs of prayer should flow responsive to the sweet movings of His Spirit within you.

There are springs of joy that must not be clogged for a moment. Never be despondent because everything around is forbidding. Your joy is heavenly joy.

2. Achsah received also the nether springs. They typify the blessings of temporal life – the grace we need in our earthly spheres.

First, there are the springs of health for the body. He has promised that "our health shall spring forth speedily." When His physical life becomes a part of ours the feet are ready to fly, the hands become strong for daily work, and the whole system receives new vigor and energy. God has Achsah's blessing for you, beloved, too.

Then there are springs of joy and blessing which God lets down into the common experiences of everyday life, which to most of you is one of toil. There are men's hands here which are brown with toil, and women's hands which are tired with labor. Blessed be God, all this can be done in gladness. God is able and willing to meet you there and fill you with freshness and joy in the midst of all your work, so that life shall be full of zest no matter what the occupation.

The springs of joy need not be disturbed by the variety of the vessels into which they pour. The joy is not in yourself or your calling at all. The joy is in the heart, because God is there and nothing can disturb it. You may come in contact with painful, grieving, disheartening things, but the joy will be undisturbed. Learn to pray the prayer of Jabez, "Keep me from evil that it may not grieve me." Then you will go forth with a coat of mail. The places where you walk may smell of brimstone and fire, but your shoes are of iron and brass and you will walk safely through them. The air may be thick around you with the fumes of hell, but you will be safe, for you are breathing the upper air, and while that lasts you need fear no evil.

Have you got all these springs, beloved? Have you taken Hebron? Have you won Kirjath-sepher? Or, have you got Achsah's heritage, a south land bending to the hot sun, and dry and scorched for want of water, but divinely irrigated by the upper and the nether springs. If Jesus is with you in that land it will be turned into a paradise. Wells of living water will be there, and it will blossom like a heavenly garden. Let the water in. Let God come into the heart, and the Artesian springs will flow forth abundantly.

Many of you have not got a great deal to fill your hearts and lives, but if you have got God you can go forth claiming victory.

"I ask Thee for the daily strength,
To none that ask denied,
A mind to blend with outward things
While keeping at Thy side.
Content to fill a little place
If Thou be glorified.

"There are briers besetting every path
That call for patient care;
There is a crook in every lot,
And a constant need for prayer;
But a loving heart that leans on thee
Is happy anywhere."

CHAPTER VIII.

LESSONS ABOUT SERVICE.

"Wherefore we, receiving a kingdom that cannot be moved, let us have grace, whereby we may serve God acceptably, with reverence and godly fear." – Heb. 12:28.

THE book of Joshua teaches many choice lessons respecting Christian service, as one of the elements in a consecrated life. Joshua himself is introduced to us, in the earlier notices of his history, as Moses' servant. He had to serve to learn before he could command. Moses also is called the servant of the Lord. Joshua, however, stands as the type of a higher service, inasmuch as the service of the gospel is higher than that of the law. And in the life of full consecration our service for Christ is freer, nobler, and more effectual than we can ever know in the wilderness.

I. SERVICE WITHOUT ENTIRE SANCTIFICATION.

The first lesson we learn from this book of object lessons is that it is impossible to do much service for God without ourselves fully entering into the experience of entire consecration. We have a striking illustration of this in the case of the two tribes of Reuben and Gad, and the half tribe of Manasseh, who chose their inheritance on the wilderness side of Jordan, leaving their families there, and afterwards returning themselves; but, at the same time, sharing the struggle of their brethren, and fighting the battles of the Lord through all the years of the conquest.

They seem to be the types of the many Christians who choose their inheritance also on the borders of the world, and are not wholly separated themselves, still less in their families and possessions, from the world, by the dividing line of a real experience of death; but who, at the same time, do much real service for the cause of Christ and for the help of others. Like these three tribes they have visited the Land of Promise, and can tell you very much about it. They have even helped to lead many others into it, and fought nobly for the testimony of God concerning full salvation, and for His cause in every way. But this good land is not their personal and permanent home.

They will frankly confess that they do not live there in the fullest sense, and that to them, to a great extent, this higher teaching is a beautiful theory. Indeed, they do not altogether desire to make it their exclusive abode; they prefer the pastures on the plains of Gilead, and the rich possessions on the earth side of Jordan; and they do not think it best to require their families to go through the sacrifices, self-denials and privations that would be required in crossing the Jordan. Their short-sighted vision does not perceive the perils of their choice, and the future trials that are to come from their situation in the very midst of worldly foes, and on the battleground of coming ages, when their beautiful estates are to be trodden by the feet of Assyrian and Babylonian conquerors, and their lovely homes desolated by heathen foes, or they, still worse, enticed into forbidden alliances with the sons and daughters of an idolatrous and godless world.

Thousands of professing Christians are living in just such circumstances, and being blighted by such influences; and yet the husband and father, and even the mothers and sisters of many such homes, are doing much earnest work for Christ, and fighting many of the battles of the Lord. Joshua recognized the services of Reuben and Gad, and gave them the full share in the spoils of victory, and sent them back with honorable appreciation, reward and blessing.

And so, still, God accepts the services of many of His children, who are like them, and rewards them as far as He can; and yet He sees how sad and foolish is their choice, and how much higher the blessing and reward of a wholly-consecrated life. Let us not only visit the Land of Promise, but let us choose it as our inheritance. Let us live in it ourselves and stay there, and let us not only enter it for ourselves, but let us never rest until those we love have their full and permanent inheritance within its safe and happy confines.

There is no place so dangerous as on the borders of the world and the threshold of the kingdom. The borderland is always Satan's very battleground and the Christian's place of extremest peril. It is possible to sail so close to the whirlpool as to be sucked into the vortex; so near to the burning breath of the pit that our sails shall be scorched and consumed by the fiery winds, and we left helpless to return.

II. CONSECRATED SERVICE.

In contrast with the two and a half tribes referred to, we have the beautiful picture in Joshua of the inheritance of the Levites, in their forty-eight cities, distributed throughout all parts of the land. The Levites stand as the special types of service, a service that springs from separation and entire dedication to God. Selected as the substitutes of Israel's firstborn, they represented, emphatically, the idea of redemption; and separated from all earthly aims by the fact that they possessed no distinct inheritance or land, the Lord Himself was their inheritance, and the choicest cities of all the tribes were assigned to them as their permanent homes. They were specially fitted to emphasize the truth – that true separation to God and a really consecrated life brings us into the possession of all things in Him.

There was not a district of Canaan where the Levites did not have the choicest cities. There was not a tribe but they shared, in some sense, in its inheritance, and in return, diffused among them the hallowed influence of their presence, example, and service; for they were the teachers of the nation, and the leaders of all true service for God.

Their distribution and inheritance teach us.

1. That God wants the principle of entire consecration exemplified in every part of our Christian life. Therefore, He sent the Levites through every part of Canaan and located them among all the tribes of Israel that there might be no region where this supreme thought of dedication to Himself would not be constantly set forth in their example. And so he wants the spirit of the Levites manifested in every part of our Christian life: not only in our temple service, but in our secular callings and domestic enjoyments and affections; from the Dan to the Beersheba of our entire existence.

2. The principle of true separation to God will bring to us the largest inheritance, and like the Levites, we shall not have one portion only, but shall possess the whole land in its choicest cities, and shall enter into all that is precious, even in the experience of others and the fellowship of God's elect. Of such a soul it is indeed true, "All things are yours, whether Paul, or Apollos, or Cephas, or the world, or life, or death, or things present, or things to come;" and the reason is not that Christ is yours, but that in the true spirit of Levitical consecration "ye are Christ's and Christ is God's."

3. Closely related to this is the truth that we can serve God in every part of our life, and in every situation where He may place us in His providence. The Levites not only ministered in the tabernacle at Shiloh, but in the remotest cities of Canaan; and so the most commonplace occupation, the most secular calling, the most trifling act of earthly duty may involve the highest ministry for Christ.

The poor nurse-girl may be training a prince for the Church of God. The toiling household-servant may be ministering along with angels to one of God's children. The ox goad of Shamgar, or the needle of Dorcas, are as sacred as the harp of David, the tongue of Paul, and the blood of Stephen. When James, the apostle, died, the church could spare even him, but when Dorcas was taken away her place could not be supplied, and she was even raised from the dead. It is the glory of the sun that it can illuminate a crumb of broken glass until it shines like costly brilliants. And it is the highest testimony to Christ when we can reflect His image from the most trivial and commonplace things of our daily life.

Therefore, the chapter which summons to the highest consecration, Rom. 12, immediately descends with us into the arena of our common life and adds, "Not slothful in business, fervent in spirit, serving the Lord." "Mind not high things, but condescend to men of low estate." "Bless them which persecute you, weep with them that weep."

III. SPECIAL SERVICE AND REWARD.

The highest recompense and the choicest possessions are to be won by brave and faithful service.

And he who would attain to the highest place may have all that he will dare to claim and occupy.

This lesson is finely brought out in the account of the two tribes of Ephraim and Manasseh – Josh. 17:14-18. After they had received their inheritance they came to Joshua and claimed, on account of their preeminence among the tribes of Israel as the family of Joseph, that they should receive a special and double inheritance. "Why hast thou given me but one lot and one portion," they ask, "seeing I am a great people, forasmuch as the Lord has blessed me hitherto?"

The reply of Joshua is particularly fine. He does not dispute their claim or preeminence, but he demands that they shall make it good by some proof of their prowess, and he promises that they shall have whatever additional territory they can conquer from the foe. "If thou be a great people, then get thee up to the wood country, and cut down for thyself, there in the land of the Perizzites and of the giants, if Mount Ephraim be too narrow for thee." Then, as they take him at his word, he adds, "Thou art a great people and hast great power, thou shalt not have one lot only, but the mountain shall be thine; for it is a wood and thou shalt cut it down and the outgoings of it shall be thine: for thou shalt drive out the Canaanites, though they have iron chariots, and though they be strong."

This is still God's message to those who are dissatisfied with their limited sphere, and tempted to talk of their special gifts and qualifications for higher service, if a better opportunity were afforded. For all such there is ample room in this great world of sin and sorrow, and if they do not have opportunities made ready to the hand, they have but to make them by going out into the ranks of evil and conquering for themselves as large an inheritance of service and blessing as their faith and love can claim. Great souls prove their greatness by making opportunities where others only have complaints. True power will turn the most formidable difficulty into an occasion of victory, and take the boldest adversary prisoner and make him fight in our own ranks.

Joseph's greatness grew out of his prison cell, and had he not been truly great as a slave, he would never have been as a prince. Paul found as good a pulpit when chained to his keeper in a Roman dungeon, or going as a prisoner on shipboard to Rome, as when standing before Agrippa, or preaching among his friends at Troas. It is as impossible for true spiritual power to be lost for lack of opportunity, as it is to stop the sun from shining, or the fountain from flowing. True life and force must find an outlet, and God proves His princes to be of royal birth just where He finds them before He gives them their crowns.

All around us there are ample fields for the exhibition of the noblest Christian heroism, and the proving of all the fullness of Christ's grace and power. Mary Lyon found such a field in the Young Ladies' Seminary. John Pounds found it over his shoemaker's last, among the ragged boys that gathered around him on the streets. Harlan Page found it among his fellow-workmen, as a common carpenter; Jerry McAuly, among the tramps of New York; David Livingstone, in the swamps of Africa; William Duncan, among the Indians of Metlakhatla.

And for each of us there is ample room among the wooded heights and iron chariots of our difficult surroundings, for brave endeavors and holy triumphs, which will thrill the pulses of heaven and crown us with the unfading glory of Christian heroes. And just as the hardest rocks of earth are the hiding places of the veins of gold and the most costly gems, so we shall find that the most difficult and unpromising situations like the ancient forests of Beth-shean, contain the very soil out of which shall grow the most precious fruits of our service and reward, and issues as blessed as the beautiful valley of Jezreel, which became the great inheritance of Ephraim, and the reward of the very exploit described in this passage.

To be the instrument in God's hands of reclaiming for Christ some utterly wretched and ruined life, or transforming, as grace has done so often, through some lowly Christian, a poor street-waif into a Robert Morrison, or a wretched African captive into the apostle of the Niger; to change some godless neighborhood, or some benighted heathen region into a moral paradise, as a single brave worker has often done; and to wring from the very grasp of difficulty and failure the triumph of truth and righteousness, when it seemed like a forlorn hope – surely, this is a higher nobility, and will win a grander prize than to wait in easy indolence for opportunities that cost no effort, or even to fill with reasonable fidelity some place of influence, where every circumstance is favorable to our success, and faith and courage have little occasion for heroic daring or enduring.

Let us, then, not look so much for promising opportunities, as we find them in the very midst of our present situation, and in the very bosom of our most formidable difficulties.

IV. SERVICES FOR THE SINFUL AND LOST.

It is the property of water to run to the lowest depths and to find its way to the deepest channels. Like its beautiful earthly type, the living water runs downward. The more of divine grace there is in any heart, the more will it prompt its possessor, like the Son of Man, to seek and save that which is lost.

The highest Christian life should ever be found in contact with the lowest sinfulness and the deepest need. They who have got too high in Christian attainment to feel called to work for sinners, have probably got too high for the companionship of the Good Shepherd. The more of His spirit we cherish, and the more of His likeness we possess, the more will we be found, like Him, in the midst of publicans and sinners, seeking "if, by any means, we may save some."

All this is finely set forth in the book of Joshua. Almost the first picture in that beautiful manual of the Higher Christian Life is the story of the salvation of poor Rahab, the harlot of Jericho. Her condition was, undoubtedly, one of great wickedness and deep degradation. The Canaanite nations were infamous for the most unnatural and abominable depravity, and she was, probably, a true type of the most abandoned of her race and her sex.

But when the messengers of Israel came to her doors she received them kindly, believed their tidings, and earnestly asked for their protection when the hour of her country's ruin should have come. They gave her a simple token, by which her home could be recognized – a crimson cord suspended from her window, suggesting, if not typifying the blood of Calvary, through which still the sinful soul is saved, and promised her that the token should be respected in the hour of danger, and all who took refuge under it be saved.

And when that hour came and Jericho fell with a crash of doom and a shriek of terror; amid all the confusion of that awful day, the falling walls, the shout of Israel's camp, the cries and shrieks from the doomed city, the groans of the dying inhabitants, and the wild excitement of the victorious army rushing in and destroying all before them, that crimson token was not forgotten. That little section of the walls of Jericho with its scarlet banner flying from the ramparts, remained unshaken, and every soldier of the Hebrew camp strictly ordered to respect the signal and to spare the confiding woman and all her household.

Beautiful foreshadowing of the coming gospel and the great redemption through the blood of Christ; proclaiming to the most lost and vile, eternal security from the judgment of God, and amid the wreck of a dissolving world, for all who put their trust in the cross of Calvary and the atoning blood. Beautiful lesson, too, to the consecrated hosts of God; that amid all the victories of faith, and all the higher attainments of the land of promise, they are not to forget as one of their chief concerns, the sinful and the lost, and the blessed and heavenly work of winning them to Jesus and sheltering them beneath His cross.

Nay, the lesson is higher still, for not only was Rahab saved from destruction, but she was received into the very household of Israel and became one of the most honored names in the very ancestry of their kings, and still more, of the very Redeemer Himself. For, when we come to trace the genealogy of the Son of Man, according to the flesh, we find in His wondrous pedigree, not only the illustrious name of David and Abraham, but also, Ruth, the Moabitess, and Rahab, the harlot.

And so, still, God is calling the princes of His kingdom from the very ranks of deepest degradation, saying to the sons and daughters, once of sin and shame, "This is my brother, my sister, and my mother"; and waiting to raise the most helpless of our fallen race to that glorious company who shall yet shine like a cloud of splendor around the throne of heaven, of whom admiring angels will ask, "Who are these, and whence come they!" and the answer shall be, "These are they that came out of great tribulation, and they have washed their robes and made them white in the blood of the Lamb."

The same beautiful lesson is taught still more emphatically in the closing incidents of the Book of Joshua. While it opens with the story of Rahab it concludes with the appointment of the Cities of Refuge, teaching the same lesson in a still more vivid and glorious manner.

These six cities were sat apart in all sections of the land of Canaan, as places of refuge for the manslayer when pursued by the Goel, or avenger of blood. They were within easy approach of every part of the land. Public roads were provided leading directly to them, kept constantly open and in good repair at the expense of the government. Every torrent was bridged, and every obstacle removed; and wherever the crossroads might render the way uncertain, finger posts were erected, opening to the refuge and preventing all possible mistake. Ample provision was made within the city for the supply of all the wants of the fugitive; the gates were ever open, and no weapon was permitted within the enclosure. There the unhappy man could rest in perfect safety until his case was formally adjudicated upon, or until the death of the high priest, when he was free to return to his home in perfect safety, and no one dare molest him. This was not a refuge for willful murderers, but for those who had unintentionally committed manslaughter.

This merciful provision was a significant type of Jesus Christ as the sinner's refuge. He is not the refuge of those who desire to continue in sin, or sinfully reject or disobey Him, but for the abandoned soul that is willing to leave his sin and turn to Him. His mercy is ever open and free. Like the ancient refuge, He is near to the most hopeless and helpless. The way to His feet is ever open and close at hand. There are no barriers across the path; "Whosoever will may come," and come at once and find an instant and gracious welcome, and ample provision for all his future need. Not only so, His own death as our great High Priest has settled all claims against us, and given us a full and eternal freedom from all the charges of the law and the judgment of God on account of our sin.

The very names of these ancient cities were suggestive of the fullness of Christ's provision. Kadesh, the first on the west of the Jordan, signifies "righteousness," and suggests the provision we find in Christ for our complete justification and cleansing. Shechem, the second on the west, literally means a "shoulder," and represents the Almighty strength which Christ supplies to the helpless sinner, and with which He upholds our weakness, and carries us upon His shoulders with all our needs and burdens. Hebron, the third of these cities, means "friendship" and "fellowship," and it tells of the love and communion into which we come when we receive Jesus; not only justified, sanctified and strengthened, but we are loved even as He is loved, and enter into His perfect fellowship and everlasting friendship; finding also in Him the high and holy companionship of His people, and intimacies and mutual bonds and blessings of the household of faith.

Crossing to the east of the Jordan we first come to Bozrah, whose name signifies "security," and is significant of the eternal security into which Christ receives His trusting children, bound to them by His covenant and oath, declaring, "They shall never perish, nor shall any man pluck them out of my hand." Ramoth, midway on the eastern side of Jordan, means "lofty," and it typifies the exalted place of privilege, honor, blessing and progress to which Christ receives us, lifting us up from our degradation, exalting us to share His rights and glories, and calling us on from strength to strength, and from grace to glory. "He hath raised us up together with Him and made us sit with Him in heavenly places in Christ Jesus."

The last of the cities of refuge, Golan, means "a circle," and represents the completeness and eternity of our redemption in Christ. All these together present the sublime picture of the fullness of Jesus as the refuge of the unworthy and the lost. And such a chain of living monuments of the divine mercy in all parts of the land could not fail to afford the most emphatic and continual witness to the gospel of the coming redemption.

So, in our Land of Promise, there should be the constant witness Christ as a Saviour, held up so vividly and so universally that men never can lose sight of it. Not a holiness so cold and inaccessible that poor sinners will feel that it is too high for their attainment, and too hard for their helplessness to reach; but a gospel, holding out to all classes and conditions of sinful men the constant proclamation of a Saviour, as complete and wonderful as these ancient names set forth.

But the very climax of our lesson is seen in the fact that all these cities of refuge were Levitical cities, and were committed wholly to the administration of that class of Israel's officials whom, as we have seen, God appointed as the special types of entire consecration. It was to the Levites' hands that the sinner was committed. It was the Levite who met him with open arms at the open gate, and ushered him into his place of security, and tenderly provided for all his needs; and it teaches us, with singular power, that those who are most fully consecrated are the very ones to whom the master looks to "rescue the perishing, care for the dying," and "snatch them in pity from sin and the grave."

Oh, that every consecrated heart, every circle of professed holiness might be a city of refuge, where poor sinners would know that they would ever find a welcome. This is the service to which Christ is calling His consecrated people. "Lovest thou me?" He still tenderly asks. "Then, feed my lambs, my sheep, and my feeble, wandering ones." Let not only the Spirit, but also the bride say, "Come!" and her tender voice," her beckoning hand, and her gentle face ever seem to echo the inviting call: "Whosoever will, let him take the water of life freely."

A Christian lady had become worn in her life-work and longed for rest. One night she dreamed that she was floating up to the gates of heaven on a crystal sea without a ripple of fear. Just before her were the shining gates and she could see already the forms of the blessed, and hear the distinct echoes of their harps and songs. Her soul was filled with rapture, the anticipation of eternal rest. Eagerly, she pressed forward to reach the heavenly haven. Suddenly, she heard a cry behind her, and looking back she saw a sinking child struggling amid the waves; she turned to rescue it and instantly it seemed that a cord from her heart-strings fell behind her and became a little cable to which the lost one clung as she drew her gently along, feeling at the same time a pang of pain from the pressure of her burden.

A moment later, there was another cry, and lo! a drowning woman was calling for her help, and all around her she now beheld the sinking forms of helpless human beings, all looking to her for rescue. She turned her back upon the glorious city, reached out her hands to the struggling ones, and each in turn fastened to her very heart, by the cords of her own life, a burden of living agony and love. But the burden was more blessed than even the glory which she had just been entering. Lifting up her voice to heaven, she cried, "Father, not yet, I ask no more for rest; a little longer let me suffer and toil for these, and bring them with me when I come, the joy of my heaven will be a hundred fold more because of their salvation."

Yes, this is the purpose of our consecration. Not that we may be happy, nor even that we may be fit for service, and clothed with heavenly love and power, does the Master call us to a consecrated life, in the Land of Promise. "Wherefore we, receiving a kingdom which cannot be moved, let us have grace whereby we may serve God acceptably, with reverence and with godly fear."

"Not now; for I have wanderers in the distance,
 And thou must call them in with patient love;
Not now, for I have sheep upon the mountains,
 And thou must follow them where'er they rove.

"Go with the name of Jesus to the dying,
 And speak that Name in all its living power;
Why should thy fainting heart grow chill and weary?
 Canst thou not watch with Me one little hour?

"One little hour! and then the glorious crowning,
 The golden harp-strings, and the 'victor's palm;
One little hour! and then the hallelujah!
 Eternity's long, deep, thanksgiving psalm!"

CHAPTER IX.

Christ Himself our True Inheritance.

"The Lord is my portion, saith my soul; therefore will I hope in Him." – Lam. 3:24.

THE highest Christian life is not the experience of holiness, or even of the richest gifts and graces of the Holy Spirit, but the life of Christ Himself manifest in our mortal flesh; that complete and perfect union with His person expressed by the apostle in the words, "Ye are dead, and your life is hid with Christ in God; when Christ, who is your life shall appear, then shall ye also appear with Him in glory"; and again, in His own personal testimony, "When it pleased God who separated me from my mother's womb, and called me by His grace to reveal His Son in me," etc.

This is the true substance and supreme inheritance of the Land of Promise. And this is the truth vividly set forth in the Book of Joshua. The very name of Joshua is substantially the same as that of Jesus; and that brave and faithful captain was, no doubt, designed to be the type of the Captain of our salvation, whom God hath set forth as a Leader and Commander to the people. It is He who brings us into the promised land as Moses never could have done. It is He who becomes our victorious Leader in the good fight of faith. It is He who divides to us our inheritance of spiritual blessing.

There are four passages in this remarkable book which set forth very definitely and strikingly the person of Jesus in connection with the experience illustrated in this book.

I. THE PROMISE OF HIS PRESENCE.

The very first assurance of God to His servant, was His own personal presence. This was to be the antidote to every fear and the ground of every confidence. "There shall not a man be able to stand before thee all the days of thy life; as I was with Moses so I will be with thee. Be not afraid, neither be thou dismayed, for the Lord, thy God, is with thee wheresoever thou goest." It was for this that Moses had specially pleaded, and refused the presence of the mightiest angel in comparison. "Wherein shall I and my people be separated from all other people of the earth except in this that thou goest with us." And this was to be the secret of Joshua's success. Indeed, this is the one transcendent promise of the Old Testament and the New.

To Abraham, God's great promise was, "Fear not; I am thy shield and thy exceeding great reward." Abraham did not know anything but God. When he was told to go out from his country he went leaving much behind him, but he had God. So Isaac was driven from place to place by the Philistines, but he, too, had always the promise, "Fear not, for I am with thee and will bless thee."

When Jacob was flying, a fugitive from home and land, God appeared to him saying, "I am with thee, and will keep thee in all places whither thou goest, and will bring thee again unto this land." When Moses hesitated to undertake the great work God had given him, because of his stammering tongue, the word of the Lord that came to him was, "Certainly I will be with thee and with thy mouth." He did not promise to make Moses eloquent and he never did, but he promised to be with him and in that power Moses prevailed.

When Balaam looked over the host of Israel, though greatly longing to curse them, he was compelled to recognize the presence of God with them. "The Lord his God is with him, and the shout of a King is among them."

Caleb, when the heart of the people melted because of the false report of the land, earnestly pleaded with them to go up at once and possess it, saying, "If the Lord be with us we be well able to overcome them."

David's source of comfort in his great trials was the presence of God. It was not a principle nor an idea of Him that possessed him but it was the consciousness of One of whom he could say, "Whom have I in heaven but thee? And there is none upon earth that I desire beside thee."

The prophecies of Isaiah are full of the same precious promise. The coming of the Lord Himself among His people was the constant burden of Isaiah's message. "Fear thou not; for I am with thee; be not dismayed; for I am thy God: I will strengthen thee; yea I will help thee; yea, I will uphold thee with the right hand of my righteousness."

The prophets of the restoration echo the same message. God spoke to Haggai commanding the people to rebuild the temple, and encouraging them in their work with the simple promise, "I am with you, saith the Lord." That was all. Months passed away and there came not another whisper even from Him; yet the people went forward with their work. Then He spoke to Haggai the second time, saying, "Be strong and work; for I am with you, saith the Lord of hosts."

The Old Testament closes with a glorious prophecy of the immediate appearing of the Lord among His people in bodily form, "The Lord, whom ye seek, shall suddenly come to his temple, even the messenger of the covenant, whom ye delight in, behold, He shall come, saith the Lord of hosts."

In the New Testament this promise of the divine presence is repeated with new definiteness and fullness. Jesus talks always about Himself. "Be of good cheer. I have overcome the world." "It is I, be not afraid." "I will love him and manifest myself unto him." "I will not leave you comfortless; I will come to you." "Lo, I am with you always, even unto the end of the world. Go ye therefore and teach all nations." He adds also the presence of the Comforter to these promises. "He dwelleth with you and shall be in you." "He will teach you all things."

There is this difference between the Old and New Testament on this subject. The Old promises God's presence with His people. The New promises His presence in them. Joshua, Moses and David never said the Lord was in them, but always spoke of His presence in them. It is possible in this dispensation to have the very nature of God put into the soul. We may be as closely united to Him as branches are to the vine, so that our brain, our heart, our hands and feet, indeed every part of our being shall feel the presence of God within us. Christ may be so one with us as to put His life into our entire being and influence our volitions, our choices, our desires, and the very affection of our hearts.

In the book of Revelation Jesus is pictured as standing and knocking at the door of the heart asking His children to let Him in; His chief complaint against them, that they are satisfied without Him.

This blessed promise of God's presence runs from the beginning to the end of the Bible. It seems as though there was nothing in the Revelation but God, or in Christianity but Christ. Christian life is just Christ life. The land of promise is the land where Jesus is revealed in all His fullness.

II. JOSHUA'S VISION – CHRIST A MANIFESTED PRESENCE.

Just after they had crossed the Jordan, and before their first conflict with Jericho, the Lord Jesus Himself suddenly appeared to Joshua as a mighty soldier with drawn sword across his path. Instantly, the brave warrior demanded "Art thou for us or for our adversaries?" And the answer prostrated him on his face in veneration and worship. "Nay, but as the captain of the Lord's hosts am I now come."

From this time Joshua understood, as never before, that there ever walked before him and beside him a personal presence, no less than the very Son of God Himself. Joshua was no more to count himself as captain, but to follow his Leader, and to know that where He led it must be victory. He had received the promise of His presence before, but now the Lord came visibly and personally to meet him. So Jacob chose the covenant blessing and stepped out in faith, leaving the land which he knew was to be his. As he lay down to rest at Bethel, Jehovah met him in the silent night. And after that vision at Bethel His presence was henceforth real to him evermore.

Has God thus become manifest to you, beloved? Has the Holy Ghost made the presence of Christ "a living bright reality" to your consciousness? He will reveal Himself to the sincere and seeking heart. You cannot lift up the cry, "I would see Jesus," in vain. The Holy Ghost will make His presence real. Don't be satisfied until you know His appearing.

The apostle John uses two words with reference to the apprehension of Jesus. He sometimes speaks of believing Him, but He often uses the word "know." Do you know Jesus? Has the captain of the Lord's host appeared to you? All through the wilderness Joshua had not seen Him. We must enter the land of promise and cross the Jordan before we can see Jesus.

In California there has been erected upon Mt. Hamilton the most wonderful observatory and telescope in the world. They did not put it down in the valley of San Jose, but away up on the mountain height where there would be no mists or fogs to obstruct the view, but in the clear, transparent light of those upper regions, unclouded views of the celestial world could be obtained. So, dear friends, we must get on the high ground of the land of promise if we would reach the place of heavenly vision. There we shall see Jesus. When Abraham was living his life of human contrivance and unbelief, God did not come to him at once. During the years of his connection with Hagar, and while he was trying to help God fulfill His promises, he never had a sight of God. We cannot see Jesus if we are not in the place of simple faith and obedience.

The effect of seeing Jesus will be the manifestation of His victorious power.

1. It will put your own self-strength out of the way. The spirit of self is never put away until there has come to the soul this vision of Christ. Joshua was thoroughly dead to every evil thing at this time, but he was still conscious of himself. He was to do the work and fight the battles. But God stepped across his path and said, "No, Joshua, it is not your work at all. I am to be leader and do the planning and fight the battles. You must simply follow me." Joshua had to take the position of a servant. This changed the position of things altogether. It altered the very center of his life. When we reach this place, things will be put in their true order. The burden will be upon His shoulder, and we will have no care or struggle.

This is the highest form of spiritual dying – to cease from our own leadership, wisdom, strength and responsibility, and to let the Lord Jesus be made unto us of God, wisdom, righteousness, sanctification, redemption, and all in all. This will prove to us the very secret both of courage and of victory; our enemies do not fear us, but before Him none dare to stand. We may have few associates and feeble resources, but if we have the Lord we must prevail. This was the spectacle that filled Balaam with admiration as he gazed on the tents of Israel. "The Lord, his God, is with him, and the shout of a king is among them." This was the dying shout of Wesley, "The best of all is, God is with us."

When the Duke of Wellington had no reinforcements to send to one of his outnumbered battalions, he galloped to the field himself, accompanied by his staff; and the hard-pressed veterans, as they saw him, shouted, "Here comes the Duke himself – better than a whole brigade." Oh! if we could but realize who it is that goes before us in our hardest places, and the myriads of angelic hosts that await His bidding, how little would we fear our strongest foes, and hope exclaim in triumph in the darkest hour:

> "I fear no foe with thee at hand to bless;
> Earth hath no ills, and tears no bitterness.
> Where is death's sting, where, grave, thy victory?
> I triumph still if thou abide with me."

III. THE LEVITE'S INHERITANCE, OR CHRIST OUR POWER.

We have already seen that the Levites had no portion in the division of the laud among the tribes, and the reason was, that the Lord was their inheritance. If the inheritance of the tribes is expressive of the special gifts and graces of the Spirit, or of the blessings of God's grace and providence, then the special inheritance of the Levites must imply that God Himself is better than any or all of His gifts. Especially is this truth connected with the idea of service, of which the Levites were the expression.

Christ Himself is our strength and wisdom for all the service for which He calls us. He does not require us to supply the resources for our Christian work from our own talents, or strength, or qualifications, but, in absolute dependence upon Himself. He bids the weakest go forth and accept Him, to use their helplessness, and through His strength, make it effectual to the pulling down of strongholds.

Therefore, we read again and again, that "God hath chosen, by an actual preference the weak things of this world to confound the wise, and base things, and things that are despised, hath He chosen, yea, and things that are not, to bring to nought things that are." He used the rod of Moses to humiliate the pride of Pharaoh, simply because He was behind it. He used the ram horns of Israel to beat down the walls of Jericho, simply because He followed up the faith and obedience of His people. He could not use Gideon's thirty thousand until they were reduced to three hundred, and weak enough for God to be glorified in the victory. David's sling was stronger than Goliath's sword because it was used in the name of the Lord.

Five barley loaves and two small fishes were sufficient for five thousand when Jesus blessed them, and so the humblest laborers and the most limited resources have usually been honored of God in the accomplishment of the greatest results in His work. Consecrated faith, humility, and earnestness, are mightier weapons in the aggressive work of Christianity, than human learning and magnificent religious forms.

If we would be true Levites, and are but willing to let the Master use us, we may find in Himself and the indwelling fullness of His Holy Spirit, all the resources of faith, wisdom, love and power, which our work requires. The baptism of the Holy Ghost includes every quality essential for spiritual power – the faith that claims divine results, the power of prayer, by far the mightiest of spiritual forces, the love which will win the lost, the tact and wisdom that will speak the word in season, or do the fit act in the appropriate time, or stand still when God is more glorified by our silence than by our officiousness.

The history and condition of Christianity today teems with illustrations of the marvelous usefulness which God can give the humblest instrumentalities that are wholly consecrated to the glory of Christ, and baptized with His spirit and fullness.

IV. TIMNATH-SERAH, OR CHRIST OUR PORTION.

This word means, literally, the City of the Sun. It may well denote the spiritual inheritance of which Christ

Himself is the substance and the glory. "I am the light of the world," the Lord Jesus has said "he that followeth me shall not abide in darkness, but shall have the light of life." "If we walk in the light, as He is in the light, we have fellowship one with the other, and the blood of Jesus Christ, His Son, cleanseth us from all sin." This is the city of the sun; the life of intimate and unclouded fellowship with the Lord Jesus Christ. Glorious things are spoken of this city of God.

1. It is an abode of delightful happiness. "Happy are the people that know the joyful sound; they shall walk, O Lord, in the light of thy countenance; in thy name shall they rejoice all the day." "For with thee is the fountain of light; in thy light shall we see light." "In thy presence there is fullness of joy, and at thy right hand there are pleasures forevermore."

2. It is a place of abundant grace. "For the Lord is a sun and shield; He will give grace and glory, and no good thing will He withhold from them that walk uprightly." Here are found, as in some sunny land of boundless fruitage and luxuriance, all the rich and abundant fruits of the Tree of Life; grace so rich and full that it sometimes rises even to the heights of glory, as through the rent vail the brightness of the inner chamber streams around us, even in the earthly sanctuary. They who dwell in this happy city have all things that divine love and wisdom can bestow.

"No good thing will He withhold from them that walk uprightly." "My God shall supply an your need according to His riches in glory by Christ Jesus." This is not only the riches of grace, but He draws even upon the reserve fund laid by in heaven, and grants according to the riches of His glory, for Jesus said, "The glory that thou hast given me I have given them."

3. They who dwell in the city of the sun enjoy the constant manifestation of the presence of Jesus. The King is among them and His presence is constantly manifested, for He has said, "If a man keep my words, I

will manifest myself unto him." And the word manifest means literally, "I will shine forth gloriously" unto him.

4. The city of the sun is a place of healing, and they who dwell in this favored abode enjoy immunity from the over-mastering physical evils of life. "For unto you that fear my name shall the Sun of Righteousness arise with healing in His wings, and ye shall go forth and grow up as calves of the stall." Even physical light is healing, but the light of Jesus and the life of Jesus are the very strength of our physical vitality; and they who abide with Him "renew their strength, shall mount up as with wings of eagles, run and not be weary, walk and not faint."

5. The city of the sun is a place of delightful guidance. "He that followeth me shall not walk in darkness, but shall have the light of life; he that walketh in darkness stumbleth, for he knoweth not whither he goeth." They who thus abide with Christ have the delightful sense of His constant direction and walk in His personal guidance, in the sound of His voice, and the print of His footsteps.

6. This is an abode of unclouded and everlasting light and blessedness. "Their sun shall no more go down, nor shall their moon withdraw itself, but the Lord shall be their everlasting life, and the days of their mourning shall be ended." True, they are not free from the trials and temptations of earth, but they have learned the secret of rising above them and dwelling in the light of a higher sphere.

There is an altitude where no cloud can reach us and no mist obscure our everlasting sunshine; and for those who have risen with Christ, "the way of life is above, to depart from hell beneath." The sorrows are still there, but we are looking at them from the throne, where we already sit with our victorious Christ. There is a fellowship with Jesus even on earth that need never be interrupted; a sunlight that need never be withdrawn; a peace that need never be broken by a ripple of unrest: and there are souls on earth that walk in everlasting light, their feet treading the troubled waves, their forms often lost to sight amid the clouds that encompass them, but their heads ever in the unclouded light of the everlasting sunshine.

Have we entered into this delightful abode? Have we claimed our citizenship in Timnath-serah? Can we sing with the psalmist, "The Lord is my light and my salvation; whom shall I fear; the Lord is the strength of my life, of whom shall I be afraid?"

The only secret of it is, to seek and find our all in God. Joshua's inheritance may have had nothing else, but it had infinite sunshine. The land may have been barren, the springs may have been dry, the houses may have been humble, the revenues may have been small, but he had the sun, the whole sun, the sun in unclouded and unceasing effulgence and glory; and when we are satisfied with the smiles of His face, the light of His love, and do not look so much to our surroundings, or even our spiritual emotions and conditions, as to His unceasing presence, we, too, shall find that life has risen above its most trying variations, and that we have reached a country which might also be called, like the strange day of northern Norway, "The Land of the Midnight Sun."

I have seen Christians who were living in the land of the midnight sun, tranquil and happy in the light of Him who was more to them than their surroundings. They are like the martyr Cyprian who, when asked to recant or his fortune would be taken from him, replied, "You cannot do that, for my treasure is laid up in heaven." Then he was threatened with separation from all his friends. The noble hero replied, "You cannot do that either, for my affections are placed on things above where Christ sitteth at the right hand of God." "Then," replied his persecutors, "we will take your life." Cyprian answered, "That, too, is beyond your reach, for I am dead and my life is hid with Christ in God."

Let us get into the city that is above the clouds, and the land whose sun no more goes down and the song that echoes the loudest in the night of sorrow, will be our refrain.

"I've found a joy in sorrow,
  A secret balm for pain,
A beautiful tomorrow
  Of sunshine after rain.

"I've found a branch for healing,
  Near every bitter spring,
A whispered promise stealing
  O'er every broken string.

"I've found a glad hosanna
  For every woe and wail,
A handful of sweet manna
  When grapes of Eschol fail.

I've found the Rock of Ages,
  When desert wells are dry;
And after weary stages,
  I've found an Elim nigh.

An Elim with its coolness,
  Its fountains and its shade;
A blessing in its fullness,
  When buds of promise fade.

"O'er tears of soft contrition
  I've seen a rainbow light;
A glory and fruition
  So near! yet out of sight.

"'Tis Jesus, my portion forever,
  'Tis Jesus, the First and the Last,
A help very present in trouble,
  A shelter from every blast."

To those who set their hearts thus supremely on Him, He reveals, in all its fullness, the light and glory of His presence. And can we look even at yonder material sun with its dazzling glory, and realize that God has filled it with its fire, and kept it burning and shining for many thousand years, and not feel that He who did so much for a mere material ball will do far more for the soul that Christ redeemed, and in which he has actually come to dwell?

Let us open all the windows of our being and receive Him with that confidence which is the condition of His manifested love and presence. And receiving Him with a surrendered and trusting heart, let us go forth to walk in His light, and so shine, in His reflected glory, that "others shall see our good works and glorify our Father which is in heaven."

The gospel which the world needs most, is not a new creed, but a new life; not new truths, but new and living realities; not better ideas, but more strength to fulfill them. The only way to make this real to the men around us, is to live it; yet, not so to live it that they shall see our character, but rather so that they shall see Christ behind us, and reflected through us, in so definite and personal a manner that it will become to them also a possibility, for their discouraged and failing lives.

Merely to see our excellencies might only discourage them by the contrast with themselves, but to see behind us, as the inspiration and support of all our victories, the real and all-sufficient presence of One who is just as willing to become for them the source of strength and constant health; to hear us say, "I am conscious of being as weak and helpless as my brethren, and yet I can do all things through Christ who strengtheneth me," this is indeed a living gospel and will lead them to hunger and thirst until they find their rest and satisfaction in Jesus for themselves.

God does not want temples of stone, or even of gold, from which to reflect His glory, but, like the ancient prince, in the oriental fable, who built a temple for the sun, He wants His sanctuary of transparent glass so that He can shine into every part, and our glory be that we are ourselves invisible, and our only mission is to receive, transmit, and reflect, the light of His glory and grace. Thus, each of us can be in ourselves a Timnath-serah, and as the world beholds us, it will say, "Come ye and let us walk in the light of the Lord."

Have we this blessed presence? We cannot seek it in vain. He who cannot lie, has said, "I will not leave you comfortless – I will come to you." O, let us claim the promise with a persistent faith, that like wrestling Jacob will not let Him go except He bless us. It is said that one of the Scottish pastors of Covenanting times was slow in coming to his pulpit, one day, and the sexton was sent to the vestry to enquire. He returned, saying, "I fear he winna come the day, for I aye heard him speakin' to One and saying he wadna come withoot Him; and when I left the other hadna spoken a word, and so I fear he willna come this morn." Yes, that is the way these men were mighty through God to the pulling down of strongholds.

Still, as at Emmaus, He often makes as though He would pass by. But let us constrain Him. He only waits your whole soul's invitation. O, beloved, let Him in. He is the Land of Promise, He is the Sun of Timnath-serah, and the Light and Glory of the City that has no need of the Sun.

"Christ to trust and Christ to know
Constitute our bliss below;
Christ to see and Christ to love
Constitute our bliss above."

CHAPTER X.

The Danger of Declension.

"Now the just shall live by faith; but if any man draw back, my soul shall have no pleasure in him. But we are not of them who draw back unto perdition, but of them that believe to the saving of the soul." – Heb. 10:38.

"Take heed, brethren, lest there be in any of you an evil heart of unbelief, in departing from the living God." – Heb. 3:12.

"And the people served the Lord all the days of Joshua and all the days of the elders that outlived Joshua, that had seen all the great works of the Lord that he did for Israel. And there arose another generation after them which knew not the Lord, nor yet the works which He had done for Israel. And the children of Israel did evil in the sight of the Lord, and served Baalim. And they forsook the Lord God of their fathers, which brought them out of the land of Egypt, and followed other gods, of the gods of the people that were around about them, and bowed themselves unto them, and provoked the Lord to anger. And the anger of the Lord was hot against Israel, and he delivered them into the hands of the spoilers that spoiled them, and he sold them into the hands of their enemies round about, so that they could not any longer stand before their eneroies." – Jdg. 2:7-14.

SUCH is the sad story of Israel's declension. It is all the more sad because it follows the wonders and triumphs of the Book of Joshua. It is far more sad even than the earlier record of their failure in the Book of Numbers. Israel's unbelief in the wilderness was not so aggravated, nor so long and bitter in its effects, as Israel's declension after entering the Land of Promise. The first arrested their progress for a generation, but the second plunged them for four hundred years into bondage, misery and shame. And so there is a backsliding in Christian life after conversion, and before entire consecration, which leads to much loss and sorrow, and retards the progress of the soul, often for many years.

But there is another backsliding, after the experience of consecration and the baptism of the Holy Spirit, which is far more inexcusable, and leads to more terrible consequences. It would seem to be against this that the warnings of the Epistle to the Hebrews are specially directed. The teaching of the Book of Joshua, and especially of the Book of Judges, seems to make it certain that such a declension is indeed possible.

After all the divine manifestations of Joshua's life and leadership, after all the victories of Jericho, Beth-horon and Merom, after all the kings of Canaan had been subdued, and their land divided into Israel's inheritance, and notwithstanding Joshua's parting charges at Shechem, Israel went back, in the third generation, into idolatry and sin, forsook the covenant of their God, became subject to the tribes that they had formerly subdued, and were overrun by foreign invaders, placed under tribute to all the surrounding nations, and reduced to a condition of such pitiful humiliation and helplessness, that, in the days of Saul, they were not even permitted to have a grindstone to whet their very ploughshares, lest it should be used to sharpen their swords for war. The Book of Judges is a melancholy picture of their degradation and well-nigh apostasy.

A picture as sad, and almost perfectly parallel, can be found in the story of primitive Christianity. The apostolic age of the church was marked by faith as bold, obedience as implicit, and victory as splendid as the conquest of Joshua. But, alas! before the third generation had come, the spirit of declension had already appeared, and another and darker period of idolatry in the very church of God. Conformity to the spirit of the world, and humiliating failure in the conflict with sin and Satan filled up more than thrice four hundred years of the dark ages of mediæval Christianity, until the very church seemed to have become apostate; and, like Deborah, Barak, Gideon, Samson and Jephthah, only a little remnant of faithful ones could be found here and there in the whole Christian world.

And, in like manner, it is to be feared that there are many examples in individual Christian life of promising beginnings in the life of consecration, sealed it may have been by the most real and glorious manifestations of the divine presence, grace and power, that have afterwards been followed, through lack of vigilance and holy obedience, by gross error, spiritual declension, soul deceiving sin, and even open disobedience, worldliness, weakness, and what seemed to threaten even final apostasy.

Thanks to the infinite mercy of God, the resources of God's grace and discipline are sufficient for the restoration of even such a soul. But the danger is not less real or the warning less solemn and emphatic. Therefore, we find the New Testament epistles, where they speak of the very highest possibilities of Christian experience, most urgently warning the believer against the danger of backsliding, calling us to ceaseless vigilance and constant obedience. Even where God's eternal faithfulness is most securely pledged to keep us, we are called upon all the more to exercise a spirit of watchfulness and constant dependence on His all-sufficient grace.

Hence, we find John saying in one breath, "The anointing which ye have received of Him abideth in you," and yet, in the next, "Now, little children, abide in Him." We find Jude pointing us to Him that is able to keep us from falling, and yet enjoining us to "keep ourselves in the love of God, looking for the mercy of our Lord Jesus Christ, unto eternal life."

We find Peter saying, "The Lord knoweth how to deliver the godly out of temptations," but adding in the same epistle, "Beloved, beware lest ye also be led away with the error of the wicked and fall from your own steadfastness," and again assuring us that "His divine power hath given us all things that pertain to life and godliness," but also charging us to give diligence, to make our calling and election sure, "for if we do these things, we shall never fall."

We find the epistle of the Hebrews, most solemnly of all, flashing before us the terrific picture of a soul once enlightened, and tasting of the heavenly gift, and then becoming so apostate as to put the Son of God to an open shame; and yet adding immediately, "we are persuaded better things of you, and things that accompany salvation, though we thus speak," and then adding, "to keep the balance of hope and fear perfectly adjusted." "We desire that everyone of you do show the same diligence to the full assurance of hope to the end."

So, again, in the tenth chapter, the fearful picture of the soul that hath "trodden under foot the Son of God, and hath counted the blood, wherewith he was sanctified a common thing and hath done despite unto the Spirit of grace," is accompanied by the warning, "If any man draw back, my soul shall have no pleasure in him," but the gracious encouragement is added, "But we are not of them that draw back unto perdition, but of them that believe to the saving of the soul."

The same striking antithesis of warning and promise runs throughout Paul's epistles. His letter to the Ephesians lifts us up to the heavenly places, but it also looks down into the deep gulf below and warns us, as no other epistle, against the real danger of ungodliness, uncleanliness, untruthfulness, dishonesty, sinful anger, strife, covetousness, drunkenness, and all the wiles of the devil.

And while Paul can exclaim, in the language of the sublimest confidence, "I know whom I have believed, and I am persuaded that He is able to keep what I have committed to Him, against that day;" yet, he also charges Timothy in the same epistle, "That good thing that was committed unto thee keep by the Holy Ghost that dwelleth in thee." "Watch thou in all things, endure afflictions, do the work of an evangelist, make full proof of thy ministry." With what fine effect these two sides of this holy teaching are set over against each other in his letter to the Corinthians. On the one hand there is the touch of caution, "Wherefore let him that thinketh he standeth take heed lest he fall." But lest this should be too strong it is followed by the word of assurance, "God is faithful and will not suffer you to be tempted above that ye are able; but will with the temptation also make a way to escape, that ye may be able to bear it." And then the balance is made complete by the final word of gentle warning, "Wherefore, my dearly beloved, flee from idolatry." There is no discouragement, but there is no presumption; the danger is real, but the security is ample; not, however, for blind, presuming rashness, but for watchful, humble, holy, and persevering obedience.

We find the same spirit of mingled warning and encouragement in all the teachings of the great Master. "My sheep," He says, "shall never perish, nor shall any man pluck them out of my hand;" but just as truly does He also teach, "My sheep hear my voice, and they follow me." Again He exclaims, "Ye have not chosen me, but I have chosen you and ordained you that ye should go and bring forth fruit, and that your fruit should remain." Surely no promise could be stronger, and no purpose more steadfast, yet in this very connection we have the tender admonition, "Abide in Me and I in you." "If ye keep My commandments ye shall abide in My love." "If a man abide not in Me, he is cast forth as a branch and is withered, and men do gather them and cast them into the fire, and they are burned."

When the pilgrims were introduced to the "Palace Beautiful," the interpreter showed them many beautiful pictures, some full of alluring loveliness and transporting hope, some full of dark and awful warning. On the one side were the visions of grace and glory, on the other the prisoner of despair in the iron cage, and the awful dream of the judgment day. And, as Christian came forth he said to his kind interpreter, "These things make me both hope and fear."

So God still teaches us. The Bible is no system or cast-iron dogmas, but the wise, firm and gentle hand of a loving teacher and guide; adjusting its messages to our situation and condition, whether of depression or false security. If in an attitude of willful disobedience, it has no absolute promise of unconditional security, but words of stern and terrible awakening and warning; but for humble trust and watchful obedience it has nothing but encouragement and the assurance of God's everlasting faithfulness and love.

It speaks to us, therefore, in many tones and from many standpoints, and is indeed "profitable for doctrine, for reproof, for correction, and for instruction in righteousness; that the man of God may be perfect, thoroughly furnished unto all good works."

There is, then, real danger of declension, even on the part of a consecrated Christian, should he for one moment become separated from Christ, or relax His vigilance and constant dependence. Sanctification is not a state of infallible holiness, but a place of dependence upon Christ and abiding communion with Him. "He that abideth in Him sinneth not," but "apart from Me ye can do nothing." And the strongest saint will, like Simon Peter, make the most desperate failure whenever he trusts his own strength, or attempts to stand alone.

Indeed, we are never truly safe till, like Peter, we have learned our constant danger and our need of Jesus every moment. Nor let us forget that declension after consecration would be for us a fearful thing. The most terrific delusions of the world's history have usually originated with those who have had much light before.

And failure, after all that the Lord has brought us into, would be utterly sad and unutterably disastrous.

Beloved, let us abide in Him; let us put on the whole armor of God, that we may stand against the wiles of the devil; let us adhere faithfully to His holy Word, and walk in obedience to all His commandments; and above all, let us depend implicitly upon His keeping, fearing to take one step alone. We fear not while He holds our hand and leads us safely in the most difficult paths, and make us "walk upon our high places."

II. THE CAUSES OF ISRAEL'S DECLENSION.

1. The first of these seems to have been a superficial experience and knowledge of God. The language in which their declension is introduced implies that much of their piety arose from the influence of Joshua and the generation that had accompanied him, and that, when he and they had passed from the stage, the nation returned to its deeper and truer spirit, and simply manifested the disposition that had been there before, but had been kept in check by the predominant influence of others.

There are many persons whose religious condition is a reflection of the influence of others, to a far greater extent than they dream. Like young Joash, who served the Lord during all the days of his godly adopted father Jehoiada, but who immediately turned back to evil when he was gone, so they manifest much sympathetic goodness under the influence of favorite teachers, and in seasons of deep religious excitement may even seem to pass through a real experience of spiritual life, with its accompanying emotions, and many of its fruits; but it is possible that much of this may be seated in the emotions, and may be the result of influence and feeling rather than radical conviction and transformation of character.

The test will come to such souls, when these favorable influences are withdrawn, when they are no longer pressed forward by stronger spirits, and upheld by helpful surroundings, but are met by opposition, misunderstanding, persecution, perhaps, and uncongenial associations of every kind. Then it will appear whether this purpose is rooted in God, and their spirit truly united with a living Christ, and abiding in Him as the source and strength of life and holiness. If this be so, they will continue even amid isolation and opposition, to stand steadfast to the truth and will of God, and, like Jeremiah's picture of the man that trusts in the Lord, and whose help the Lord is, "They shall be like a tree planted by the waters, and that spreadeth out her roots by the river, and shall not see when heat cometh, but her leaf shall be green; and shall not be careful in the year of drought, neither shall cease from yielding fruit."

The secret of Joshua's victory was that he had long before learned to stand alone; when the faithless spies, and the whole congregation refused to follow and even threatened to destroy him, with his solitary companion he stood steadfast to God and principle; and therefore, when the multitude afterwards followed, his purpose was not affected by their favor or faithlessness, but he could look them in the face and say, "Choose ye this day whom ye will serve, but as for me and my house, we will serve the Lord."

This must be the secret of steadfastness in every consecrated life. Dear brother, you must know the truth for yourself and commit yourself to it even if you have to stand alone. You must be so persuaded of it that you cannot surrender it even if you die. And you must so know the Lord, for yourself, and not for another, that even if all the Christians in the world should fail, you could still stand exclaiming, "Christ is true, and Christ is mine, and I know Him whom I have believed."

If you have thus learned Christ the presence or the absence of people will not affect your life and testimony. Men may come and men may go, but you will go on forever. You will be able to say, like the heroic men of Babylon, "O king, we are not careful to answer thee in this matter; if it be so, our God is able to deliver us out of the burning fiery furnace, and He will deliver us out of thy hand, O king; but if not, we will not serve thy gods, or worship the golden image which thou hast set up."

2. The second cause of Israel's declension was their failure to do thorough work, especially in separating from and exterminating their enemies. We read in the beginning of the Book of Judges of many of the tribes of Canaan whom they should have thoroughly subjugated, that the children of Judah could not drive out the inhabitants of the valley. 1:19; and that the children of Benjamin did not drive out the Jebusites that inhabited Jerusalem. 1:21; nor did Manasseh drive out the inhabitants of Beth-shean and her towns, but the Canaanites would dwell in the land; verse 27; nor did Ephraim drive out the Canaanites in Gezer, but Canaanites dwelt in Gezer among them, and so of many of the other tribes. Not only so, but Israel, in some cases, put the Canaanites to tribute, chapter 1:28-30: making it even a profitable business, and a source of income, to have them remain, when the Lord had commanded their utter extermination.

And still worse, we find them even entering into forbidden alliances with them, and also intermarrying among their sons and daughters. Chapter 3:5-6. God's command to them had been, "Thou shalt make no covenant with the inhabitants of this land, thou shalt throw down their altars; thou shalt smite them and utterly destroy them; thou shalt make no covenant with them, nor show mercy unto them, nor shalt thou make marriages with them; thy daughter thou shalt not give unto his son, nor his daughter shalt thou take unto thy son." Deut. 7:2-3.

But here we read "the children of Israel dwelt among the Canaanites, Hittites, Amorites, Perizzites, Hivites, and Jebusites; and they took their daughters to be their wives; and they gave their daughters to their sons, and they served their gods." Israel had become content with the victories which had subdued their more formidable foes, and given them the chief strongholds of the land, but in a thousand little places the enemy still lurked and lingered, and gradually became tolerated. The danger of their continuance did not seem very great and the trouble and cost of their extermination was greater than the courage and patience of Israel. Thus they were suffered to remain, half conquered, and for the time, wholly subordinate. In a little while it became a source of profit to collect tribute from these bold giants, and so, many of them were made tributary to Israel, contrary to the divine command.

A little later, relations of friendship and fellowship began to be established, and before long, they were intermarrying with the tribes of Israel and raising a mongrel race in which the true seed would soon be wholly extinguished; and to crown all they naturally began to serve the idols of their heathen friends, and to mingle in all the abominations of their unholy religion; thus becoming in the end, really apostate from the worship of the true God altogether.

This is the sad story of the development of evil in many a life, which once seemed wholly consecrated. Little sins are left unsubdued. Like Saul, they destroy the Amalekites but spare Agag, their king, for some good purpose, as they suppose, and keep the best of the spoil with the idea that they are going to sacrifice it unto the Lord. They have not the courage to deal bravely and firmly with evil. After a while they begin to turn it to profitable account, and tolerate certain forms of sin and worldliness because of advantage. Their business interests would be ruined by too rigid a conscientiousness, for some of their investments are not wholly separated from forbidden associations; the profits, at least, will be divided with the Lord, and the end will sanctify the means. A thousand specious and plausible excuses are made for things that ought to be thoroughly put aside, and which, like the Canaanites, they put under tribute, and try to justify because of some advantage that can be brought out of them.

By-and-by, the social element is introduced. Families that were separated from unholy friendships and ungodly alliances, become mixed with the world in the social reception, the promiscuous dance, or perhaps in the milder form of the church entertainment. If the old people still retain their separation, yet they let their sons and daughters mingle with the Canaanites; and they do not shrink from even permitting the marriage of a Christian girl with the godless man, or receiving into this consecrated home, as the bride of a son, devoted in infancy to God, some bright and fascinating daughter of fashion; who soon succeeds in subverting all the separation to God that has been left, until it is not far now to the last step of the worship of idolatry, the unrestrained career of worldly amusement, covetousness which is idolatry, and the carnival of godless selfishness and pleasure.

Dr. Livingstone tells of a singular creature which he found in Africa, called the ant-lion. It attacked and destroyed the strongest victims by a master piece of strategy. Excavating a little pit in the dry sand, in the form of an inverted cone, running to a point at the bottom, it sits down at the base of its little pitfall and waits for some unsuspecting beetle or insect to tread too near the edge of the crumbling sand. The unhappy victim at last approaches, and perhaps, prompted by curiosity, looks over the edge of this strange excavation, and lo! in a moment he has lost his balance and rolls down the side of the little pit where the ant-lion waits for his prey.

Not, however, directly and instantly does the destroyer attack his victim; this might be too unequal a contest for the little strategist, but he suddenly opens his sharp little mouth, formed like a pair of powerful scissors, and with one quick movement he cuts off a limb from the unsuspecting victim, and then disappears out of sight.

Slowly the mutilated creature recovers itself and climbs up the slippery side of the pit; but just as he reaches the summit his footing slips again and he tumbles once more into the jaws of the little monster. Another quick movement, and another limb is gone; and again the wounded insect gathers up his remaining strength and makes another ascent of the side of this death-trap, but the result is the same as before; again he sinks to receive a fresh blow, and the process is repeated until at length he is so dismembered that he has not strength enough even to attempt to escape, but sinks, a bleeding, suffering mass, into the hands of his enemy, who devours at leisure the antagonist that he would not have dared to approach directly.

This, alas! is the story of many a defeated and ruined life. Some little adversary that was not even dreaded, has been the final destroyer, not by one bold attack, but by a thousand little wounds that at last have left the victim helpless to resist or return. Saul's career is a sad example of a noble beginning, ending in mournful disaster; and the saddest part of it is the very smallness of the cause where the pathway of declension and ruin began. It was simply in this very thing of refusing to deal firmly with the enemies of God. The reason of his failure was because of his deeper fear to deal firmly with the sin and self-will of his own heart.

Saul's failure to slay Agag, and his soft dealings with the Amalekite chief, were but the outward type of his tolerance of a greater giant in his own heart, even his own self-will, and the spirit of disobedience which, Samuel tells him, was expressed by his conduct in this case, and was the ground of his rejection, and the secret of his final ruin. But not all at once did Saul go down; for nearly ten years did he sit still upon Israel's throne and work out the dreadful proceeds of sin's development, leading from step to step, until at last a branded murderer, a slave of blind and furious passion, and an awful instrument of Satan's very possession, he closes his wretched life in tragedy almost as dark as the story of Judas.

Oh! let us beware how we tolerate a single sin, how we leave an enemy in the land, how we make terms with any forbidden thing, how we enter into alliances with the world, or let its spirit touch our fondest affections. "We cannot serve God and Mammon." We cannot compromise with any evil thing and remain in the Land of Promise. We cannot abide in His love without keeping His commandments. "Wherefore come ye out from among them and be ye separate, saith the Lord, and touch not the unclean thing; and I will receive you, and ye shall be my sons and daughters, saith the Lord Almighty."

CHAPTER XI.

THE CHURCH'S INHERITANCE.

"And Jesus came and spake unto them, saying, All power is given unto me in heaven and in earth. Go ye therefore and teach all nations, baptizing them in the name of the Father, and of the Son and of the Holy Ghost: Teaching them to observe all things whatsoever I have coromanded you; and lo, I am with you alway, even unto the end of the world. Amen." – Matt. 28:19-20.

THE whole story of the Book of Joshua may be applied, in a broader sense, to the people of God collectively, and especially to the New Testament church. In an important sense the whole body of Christians may be called the spiritual Israel. And the history of God's ancient people is full of interesting parallels and lessons for us, even if they may not be exact types in this respect.

1. The failure of Israel to enter into the land of promise through unbelief, had its parallel in the rejection of Christ by His own countrymen, and the consequent rejection of the Jewish people from the privileges of the Gospel. But, as for ancient Israel, there was still a period of probation and long-suffering, which lasted for forty years, affording individuals the opportunity of entering into the spiritual blessings of God's covenant, so there intervened a similar period after Christ's rejection by His own people, before the final destruction of Jerusalem, and the dispersion of the Jews. And as there were some of even the first generation of Israel who believed, so there were exceptions in the ministry of Christ and His disciples, from among even that unbelieving nation, who gladly

accepted their Messiah, and entered into their spiritual inheritance.

2. The glorious career of Joshua, the crossing of the Jordan, the conquest of Canaan, and the dividing of the inheritance among the tribes of Israel, finds its striking parallel likewise, in the death and resurrection of Jesus, the descent of the Holy Ghost, at Pentecost, and the triumphs of Christianity, when the church, to a very great extent, claimed her inheritance of power, purity, and blessing, and entered upon the conquest of the world for Christ, until there was scarcely a region of the globe where the gospel was not at least planted, and the strongholds of Satan challenged and shaken. The crossing of the Jordan may well illustrate the cross of Calvary, and the experience of death and resurrection which was so emphasized in primitive Christianity. The new covenant has its counterpart in the coming of the Holy Ghost, and the gospel of full and free salvation.

The death of Moses and the advent of Joshua, whose very name is suggestive of Jesus, suggest the transition which then actually came, from the law to the gospel. The victories of Canaan had their counterpart in the triumphs of primitive Christianity. The dividing of the inheritance foreshadowed the various gifts of the Holy Ghost distributed to the church.

The supernatural element which runs through the entire story of the conquest of Palestine, was more than realized in the first centuries of Christianity in the manifestations of the divine presence and power, in signs and wonders and mighty deeds. And the choice possessions won by Caleb, Othniel, Achsah, and others, remind us of the transcendent examples of piety, faith, love, knowledge, and holy power and usefulness, which adorned the annals of the early church.

3. The failure of Israel to enter promptly and fully into their whole inheritance, also finds its counterpart in the church of the New Testament. With all its fresh beauty

and divine glory, still there was much of human imperfection and melancholy failure.

The old cry, "There remaineth much land yet to be possessed," "How long are ye slack to go up and possess all the land which the Lord your God has given you," is echoed back in more than one of Paul's sorrowful admonitions to the churches he loved; and still more strongly in the appeals and warnings of the Son of God to the seven churches of Asia, through the last messages of the Holy Ghost, sixty years after His ascension. There we find Him saying to the strongest of these churches, "I have somewhat against thee, that thou hast left thy first love. Therefore be watchful and strengthen the things that remain that are ready to die, for I have not found thy works perfect before God." And to another, "Thou hast a name that thou livest, and art dead." And yet again, thou sayest, "I am rich and increased with goods, and have need of nothing, and knowest not that thou art wretched, and poor, and miserable, and blind, and naked."

Already, even in the lifetime of Paul and John, the primitive church had allied itself sufficiently with the world to open the door for many of the errors which afterward entered and overwhelmed the purity of the early church.

4. The fearful declension of ancient Israel, leading ere long to the dark chapter of the Book of Judges, and their shameful compromise with the heathen world and subjugation to its power, is more than paralleled in the story of the dark ages of mediæval Christianity, through the same causes, namely, the failure of God's people to separate themselves from sin and worldliness, and to enter into their full inheritance. The purity and strength of apostolic Christianity were speedily lost in the unspeakable corruptions of an apostate church, with all the errors and abominations of that anti-christian system which took the place of the Church of God for twelve hundred years, and has been well called a "baptized heathenism."

Many of the pictures of the Book of Judges might find a vivid counterpart in the story of the middle ages. The graphic picture of Micah and his mother, with its strange intermingling of dishonesty, religion and ritualism, almost seems like a parable of much of the religious life of such a period, and, indeed, is not without its parallels in our own day. Like Micah's sanctuary, many a church has been built out of ill-gotten gains, and, like Micah himself, many a formalist has folded his arms in the midst of violence and sin, and said, "Now I know the Lord will do me good, seeing I have a Levite to be my priest."

Notwithstanding this there were many exceptions in ancient Israel – a wise and patriotic Deborah, a brave and faithful Barak, a divinely-called Gideon, a single-hearted Jephthah, and a mighty Samson. And, so, even in the darkest ages of Christianity, there have not been wanting those who had not defiled their garments, and who, at times, dared to rise up for God against those that did wickedly, and shed a divine luster on their times and names. Such were the noble army of the martyrs, and confessors – a Waldo, a Wycliffe, a Huss, a Savonarola, a Bernard and a Bede.

At length the time of reformation came to ancient Israel, when Samuel, the prophet, arose to recall his people to their ancient faith, and prepare them for the coming kingdom. Such a ministry in our own time was that of Luther and the Reformation, calling back the church of God to her ancient faith, and arousing her to claim her lost inheritance. But, as even Samuel's mighty work was in a measure ineffectual, and was followed for a time by the counterfeit kingdom of Saul, and the false and worldly aims of his countrymen, which led them into a separation from God that left its effects for half a century, so even the revived Christianity of the Reformation has not been perfect; and, like ancient Israel, the church, delivered from her immediate foe, has given herself up, to a great degree, to a spirit of worldliness, and to look for her kingdom in a forbidden world. There is much today of the spirit of Saul in nominal Christianity; the pride that finds its satisfaction in earthly gifts, talents and successes, and fails to recognize the true King, who, like the rejected David, waits for His throne as the "despised and rejected of men."

The kingdom of David seems to prefigure the true triumphs of our coming King, and the ushering in of His dominion in the final victory of Christianity.

5. The peaceful and splendid throne of Solomon completes the picture of the millennial glory which is to be the consummation of the Christian age.

Then will come the full inheritance of grace and glory, both for God's ancient people and the church and the bride of the Lamb.

What, then, for us, in the church of God today, is the teaching of this ancient book?

1. It summons her to her glorious crusade of conquest against the enemies of Christ. Never was there an age more full of encouragement for the good fight of faith and the conquest of the world for Christ. The whole land is before us; every avenue of influence at home, and every missionary field abroad, is open for the church's zeal and holy enterprise. The triumphs of the gospel in the past fifty years have not been unworthy of comparison with Pentecost, or even with Joshua's campaigns. True, it has been but a small section of the nominal church that has dared to claim these victories, but the recompense has been sufficient to call forth far higher achievements and aspirations.

Especially should the near prospect of the coming kingdom arouse us to go forth and win for our glorious Captain the crown of all the world, until every citadel of heathendom, and every stronghold of sin, shall have become a monument of His grace and power.

More emphatically still, let the tender lesson of Rahab in the beginning, and the Cities of Refuge at the close, remind us that our supreme conflict is for the souls of sinful men. And beyond all the questions of dogmas, and the discussions of principles, and the undermining of systems of error and iniquity, let our objective point be individual men and women, and our highest and brightest trophies, the transformed lives of the most helpless and degraded of our race.

2. Let us, like Joshua and Israel, go in and possess all our inheritance. The church has been slack to do this, and is still slack; she has not claimed her full inheritance of knowledge and truth, nor entered into all the fullness of God's precious promises.

She has not entered into her full inheritance of holiness, but has been content to look upon a life of sanctity and devotedness as an exceptional and occasional exhibition of individual temperament rather than as the duty and privilege of every child of God.

She has not entered into her full inheritance of faith, nor recognized the power that lies latent in taking God at His word and daring to claim all that He has spoken. A life of becoming faith and remarkable answers to prayer is regarded as something special and wonderful, a sort of peculiar calling on the part of some individual of exalted piety.

She has not entered into her full inheritance of love and unity, but has been rent with strifes, divisions, jealousies and controversies, which have left Hebron in the hands of the Anakims, and her Lord "wounded in the house of his friends."

And she has failed to enter into her full inheritance of supernatural power. The gifts of Pentecost have never been recalled, but have only been imperfectly claimed, and natural talent, human learning and worldly influence have been their weak and insufficient substitutes. Let us go in and possess all the land. All power is given unto our Joshua in heaven and in earth, and lo! He is with us always.

"God hath not given us the spirit of fear, but of power, and of love, and of a sound mind." Let us, therefore, "stir up the gift of God that is in us." Let Zion hear her Master crying, "Awake, awake, put on thy strength, thy beautiful garments;" "Arise and shine, for thy light is come, and the glory of the Lord is risen upon thee."

The almighty presence of our risen Lord is sufficient for any obedient service which we will dare to attempt in His strength and name. Let us put on the whole armour of the Lord, "Be strong in the Lord, and in His power and His might," and clothed in all the fullness of the unchanging Paraclete, let the church of God go forth to the last campaign of the great conflict.

3. Let the church remember the necessity of separation from sin and the world if she would overcome her enemies and possess her full inheritance. She must cross the Jordan and let its unbridged torrents roll between her and the world. She must know the true meaning of circumcision and let Gilgal roll away the reproach of Egypt from her spirit and person. She must watch against the sin of Achan, and not let the accursed thing touch her spotless hands. She must take no tribute from the Canaanites, nor lean upon the world in the slightest measure for her support.

She must separate from forbidden alliances with the ungodly, and stand "fresh as the morning, fair as the moon, clear as the sun, and terrible as an army with banners." Alas, this is the secret of her weakness and failure; she has gone, like Israel, into a forbidden league with the tribes of the land. She has put her head, like Samson, in Delilah's lap, and her locks are shorn, and all her shaking of herself will not renew her strength until she has taken the place of the Nazarite and separated herself from a defiling and hostile world. "Come out of her, my people," is the Master's call; and as the Church obeys it, will she stand forth in her primitive purity and power and draw all men unto her Lord.

CHAPTER XII.

THE HEAVENLY CANAAN.

"But now they desire a better country, that is, a heavenly: wherefore God is not ashamed to be called their God, for He has prepared for them a city." – Heb. 11:16.

CHRISTIAN hope has always loved to link the land of promise with our heavenly inheritance. The sacred poetry of the past is full of this sweet and sacred imagery. Jordan is the swelling flood of death, and the sweet fields beyond are the images of that heavenly land.

"Where everlasting spring abides,
And never withering flowers,
And death, the narrow stream, divides
That heavenly land from ours."

The vital objection to the logic of this theory is that heaven essentially differs from the earthly Canaan in most of the features which chiefly distinguished the latter. That was a land of conflict and hard won victory, while heaven shall have no foes to overcome, and all its crowns shall be those of accomplished triumph and peaceful recompense. Heaven will have no Jericho, no Gibeon, no valley of Achor, or failure such as that of Achan, and no sad declension such as that which followed Israel's entry into Canaan. And yet there are some points in which the misinterpretation is not without its lessons. Canaan was Israel's home; their place of rest after the conflicts in the wilderness, and the realization of long deferred hopes and promises.

And so, there remaineth a rest for the people of God on the heaven side of the grave where they shall be at home, and "shall rest from their labors while their works do follow them;" and where the long deferred hopes and expectations of life shall be realized at length, and all their wanderings and trials shall forever cease. God forbid that we should abate aught of the blessed meaning of heaven, where all the ransomed wait in unspeakable felicity for the greater inheritance that lies still farther beyond.

It is of this better inheritance that the ancient Canaan was really the type; for there is a better inheritance even than heaven. Christian hope is always connected in the New Testament Scriptures, not with death and the state of the departed, but with the second coming of the Lord Jesus, and the millennial glory which is then to be ushered in. Even the earthly Canaan itself was but the transient home of the seed of Abraham; it looked forward both in type and promise to a future age when Israel shall inherit their full patrimony, and when all the children of faith shall possess, through the age of glory, their true Land of Promise.

1. Like the ancient Canaan, it is to be introduced by the true Joshua, the Lord Jesus Christ. There is no millennium promised in the Scriptures apart from His personal coming. The heavens have received him, according to the language of the apostles, "until the times of restitution of all things;" but he is coming again, and His appearing and His kingdom will be simultaneous.

2. Like the ancient Canaan, only the children of faith and obedience will possess this inheritance. Perhaps many of the ancient Israel were saved who never entered the Land of Promise; and so it is possible to belong to the people of God and yet lose much of the glory and recompense connected with the hope of His appearing. "Unto them that look for Him will He appear the second time without sin unto salvation." "They that are with Him, are called, and chosen, and faithful."

3. The millennium, like Canaan, must be conquered, too. Not without resistance shall He enter upon His kingdom. The world's greatest conflict will just precede its millennial Sabbath. The mighty captain of the millennial armies sits upon a white horse with garments dyed in blood, and a name upon His vesture and upon His thigh, King of kings, and Lord of lords, and comes forth as a mighty conqueror, treading under His feet the hosts of Antichrist and the powers of hell, and scattering His enemies, as the feet of Nebuchadnezzar's image, like the chaff of the summer threshing floors; for "He must reign until He put all enemies under His feet." The battles of Joshua and the conquests of David are the living types of the advent struggles, and the Armageddon war.

4. The Lord's coming will bring not only conflict, but victory. Joshua's campaign was an uninterrupted and complete triumph until it was finished. There was no king in all the Hittite confederacy that had not been overthrown; and so our Lord is to put down all authority and opposition and reign without a rival over the millennial earth. The day is surely coming when every evil thing that lifts its head in proud defiance shall be laid prostrate at His feet. Not forever shall right be on the scaffold and wrong upon the throne. He will "avenge His own elect."

Error shall at length cease to delude, selfishness to prey on holiness, and injustice, vice and crime to defile and destroy the creation of God. The hour is coming when the adversaries of the church and of the soul shall be remembered only as a vanished dream. We shall seek for them and they shall not be found. The proud empires of the world, the blasphemous and defiant power of antichrist, and even Satan himself, shall be cast out from God's fair inheritance, and the kingdom shall be given to the saints of God and the Prince of Peace. The conquests of Canaan were not a truce with the adversary, nor an attempt to transform their adversaries into peaceful friends, but their utter extinction.

And so the coming of the Lord is to involve the destruction of His enemies. The gospel age is the time of evangelization and the day for the world's peaceful submission and conversion, but when the Master comes it will be to "consume with the spirit of His mouth, and to destroy with the brightness of His coming," "everything that exalted itself against the obedience of Christ."

5. His coming will bring to us our inheritance. Then will Abraham and David possess the literal fullness of their ancient covenants, and the land on which their feet rested for a time shall be their own and the home of their off-spring. Then shall the disciples who followed Jesus in His days of rejection, "sit on twelve thrones judging the tribes of Israel." Then shall we possess our complete redemption, spirit, soul and body, perfectly restored to the image of God, and our lost dominion over the earth given back through our exalted Head. Then shall the saints of God receive the recompenses of their lives of service and suffering, and those who have overcome shall wear the crowns of victory and glory which He hath promised to the faithful and triumphant. Then shall each soul find its perfect sphere and enter upon the service for which its earthly training has qualified it; and doubtless there will be a Hebron of exalted fellowship and love for every brave Caleb; a Kirjath-sepher of boundless knowledge for every conquering Othniel; a fountain of life, with its upper and nether springs, for every true Achsah who has dared to claim her full inheritance; a double inheritance for every true Ephraimite that has dared to conquer it in the days of earthly battle; a city of honor and service for every Levite who has been true to his consecration; and a Timnath-serah of everlasting light and glory for every faithful Joshua.

Our full inheritance is yet to come. All we know of Jesus in His indwelling fullness and victorious life is but the type of the glory that awaits us at His advent. All we know of truth here is but through glass darkly, then "shall we know even as we are known." All we know of holiness here is but a shadow of that hour when "we shall be like Him," as we see Him as He is. All we know of physical redemption is but a prophetic foretaste of the glorious life that will thrill every frame with the resurrection joy. All we know of service for the Master is but the blundering attempt of the school boy as he learns the mere alphabet of knowledge, compared with the mighty faith and divine power with which we shall be workers together with Him, in the transformation of the Millennial earth, at the inauguration of His glorious kingdom.

He is educating us to bear a far "more exceeding, even an eternal weight of glory." Let us be apt learners, and by-and-by we shall look back with amazement to our earthly childhood and scarcely recognize the trembling and blundering beginner who once struggled and toiled through the years of time, and claimed the inheritance that was to be so much more vast and transcendent than his brightest earthly dream.

6. And best of all, He will be Himself our Eternal Inheritance. "Behold, the Tabernacle of God is with men and God Himself shall be with them and be their God."

"Hallelujah! hark, the sound,
From the center to the skies,
Wakes above, beneath, around,
All creation's harmonies.

"He shall reign from pole to pole,
With illimitable sway;
He shall reign when, like a scroll,
Yonder heavens have passed away.

"Then the end – beneath His rod
Man's last enemy shall fall.
Hallelujah! Christ in God,
God in Christ is all in all."

Made in the USA
Columbia, SC
24 December 2023

29415216R00214